Dulce

DESSERTS
IN THE
LATIN-AMERICAN
TRADITION

Joseluis Flores

with Laura Zimmerman Maye

PHOTOGRAPHS BY BEN FINK

RIZZOLI
NEW YORK

New York · Paris · London · Milan

This book is dedicated to my grandmother, Carmen, and my mother, Aurora, who both gave me the knowledge and inspiration to pursue my passion.

First published in the United States of America in 2010
by Rizzoli International Publications, Inc.
300 Park Avenue South
New York, NY 10010
www.rizzoliusa.com

2010 2011 2012 2013 / 10 9 8 7 6 5 4 3 2 1

DESIGN BY CHALKLEY CALDERWOOD
PROP STYLING BY CLAIRE PEREZ

Props provided courtesy of Saks Fifth Avenue,
Palm Beach Gardens, Florida, and private collections.

Printed in China

ISBN: 978-0-8478-3321-4

Library of Congress Control Number: 2009940173

Contents

Introduction

BY JOSELUIS FLORES

My earliest memories of food and cooking involve my paternal grandmother. She was a house manager and cook for wealthy families in Mexico City, where she was trained in many of the classical French preparations and techniques. Even at six or seven years old, I knew that her meals were something special. I loved all her food, but what I remember most vividly were her desserts: chocolate, orange, or vanilla pound cakes or génoise cakes, immaculate fruitcakes painstakingly soaked with cognac. They were amazing to me as a child and we looked forward to them as presents.

So often life's greatest challenges are what truly shape our lives and make us the people we are. And so it was with me. On September 15, 1982, Mexican Independence Day, my family waited for my father to return home from work and join us for dinner. He never came. We learned later that he had been killed by a hit-and-run driver.

My mother suddenly plunged into becoming the provider for my two sisters and me, and she eventually found a job in a local supermarket. After about a year, she convinced the manager that her cooking skills would be best utilized in the deli department or Fuente de Sodas. Her love of cooking and her determination to succeed would one day parallel my own. Now that my mother was working outside of our home, I took over preparing the daily meals for the family. It was during the next six years that my passion for cooking really blossomed.

My wife, Claudia, and I fell in love when we were sixteen years old. After I was passed over in the government lottery for attending university in Mexico, we decided to get married and start our family. The challenge of starting a family at such an early age fueled my motivation, and my family remains my most powerful inspiration to this day.

I started working where I could in a local restaurant—as a dishwasher. I continued, trying to sell my supervisor on the idea of moving me into cooking. Eventually he gave in and I joined seven women in the kitchen. These women built on what I had learned at home and taught me even more about the techniques and flavors of traditional Mexican cooking. Seeing them use bits of technique from outside of Mexico—from Italy and France—piqued my interest to learn more.

It was here that my interest in pastry and desserts took off. After my job was done, I started waiting for the later shift to arrive so that I could watch the pastry chef and her team. The desserts they prepared were very simple—plain and stuffed churros, traditional bread pudding, chocolate and vanilla *natillas* (Mexican style custards)—but with such powerful flavors.

My desire to seek ever more opportunity and to provide a better quality of life for my family led me to immigrate to New York City. I knew it would be quite a change from the small working-class suburb of Mexico City where we had grown up. But my sister Mireya had already been living in New York with her husband, Ramiro, a sous chef. I knew he could help me get a job. What I didn't know was that he worked in one of the hottest restaurants in Manhattan, China Grill.

My first days on the job were at once overwhelming and invigorating. Watching the pastry team, I felt the same awe I felt as a child when watching my grandmother prepare desserts. In those moments I fell in love with pastries and desserts and decided to focus my energy on finding my way into that station of the kitchen. I started making notes about everything—lists of ingredients with their English translation, descriptions of preparations I had never seen in Mexico, sketches of plate presentations. One day I got up enough nerve to talk to the pastry chef about my desire to work for her. I started on the pastry line and for several months spent most of my time either at work or in English classes trying to learn as much as I possibly could. The repetition and the quest for perfection were very satisfying to me.

I worked on the pastry team for the next four years and was ultimately given the responsibility of managing the team. I had five pastry assistants often serving more than 450 covers each weekend night. I finally felt that I had the opportunity to apply all of what I had learned. Now, I not only understood what everyone was saying, but also I could articulate my own ideas about desserts and pastries, both in English conversation and on the plate. I started experimenting with different flavor combinations, developing specials, and creating my own style.

In 1997 I received what ended up being a very important invitation. An ex-pastry chef from China Grill invited me to a "research and development" dinner at one of the city's hottest Latin restaurants, Patria. The chef, Douglas Rodriguez, was at the forefront of what was being called Nuevo Latino cuisine. Dining at Patria sealed my decision to concentrate on bringing my Latin roots into my cooking. As we left that night, I thought, "One day, I'm going to work here."

Just a few months later, Douglas was looking for a new pastry chef, and I wasted no time. Douglas loved everything I made during my interview and said they were some of the best Latin desserts he'd ever tasted. By the following week, he had invited me to discuss the details of a job offer. I remember walking through the back kitchen door around eight in the evening. When Douglas spotted me, he put his arm around me, smiling and shouted to the whole kitchen, "This is the new pastry chef, Joseluis. He's taking over!" I was twenty-four years old then. My adventures in Latin desserts haven't stopped since. I invite you to share in the adventure.

1

FLANS AND PUDDINGS

Flanes y Puddines

In This Chapter

TRADITIONAL FLAN
Flan Tradicional

Unfortunately for many, flan is the only Latin dessert that is easily recognizable. But flan is just the beginning of the sweet side of the Latin kitchen. And what a beginning it is. Called crème caramel in Europe, flan is a silky custard bathed in creamy melted caramel, as opposed to its close cousins, crème brûlée or *crema catalana*, which have crisp caramelized tops. Crème brûlée and *crema catalana* are also typically made only with egg yolks, lending a creamier consistency and requiring these custards to be served in their baking vessels, rather than being unmolded like flan.

Think of flan as the American equivalent of chocolate cake or apple pie. One taste and I'm transported back to the countless little towns I've visited in Mexico: Cuernavaca, Pachuca, Morelia, or Querétaro, where I grew up. I can still hear the voice of *la señora de los dulces* who would sell fresh sweets door to door.

You will notice that I do not cook the eggs in the milk mixture on the stovetop before baking the flans. I find that this "cold" method results in a lighter, more delicate flan.

SERVES 8

1 recipe Caramel for Flan (page 234)

4 cups heavy cream   950 MILLILITERS

1½ cups whole milk   360 MILLILITERS

1¼ cups granulated sugar   250 GRAMS

2 vanilla beans, halved lengthwise, seeds
    scraped out and reserved
    (or 3 tablespoons vanilla extract)

1 cinnamon stick

6 whole eggs

4 egg yolks

◉ In a microwave oven, bain-marie, or pan set over gently simmering water, slightly reheat the caramel until just pourable. Pour ⅛ inch into the bottom of each of 8 (6-ounce) ramekins.

◉ Preheat the oven to 350° F.

◉ In a medium saucepan over high heat, bring the cream, milk, sugar, halved vanilla beans (including seeds) or extract, and cinnamon stick to a boil, whisking constantly, being careful not to burn. Remove from the heat, and chill in the refrigerator until completely cooled, about 30 minutes.

◉ In a large bowl, whisk together the eggs and yolks. Continue whisking and slowly pour the cooled cream mixture into the egg mixture to combine. Pour the custard through a fine sieve into a clean bowl, preferably one with a spout, to remove any bits of egg. Pour the custard over the caramel in the ramekins (fill to about ⅛ inch from the top), place them in a water bath (see page 6), and cover the whole pan with aluminum foil.

⑨ Put the pan in the oven, set the oven temperature to 325° F, and bake for 30 minutes, or until the custards are set (a knife inserted in the center should come out clean). The center will still look a little loose, but the custards will continue cooking after they are removed from the oven. Carefully remove the baking dish from the oven, lift out the ramekins, using tongs, and let them rest for at least 20 minutes. Move them to the refrigerator and chill for at least 4 hours, preferably overnight.

⑨ When ready to serve, invert a ramekin onto each serving plate and gently tap the bottom with the end of a butter knife to help unmold.

Adorno Especial

Sobre Piña y Queso de Cabra

1 medium pineapple, peeled, cored, and diced or thinly sliced into rounds
4 ounces fresh goat cheese 115 GRAMS
Freshly ground black pepper to taste

Unmold each flan onto a slice of pineapple or surround with diced pineapple.
Top with crumbled goat cheese and a few grinds of black pepper.

Sweet and Savory

YOU WILL LOVE THE COMBINATION OF SWEET AND SAVORY IN LATIN desserts. Though the concept has taken off in the United States only in the last decade, it has been around forever. For example, my Chocolate Flan with Yellow Corn Foam and Chocolate Sauce (page 143) takes its lead from the Aztecs, who used to melt chocolate together with ground corn. The first time I tried a sweet and savory dessert duo, I was just a young boy. My grandmother had taken me with her to work—the home of a wealthy family for whom she cooked. As I sat in the beautiful kitchen watching her, I ate one of her amazing creations, a poached pear stuffed with creamy goat cheese. I will never forget that combination. At home, things weren't quite as extravagant, but they were just as delicious. Slices of toasted bread spread with prune marmalade and duck liver pâté, or the classic Spanish combination of quince paste and cheese. There are endless brilliant flavor combinations out there if you remain open-minded. For a list of all the sweet and savory combinations in this book, see the Index.

ALMOND FLAN
Flan de Almendra

Sliced, toasted almonds and almond extract infuse this flan with an intense nutty flavor. Since the nuts are blended into the flan mixture, the flan retains a beautiful silky texture.

SERVES 6

1	recipe Caramel for Flan (page 234)	
2¼	cups heavy cream	540 MILLILITERS
¾	cup whole milk	180 MILLILITERS
¾	cup granulated sugar	150 GRAMS
1½	cups sliced almonds, toasted	190 GRAMS
1	pinch salt	
1	teaspoon almond extract	
5	whole eggs	
3	egg yolks	

In a microwave oven, bain-marie, or pan set over gently simmering water, slightly reheat the caramel until just pourable. Pour ⅛ inch into the bottom of each of 8 (6-ounce) ramekins.

Preheat the oven to 350° F.

In a medium saucepan over high heat, bring the cream, milk, sugar, 1¼ cups of the almonds (reserve ¼ cup for garnish), the salt, and almond extract to a boil, whisking constantly, being careful not to burn. Remove from the heat, and chill in the refrigerator until completely cooled, about 30 minutes. Place the mixture in a blender and blend on high speed until smooth, about 3 minutes.

In a large bowl, whisk together the eggs and yolks. Continue whisking and slowly pour the cream mixture into the egg mixture to combine. Pour the custard through a fine sieve into a clean bowl, preferably one with a spout, to remove any bits of egg. Pour the custard over the caramel in the ramekins (fill to about ⅛ inch from the top), and place them in a deep baking pan. Make a water bath (bain-marie): Fill the baking pan with water to reach one-quarter of the way up the sides of the ramme-kins. Cover the whole pan with aluminum foil.

Put the pan in the oven, set the oven temperature to 325° F, and bake for 30 minutes, or until the custards are set (a knife inserted in the center should come out clean). The center will still look a little loose, but the custards will continue cooking after they are removed from the oven. Carefully remove the baking dish from the oven, lift out the ramekins, using tongs, and let them rest for at least 20 minutes. Move them to the refrigerator and chill for at least 4 hours, preferably overnight.

When ready to serve, invert a ramekin onto each serving plate and gently tap the bottom with the end of a butter knife to help unmold. Garnish with the reserved almonds.

Adorno Especial

Nieve de Morir Soñando y Tejas de Coco

Citrus and almonds make a great flavor combo. This ice cream has a gelato-like texture that makes the creamy flan even more decadent.

"To Die Dreaming" Ice Cream

1 recipe (page 209)

Coconut Tuiles 1 recipe (page 62)

Unmold the flans. Place a quenelle or small scoop of the ice cream next to each flan and stick one of the tuiles into the ice cream and/or flan.

CHEESE FLAN
Flan de Queso

This dessert was born out of my desire to make a more nontraditional, cheesecake-inspired dessert with a Latin twist. I like to serve it with Guava Foam (page 243) and Candied Almonds (page 250). The guava and cheese combination is a favorite in Cuba. You'll find it in empanadas, in pastries, or simply on its own—a piece of cheese topped with a slice of fresh guava, guava paste, or *cascos de guayaba*, fresh poached guava scented with cinnamon and cloves. This dessert was also inspired by the tradition of finishing a meal with a cheese course, pairing the cheese with fruit as well as nuts, hence the addition of the candied almonds. Serve the flan on its own or pair it with your favorite fresh fruit and a sprinkling of toasted nuts.

SERVES 8

1 recipe Caramel for Flan (page 234)

2 (8-ounce) packages softened cream cheese   455 GRAMS

7 eggs

1 (12-ounce) can sweetened condensed milk   360 MILLILITERS

1 cup whole milk   240 MILLILITERS

½ cup heavy cream   120 MILLILITERS

1 tablespoon granulated sugar

1 tablespoon vanilla extract

◎ In a microwave oven, bain-marie, or pan set over gently simmering water, slightly reheat the caramel until just pourable. Pour ⅛ inch into the bottom of each of 8 (6-ounce) ramekins.

◎ Preheat the oven to 350° F.

◎ In a food processor or blender, puree the rest of the ingredients until smooth. Pour the mixture through a fine sieve into a clean bowl, preferably one with a spout, to remove any bits of cream cheese or egg. It will be thinner than a traditional cheesecake mixture. Pour the custard over the caramel in the ramekins (fill to about ⅛ inch from the top), place them in a water bath (see page 6), and cover the whole pan with aluminum foil.

◎ Bake for 30 minutes, or until the custards are set (a knife inserted in the center should come out clean). The centers will still look a little loose, but the custards will continue cooking after they are removed from the oven. Carefully remove the baking dish from the oven, lift out the ramekins using tongs, and let them rest for at least 20 minutes. Cover and refrigerate for at least 4 hours, preferably overnight.

◎ When ready to serve, invert a ramekin onto each serving plate and gently tap the bottom with the end of a butter knife to help unmold.

Guayaba

THE *GUAYABA* IS ONE OF THE WONDERS OF LATIN AMERICAN FRUIT, NOT only for its taste and intoxicating aroma, but also for its exceptional nutritional value and medicinal qualities. Thought to be native to southern Mexico and Central America, the guava is now grown in South America, the Caribbean, the tropics, and even in some parts of the United States. Although it is an extremely adaptable plant, it has never caught on in the commercial world fruit trade. But this "poor man's apple," as it is sometimes called, is worth seeking out. You'll find guava paste or marmalade, canned guava juice, or frozen guava puree at most Latin American markets, or in the imported foods section of your local supermarket, but, depending on the climate you live in, you may have to search a bit harder to find fresh guavas.

The guava is entirely edible, from its skin to its seeds. It looks somewhat like a cross between an apple and a pear, with a thin yellow to green rind and white to pale pink or bright orange-pink flesh speckled with light-tan-colored seeds. There are many varieties, but the two most commonly found are the pink guava and the yellow or white guava. The pink variety is most often used to make *pasta de guayaba* (guava paste), *cascos de guayaba* (guava in syrup), and milkshakes. The yellow or white guava is the one typically eaten raw because it has a more tender flesh and higher water and sugar content. However, it is the pink guava that is more readily found in the United States, as it is less delicate, resistant to temperature variation, and has a longer shelf life.

The fruit of a flowering evergreen shrub or small tree, guavas have been called "superfruits" for their exceptional nutritional value. They are high in vitamins A and C, polyunsaturated fatty acids, and fiber. Even the wood of the guava tree is used to make kitchen tools and toys in Mexico, and my family used to use the leaves as healing skin patches for cuts and rashes.

I grew up eating guavas. In Mexico and throughout Latin America they are as popular as apples and oranges are in the United States. My mother used to have them on hand to eat as snacks or to make agua fresca, fresh juice. Guavas taste pleasantly acidic, sweet, and perfumed, with a musky fragrance reminiscent of rose petals, apples, and strawberries. They are the perfect antidote to the richness of cheese or nuts, as in my Goat Cheese and Guava Empanadas (pages 116–117).

COFFEE BEAN FLAN
Flan de Café

This dessert is the perfect combination of two of my very favorite flavors: coffee and caramel. I love it so much as is, I would suggest garnishing it only with plain whipped cream and perhaps a few chopped chunks of *panela*—a candylike brick of golden brown sugar made from boiled sugercane juice (see page 13)—for a nice contrast of textures: the richness of the silky, smooth flan custard with the sweet, crunchiness of the panela. If you can, use freshly crushed coffee beans in this recipe rather than ground coffee, as they retain more of their flavorful oils and produce a less bitter coffee taste. Crushing them is easy: simply put the beans between two dishtowels and use the back of a pan to break them into smaller bits. It seems fitting to serve this flan in a coffee cup. When entertaining at home, it creates an impressive presentation that is easy and convenient to make and to serve.

SERVES 10

1 recipe Caramel for Flan (page 234)

1 (12-ounce) can evaporated milk — 360 MILLILITERS

4 cups heavy cream — 950 MILLILITERS

1¼ cups granulated sugar — 250 GRAMS

2 cups crushed coffee beans — 130 GRAMS
(or 1 cup/100 grams ground coffee, or ¼ cup/60 milliliters coffee extract or brewed espresso)

1 vanilla bean, halved lengthwise, seeds scraped out and reserved
(or 1 to 2 tablespoons vanilla extract)

8 whole eggs

4 egg yolks

◎ In a microwave oven, bain-marie, or pan set over gently simmering water, slightly reheat the caramel until just pourable. Pour ⅛ inch into the bottom of each of 10 (6-ounce) ovenproof coffee cups or ramekins.

◎ Preheat the oven to 350° F.

◎ In a medium saucepan over high heat, bring the evaporated milk, cream, sugar, coffee beans, and halved vanilla bean (including seeds) or extract to a boil, whisking constantly, being careful not to burn. Remove from the heat, and chill in the refrigerator until completely cooled, about 30 minutes.

◎ In a large bowl, whisk together the eggs and yolks. Continue whisking and slowly pour the cooled cream mixture into the egg mixture to combine.

⊙ Pour the custard through a fine sieve into a clean bowl, preferably one with a spout, to remove the coffee beans or grounds and any bits of egg. Pour the custard over the caramel in the coffee cups or ramekins (fill to about ⅛ inch from the top), place them in a water bath (see page 6), and cover the whole pan with aluminum foil.

⊙ Put the pan in the oven, set the oven temperature to 300° F, and bake for 30 to 35 minutes, until the custards are set (a knife inserted in the center should come out clean). The center will still look a little loose, but the custards will continue cooking after they are removed from the oven. Carefully remove the baking dish from the oven, lift out the ramekins using tongs, and let them rest for at least 20 minutes. Move them to the refrigerator and chill for at least 4 hours, preferably overnight.

⊙ When ready to serve, invert a ramekin onto each serving plate and gently tap the bottom with the end of a butter knife to help unmold. If serving in a coffee cup, don't bother unmolding. Just make sure to dig deep for the delicious caramel at the bottom of the cup.

Adorno Especial

Crema Batida y Panela

1 cup chopped *panela* (see page 13)
1 recipe Whipped Cream (page 235)

Unmold the flans. Garnish each plate with a spoonful of the Whipped Cream and some chopped *panela*.

Café

WE DRINK A LOT OF COFFEE IN LATIN AMERICA. ALTHOUGH THE BEANS are native to Ethiopia, they are grown extensively throughout Latin America, where they prosper in volcanic highlands. Brazil is the world's largest producer, but, in terms of quality, Colombia reigns supreme. Beans from Venezuela and Jamaica are also prized.

Unlike children in the United States, many Latin American children grow up drinking coffee from a very young age. It's a flavor I have loved ever since I can remember. The coffee I grew up drinking in Mexico (Café Legal was the big brand, but the similar Café Bustelo is easy to find here in the United States) is different from American coffee, mostly because of the way it is brewed.

My grandmother used to brew coffee on the stovetop rather than in a modern coffee maker. It was almost ceremonial in the way it marked the start of each day. My grandmother would wake at about 5 o'clock in the morning to water the plants and begin the housework. The first order of business was putting the water for the coffee on the stove. She used a traditional stone pot with two handles and a spout to boil the water. She'd add crushed coffee beans and some-times a cinnamon stick, letting that boil for a few minutes to release the flavors, then taking it off the heat to steep for a few more minutes. She'd reheat it for us when we got up, straining it into individual cups. The clay of the pot actually gave the coffee a distinct flavor. We would create our own concoctions with milk, milk powder, chunks of *panela* (page 13), white granulated sugar, or chunks of Ibarra or Abuelita chocolate.

Although her homemade coffee is my favorite, I was also a fan of instant coffee—also popular in Mexico. I used to take a big tablespoon of the instant granules, plus an equal part of sugar, add just a little bit of water, and whip it up with a spoon until it was nice and foamy. Then I'd pour hot water over it and it would be just like one of those foamy instant coffees you get from a machine.

But just as with most food or drink in Mexico, coffee was just as much about gathering the family together as it was about the drink itself. We'd sit in the morning together, waking up, drinking our coffee, eating a piece of toast or a slice of *pan dulce* (Mexican-style sweet bread, see page 68), thinking and talking.

Panela

ALSO CALLED *PILONCILLO* IN MEXICO, *PANELA* IS A DENSE BRICK OF unrefined, dark brown sugar made from boiled sugercane juice. In Chile and Peru, it is called *chancaca*. *Panela* has an intense caramel taste, almost like a cross between brown sugar and molasses, and is sold in solid bricks, disks, or cones, or sometimes as a coarse powder. Broken chunks or grated pieces of *panela* used as a garnish provide the perfect contrasting texture for creamy desserts like flans or puddings. I suggest trying it on top of my Coffee Bean Flan (page 10) or Rice Pudding (page 24).

In the States, look for Goya *piloncillo* or Iberia *panelin*. You may need to use a meat mallet or hammer to break apart the large solid pieces. The resulting chunks can be crumbled with a mallet or rolling pin beneath a kitchen towel or inside a plastic bag. Or the large pieces can be grated.

Colombia is the largest producer of *panela*, where it is mostly used in the preparation of *aquapanela*, or *panela* water. The *panela* is dissolved in water, served either hot or cold, and flavored with fresh citrus juice, milk, or even cheese. Many Colombian homes even have a special rock specifically used to break apart blocks of *panela* into manageable pieces. In Ecuador, the drink is sometimes enhanced with cinnamon and a regionally produced distilled spirit called *aguardiente*, literally firewater, to make a cocktail called *canelazo*.

Panela can also be melted and made into a delicious syrup, as in the spiced syrup I recommend serving with my freshly fried *picarones*, Peruvian Sweet Potato and Pumpkin Fritters (pages 124-125). It is used in this capacity in many Latin countries not only as a recipe ingredient, but also simply to sweeten things like coffee or tea, much as Americans would use honey or white sugar.

GOAT'S MILK CARAMEL FLAN
Flan de Cajeta

This dessert is at once rich and refreshing—a great one for summer. I like to use vanilla extract here, since the color of the flan is so light and the black speckles you get from vanilla beans can diminish the effect. It's worth it to make the *cajeta* from scratch. The depth of flavor from a true *cajeta* really makes this dish. As a garnish, try Caramelized Nectarines (page 186) and Sugar-Coated Nuts (page 251), or just your choice of sliced fresh fruit and toasted nuts.

SERVES 10

1 recipe Caramel for Flan (page 234)	
1½ cups evaporated milk	360 MILLILITERS
1¼ cups whole milk	300 MILLILITERS
½ cup heavy cream	120 MILLILITERS
1 tablespoon vanilla extract	
¼ cup Grand Marnier	60 MILLILITERS
1 pinch salt	
2 cups (see page 15) *cajeta* (goat's milk caramel)	455 GRAMS
6 whole eggs	
2 egg yolks	

⊚ In a microwave oven, bain-marie, or pan set over gently simmering water, slightly reheat the caramel until just pourable. Pour ⅛ inch into the bottom of each of 10 (6-ounce) ramekins.

⊚ Preheat the oven to 325° F.

⊚ In a medium-sized saucepan over high heat, bring the evaporated milk, whole milk, cream, vanilla extract, Grand Marnier, and salt to a boil, whisking constantly, being careful not to burn. Remove from the heat and whisk in the *cajeta* until melted. Chill in the refrigerator until completely cool, about 30 minutes.

⊚ In a large bowl, whisk together the eggs and yolks. Continue whisking and slowly pour the cooled cream mixture into the egg mixture. Pour the custard through a fine sieve into a clean bowl, preferably one with a spout, to remove any bits of egg. Pour the custard over the caramel in the ramekins (fill to about ⅛ inch from the top), place them in a water bath (see page 6), and cover the whole pan with foil.

⊚ Bake for 30 to 35 minutes, or until the custards are set (a knife inserted in the center should come out clean). The center will still look a little loose, but the custards will continue cooking after they are removed from the oven. Carefully remove the baking dish from the oven, lift out the ramekins using tongs, and let them rest for at least 20 minutes. Move them to the refrigerator and chill for at least 4 hours, preferably overnight.

⊚ When ready to serve, invert a ramekin onto each serving plate and gently tap the bottom with the end of a butter knife to help unmold.

Cajeta

CAJETA IS A GOAT'S MILK CARAMEL SIMILAR TO *DULCE DE LECHE* (COW'S milk-caramel originally from Argentina) or *manjar blanco* (what they call *dulce de leche* in Peru). In Mexico, it is traditionally sold in small, thin wooden boxes, or *cajas*, on the streets or in the open-air markets. The boxes keep the *cajeta* fresh and seal in the flavors—typically either *ron* (rum), *quemada* (caramelized; it tastes like a slightly bitter burnt caramel), or vanilla. *Cajeta* is truly a staple in every Mexican home and is used for everything from a spread for toasted bread or fresh *bolillo* (like a Mexican baguette), to an ingredient for lollipops, candies, or *turrones* (nougats), to a stuffing for crêpes. The Morelianas, from Morelia, Michoacán, in Mexico, even make a deliciously thick *cajeta* mixed with pecans or almonds and wrapped in brightly colored parchment paper.

Just as goat's milk brings a certain richness and pleasant tang to some of my favorite cheeses, it also brings an unmistakable depth of flavor to this caramel. These days, it is fairly easy to track down goat's milk at some of the specialty or more organic- or health-food-oriented groceries. And it is worth the time to find it, make a fresh *cajeta*, and taste one of the traditional flavors of Mexico.

My Flan de Cajeta requires only 2 cups of this caramel, so thankfully you'll have some leftovers from this recipe. Use it just as you might Nutella as a sweet spread for just about everything: bread, muffins, waffles, pound cake, croissants, and so on. Of course, you can buy it in a jar in a pinch. One of the favorite brands in Mexico is Coronado, and it's certainly decent. You can find it and other brands pretty easily here in the United States. I still often have a jar of it at home to use for last-minute snacks.

YIELDS 3 CUPS

4 cups whole goat's milk	950 MILLILITERS
4 cups granulated sugar	800 GRAMS
1 cinnamon stick	
1 teaspoon baking soda	
½ cup glucose or corn syrup	120 MILLILITERS

In a heavy, medium-sized saucepan over medium heat, combine all the ingredients and bring to a boil. Lower the heat and simmer, stirring frequently, until thick and golden brown (1½ to 2 hours). The liquid will reduce to about 3 cups. Remove the cinnamon stick and chill the *cajeta*, tightly covered in the refrigerator, for at least 4 hours, preferably overnight. The *cajeta* can be stored in an airtight container in the refrigerator for 2 months, or even at room temperature for about 10 days.

WHITE CHOCOLATE MOCHA FLAN

Flan de Mocha

Mocha is a flavor I fell for early in life. When I was young, I would add chunks of Mexican chocolate, already scented with cinnamon and sugar, to my coffee. The aroma alone was enough to start my craving, and one taste made it official. I like that this flan combines an ingredient and a beverage that are both such a large part of Latin culture and tradition—although I've added a slight twist by using white chocolate instead of dark. Pick a good coffee for this recipe so that you end up with a refined, smooth taste, rather than anything bitter.

SERVES 8

1	recipe Caramel for Flan (page 234)	
1½	cups evaporated milk	360 MILLILITERS
2½	cups whole milk	600 MILLILITERS
¼	cup granulated sugar	50 GRAMS
1	teaspoon salt	
1	cup crushed coffee beans	65 GRAMS
	(or ½ cup/50 grams ground coffee or	
	2 tablespoons cool brewed espresso)	
1½	cups white chocolate chips,	
	roughly chopped	255 GRAMS
5	whole eggs	
2	egg yolks	

◎ In a microwave oven, bain-marie, or pan set over gently simmering water, slightly reheat the caramel until just pourable. Pour ⅛ inch into the bottom of each of 8 (6-ounce) ramekins.

◎ Preheat the oven to 350° F.

◎ In a medium saucepan over high heat, bring the evaporated milk, whole milk, sugar, salt, and coffee beans or extract or brewed espresso to a boil, whisking constantly, being careful not to burn. Remove from the heat, add the white chocolate, and stir until melted. Chill in the refrigerator until completely cooled, about 30 minutes.

◎ In a large bowl, whisk together the eggs and yolks. Continue whisking and slowly pour the cooled cream mixture into the egg mixture to combine. Pour the custard through a fine sieve into a clean bowl, preferably one with a spout, to remove any coffee beans or bits of egg. Pour the custard over the caramel in the ramekins (fill to about ⅛ inch from the top), place them in a water bath (see page 6), and cover the whole pan with aluminum foil.

◉ Put the pan in the oven, set the oven temperature to 300° F, and bake for 30 to 35 minutes, until the custards are set (a knife inserted in the center should come out clean). The center will still look a little loose, but the custards will continue cooking after they are removed from the oven. Carefully remove the baking dish from the oven, lift out the ramekins using tongs, and let them rest for at least 20 minutes. Move them to the refrigerator and chill for at least 4 hours, preferably overnight.

◉ When ready to serve, invert a ramekin onto each serving plate and gently tap the bottom with a butter knife to help unmold.

Adorno Especial

Crema Batida de Café

Coffee Whipped Cream
1 recipe (page 235)

Unmold the flans. Garnish each plate with a spoonful of the Coffee Whipped Cream.

PINEAPPLE FLAN
Flan de Piña

I have such vivid memories of pineapple from my childhood. Every time I went to the *mercado* with my grandmother or my mom (it was usually early in the morning), I remember seeing men unloading these huge trucks that were filled to the top with fresh pineapples. They are cut decoratively at the market, right on site, and sold already peeled in plastic bags alongside *agua de piña*, refreshing *agua fresca* made with pineapple. By the end of the day, almost all of the pineapples are gone.

Combining flan with the flavor of pineapple seems so natural to me. Just like the caramelized nectarines I pair with the Flan de Cajeta (page 14), the sweet, tart pineapple cuts the creaminess of the custard, making it rich, yet still light and fresh.

After peeling and coring the pineapple, save the peel and use it to make a batch of *chicha de piña*, Pineapple Punch (page 20). Or boil the core with water to make an *agua fresca* (see page 191).

SERVES 8

1 recipe Caramel for Flan (see page 234)

1 large pineapple, peeled, cored, and roughly chopped

1½ cups pineapple juice · 360 MILLILITERS

2 bay leaves

1 cup granulated sugar · 200 GRAMS

1 cup sweetened condensed milk · 240 MILLILITERS

12 whole eggs

6 egg yolks

2 cups heavy cream · 480 MILLILITERS

◉ Preheat the oven to 350° F.

◉ In a microwave oven, bain-marie, or pan set over gently simmering water, slightly reheat the caramel until just pourable. Pour ⅛ inch into the bottom of each of 8 (6-ounce) ramekins.

◉ Put the pineapple and pineapple juice in a blender or food processor and puree until smooth. Pour the pineapple puree (about 3 cups) into a medium saucepan, add the bay leaves and sugar, and bring to a boil. Reduce the heat and simmer, untouched, until the mixture has reduced by half. Chill in the refrigerator until completely cool, about 30 minutes. Pour the cooled reduction into a large bowl, preferably with a spout, and whisk in the condensed milk, eggs, egg yolks, and cream. Pour the custard over the caramel in the ramekins (fill to about ⅛ inch from the top), place them in a water bath (see page 6), and cover the whole pan with aluminum foil.

◎ Put the pan in the oven, set the oven temperature to 325° F, and bake for 30 minutes, or until the custards are set (a knife inserted in the center should come out clean). The center will still look a little loose, but the custards will continue cooking after they are removed from the oven. Carefully remove the baking dish from the oven, lift out the ramekins using tongs, and let them rest for at least 20 minutes. Move them to the refrigerator and chill for at least 4 hours, preferably overnight.

◎ When ready to serve, invert a ramekin onto each serving plate and gently tap the bottom with a butter knife to help unmold.

Adorno Especial

Fresas Frescas con Vinagre Balsamico

The garnishes here are easy enough, and any leftover strawberries and balsamic vinegar can make a store-bought vanilla ice cream look fancy and taste even fancier. If you have a good aged balsamic at home, this is the time to pull it out.

1 pound fresh strawberries, cleaned, stems removed, and quartered lengthwise
Aged balsamic vinegar reduction
1 tablespoon

Unmold the flans. Garnish each plate with the strawberries and drizzle with the balsamic vinegar.

Chicha de Piña

THE SPANISH WORD FOR PINEAPPLE, *PIÑA*, LITERALLY MEANS PINECONE, a reference to the fruit's prickly exterior and giant pineconelike shape. It is one of the most representative fruits of Latin America, and its popularity now spans the globe. In Mexico, the temperature and soil are perfect for growing pineapple. You will find fresh pineapple in absolutely every Mexican *mercado*. One of my favorite ways to enjoy it is cut into big chunks, sprinkled with chile powder and salt.

The role of the pineapple in the popular piña colada cocktail, a mixture of pineapple juice, coconut cream, and rum, is well known in America. But this tropical fruit native to southern Brazil is also the star ingredient in a flavorful fermented punch known in Mexico as *tepache* and in Cuba as *garapiña*. In Mexico, *tepache* is made at home and also sold in taquerias and markets. Surprisingly, it is not the fresh fruit itself that is used to make the drink, but rather the peel and sometimes also the core.

If you have the time, I prefer the method of letting the ingredients steep together at room temperature over a few days. This method is more traditional and produces a complex yet mild flavor. Alternatively, you can boil the ingredients together to extract their flavors. Since the latter method doesn't allow for any fermentation, I call it simply *chicha de piña*, or pineapple punch. Although *chicha* has many variations throughout Latin America, it is predominantly made with corn but can vary from alcoholic to nonalcoholic and include other fruits or grains, like rice, oats, or even yucca. If you purchase purple corn to make my Purple Corn Pudding (page 40), you might consider throwing a few ears into the recipe below to make what is known as *chicha morada*.

I love *chicha de piña* over ice, but you can also enjoy it hot in the winter months like mulled cider. It brings back many wonderful memories for me. My father used to bring my sister and me to the Tacubaya neighborhood of Mexico City about twice a month for street food and *chicha de piña*. It was served out of huge wood barrels, and we would drink it from beer mugs, which we thought was very cool and grown up (although most street vendors sell it as they do fresh fruit juices—in a knotted plastic bag with a straw). The vendors kept the *chicha* cold with huge chunks of ice that they would stir inside the barrels with oversized wooden spoons that seemed bigger than me at the time.

Peel of 1 large pineapple (you can also
   include the core)
4 cinnamon sticks
1 pound chopped *panela* (page 13) or
   2 cups packed brown sugar   455 GRAMS
2 whole cloves

Stir together all the ingredients along with
2½ quarts (2½ liters) water in a medium wood,
clay, or ceramic container. Cover with cheesecloth
or a kitchen towel and place in a dark spot. Let rest
at room temperature for at least 48 hours and up to
3 days. Stir periodically to make sure the *panela*
dissolves. Strain the liquid into a pitcher, discarding
the solid ingredients, and refrigerate for up to
3 days. Alternatively, in a large saucepan over
medium-high heat, bring all the ingredients to a boil.
Reduce the heat and simmer for 5 minutes. Remove
from the heat, strain as above, and let cool either
at room temperature or in the refrigerator. Serve
in a tall glass over lots of ice.

ORANGE FLAN

Flan de Naranja

I like to make this light and refreshing flan as an elegant finish for holiday dinners because it works especially well after a heavy meal.

You may want to double the recipe for the orange marmalade to have a stock of it in the refrigerator. It's great spread on bread or toast, but because of the addition of cardamom and chile powder it's really a hit in a vinaigrette mixed with olive oil, fresh herbs, and balsamic vinegar. Or try blending it with olive oil, garlic, and white onions to use as a marinade for pork or use it straight to baste grilled meats.

SERVES 8

1 recipe Caramel for Flan (page 234)

For the orange marmalade:

2 medium oranges, preferably Valencia

2 cups granulated sugar   400 GRAMS

¼ teaspoon ground cardamom

¼ teaspoon chile powder

For the flan:

3 cups heavy cream   720 MILLILITERS

1½ cups whole milk   360 MILLILITERS

6 whole eggs

4 egg yolks

◎ In a microwave oven, bain-marie, or pan set over gently simmering water, slightly reheat the caramel until just pourable. Pour ⅛ inch into the bottom of each of 8 (6-ounce) ramekins.

◎ Make the orange marmalade: Cut the oranges in half and remove the seeds. Cut the orange halves into medium slices and place them along with the sugar and 1½ cups water in a medium saucepan over low heat. Cook for 35 minutes, or until the orange peels are tender. Set aside to cool. Once the mixture is cool, stir through it and remove any remaining seeds. In a blender or food processor, blend it, along with the cardamom and chile powder, until smooth.

◎ Preheat the oven to 350° F.

◎ In a medium saucepan over high heat, bring the cream and milk to a boil, whisking constantly, being careful not to burn. Remove from the heat and chill in the refrigerator until completely cool, about 30 minutes.

In a large bowl, whisk together the eggs and yolks. Continue whisking and slowly pour the cooled cream mixture into the egg mixture. Add the marmalade and whisk to combine. Pour the custard through a fine sieve into a clean bowl, preferably one with a spout, to remove any bits of orange or egg. Pour the custard over the caramel in the ramekins (fill to about $1/8$ inch from the top), place them in a water bath (see page 6), and cover the whole pan with aluminum foil.

Put the pan in the oven, set the oven temperature to 325° F, and bake for 35 minutes, or until the custards are set (a knife inserted in the center should come out clean). The center will still look a little loose, but the custards will continue cooking after they are removed from the oven. Carefully remove the baking dish from the oven, lift out the ramekins using tongs, and let them rest for at least 20 minutes. Move them to the refrigerator and chill for at least 4 hours, preferably overnight.

When ready to serve, invert a ramekin onto each serving plate and gently tap the bottom with a butter knife to help unmold.

Adorno Especial

Salsa de Arandano y Macadamia Polvorones

The combination of orange and cranberry feels like fall. The *polvorones*—very flaky unsalted butter cookies popular in Mexico—are a crisp complement. But if you're short on time, bakery-bought or packaged thin unsalted butter cookies of your choice will work as well.

Cranberry Sauce 1 recipe (page 252)
Macadamia Nut Cookies
1 recipe (page 60)

When ready to serve, decorate each plate with sauce, then unmold the flans over the sauce. Garnish with a cookie or two.

RICE PUDDING
Arroz con Leche

In Latin America rice pudding is an extremely common, everyday kind of dessert. In Mexico, it is served as a hot drink or *atole* (see page 142) for breakfast or lunch accompanied by sweet bread, much as Americans might enjoy a latte with a muffin or scone. In Colombia, it is served in its pudding form sprinkled with chunks of *panela*, a hard-candy-like brown sugar (see page 13). Alternatively, it is topped with crumbled *bocadillo veleño*, a guava or *dulce de leche* nougat candy. The simple, classic version here doesn't need much adornment, except perhaps a sprinkle of cinnamon or nutmeg before serving. Valencia rice, the one often used for paella, works best, but any medium- or short-grain variety will do.

SERVES 12

2 cups Valencia rice	400 GRAMS
8 cinnamon sticks	
2 cups heavy cream	480 MILLILITERS
2 cups whole milk	480 MILLILITERS
1 (12-ounce) can evaporated milk	360 MILLILITERS
½ cup granulated sugar	100 GRAMS
1 (14-ounce) can sweetened condensed milk	420 MILLILITERS
Ground cinnamon or freshly grated nutmeg	

In a medium saucepan over high heat, bring the rice, cinnamon sticks, and 3 cups (720 milliliters) water to a boil. Reduce the heat and cook, uncovered, until the water is almost gone, about 8 minutes.

Stir in the cream, whole milk, evaporated milk, and sugar and bring back to a boil. Lower the heat and simmer, stirring occasionally to keep the rice from sticking, for about 20 minutes, until thick but still creamy. Stir in the sweetened condensed milk and simmer for 1 minute.

Remove from the heat, remove the cinnamon sticks, and let rest for 10 minutes. Spoon into serving bowls or parfait glasses, sprinkle with cinnamon or nutmeg, and serve warm. (Alternatively, chill it and serve cold; it will keep, covered and refrigerated, for a day or two. Longer than that, and the pudding will become dry and lose its creamy texture.)

LEMONGRASS AND VANILLA BEAN-SCENTED RICE PUDDING

Arroz con Leche con Infusion de Yerva Luisa y Vaina de Vainilla

I n Mexico, lemongrass is known as *te de limon* (lemon tea) and in Cuba as *caña santa* (miracle cane). In other parts of Latin America, it is called *yerva luisa*. My first experiences with lemongrass were in fact limited to tea. My mother would purchase it in huge stalks at the market, cut it down, boil it with water, and serve it to us as a warm drink at bedtime. We would enjoy any leftovers as iced tea the next day.

SERVES 12

¼ cup finely diced dried apricots	45 GRAMS
¼ cup finely diced candied pineapple	45 GRAMS
Grated zest of 1 lemon	
¼ cup dark rum	60 MILLILITERS
2 stalks lemongrass	
1 vanilla bean, halved lengthwise, seeds scraped out and reserved (or 1½ tablespoons vanilla extract)	
2 cups jasmine rice	400 GRAMS
2 cups heavy cream	480 MILLILITERS
3 cups whole milk	720 MILLILITERS
1½ cups granulated sugar	300 GRAMS
1 (14-ounce) can sweetened condensed milk	420 MILLILITERS

⊚ In a small bowl, combine the apricots, pineapple, lemon zest, and rum.

⊚ Cut the lemongrass stalks into manageable pieces. Split each piece in half lengthwise and pound with the flat side of a knife on a cutting board to help them release their flavor. In a medium saucepan over high heat, bring 5 cups (1.25 liters) water, the vanilla bean (including the seeds) or extract, and lemongrass to a boil. Reduce the heat and simmer for 10 minutes. Pour the liquid through a fine sieve into another medium saucepan (or into a bowl, and then transfer back into the saucepan) to remove the vanilla bean and lemongrass. Stir in the rice and simmer, uncovered, until the water is almost gone, about 10 minutes. Stir in the milk, cream, fruit and rum mixture, and sugar and bring back to a boil. Lower the heat and simmer, stirring periodically to keep the rice from sticking, for about 20 minutes, until thick but still creamy. Stir in the sweetened condensed milk and simmer for 1 minute.

⊚ Remove from the heat and let rest for 10 minutes. Spoon into serving bowls or parfait glasses and serve warm. (Alternatively, chill it and serve cold; it will keep, covered and refrigerated, for a day or two. Longer than that, and the pudding will become dry and lose its creamy texture.)

COCONUT RICE PUDDING

Arroz con Leche de Coco

This rice pudding, with grated coconut, is popular on the island of Puerto Rico, and it's one of my favorites. The Valencia rice plus the oil released from the freshly grated coconut really does make a difference in the taste of the pudding, but another rice and a bag of sweetened shredded coconut from the grocery will work. If you use bagged sweetened shredded coconut, reduce the sugar by ½ cup.

SERVES 12

2	cups Valencia rice	400 GRAMS
½	teaspoon salt	
2	cups heavy cream	480 MILLILITERS
3	cups whole milk	720 MILLILITERS
1½	cups granulated sugar	300 GRAMS
1	(14-ounce) can sweetened condensed milk	420 MILLILITERS
2	cups grated fresh coconut (see page 98)	150 GRAMS

In a medium saucepan over high heat, bring the rice, salt, and 4 cups (950 milliliters) water to a boil. Reduce the heat and cook, uncovered, until the water is almost gone, about 10 minutes. Stir in the cream, whole milk, and sugar and bring back to a boil. Lower the heat and simmer, stirring occasionally to keep the rice from sticking, for about 20 minutes, until still slightly loose and creamy and a line forms briefly when you pull a wooden spoon through the pudding across the bottom of the pan. Stir in the sweetened condensed milk and grated coconut, reserving a bit of the coconut for garnish, and simmer for 1 minute. Remove from the heat and let the pudding rest for 10 minutes. Spoon into serving bowls or parfait glasses, sprinkle with the reserved coconut, and serve warm. (Alternatively, chill it and serve cold; it will keep, covered and refrigerated, for a day or two. Longer than that, and the pudding will become dry and lose its creamy texture.)

Adorno Especial

Espuma de Lima y Aceitede Cilantro

Lemon Foam 1 recipe (page 245)
Cilantro Oil 1 recipe (page 256)

Remove the foam canister from the refrigerator, shake it vigorously, turn it upside down, and squeeze some of the foam onto the top of the rice pudding. Drizzle the oil around the foam and serve immediately.

27

TRADITIONAL FLAN *(Page 4)*
with Pineapple Confit (page 190)
and Goat Cheese

**MANGO CATALONIAN
CRÈME BRÛLÉE** *(page 46)*

GOAT'S MILK CARAMEL FLAN *(page 14)*
*with Caramelized Nectarines (page 186)
and Sugar-Coated Nuts (page 251)*

PUDDINGS

Clockwise from top left:

COCONUT TAPIOCA PUDDING
(page 35)
with Oatmeal Guava Bars (page 57)

MEXICAN-STYLE MAMEY CUSTARD
(page 42)
with Amaretto Cream (page 256)

QUINOA PUDDING
(page 44)
with Spiced Ice Cream (page 206)

BANANA THREE MILKS CAKE *(page 84)*
with Italian Meringue (page 236)
and Prunes in Passion Fruit Syrup (page 188)

PURPLE CORN PUDDING *(page 40)*
with Whipped Cream (page 235)

PINEAPPLE UPSIDE-DOWN CAKE *(page 88)*
with Cheese Ice Cream (page 200)

COCONUT TAPIOCA PUDDING

Puding de Tapioca con Leche de Coco

Tapioca pearls are made from the root of the yucca or cassava plant, a plant native to South America. I've been eating tapioca pudding since I was a small child in Mexico and to this day it remains one of my very favorites, especially with the addition of coconut milk.

You might have come across tapioca pearls while drinking up the latest craze—bubble tea. The pearls work in this pudding for the same reason they work in bubble teas: They provide an addictive texture and chew. You can find tapioca in the baking section of most supermarkets (near gelatin and pudding mixes), but be careful to buy tapioca "pearls" (the larger pearls are best), not instant tapioca. I like the Bascom brand.

This pudding is delicious and easy to make. You can eat it after a casual weeknight dinner at home, or you can take it out to a dinner party. Try serving it in a hollowed-out coconut (Tahitian coconuts work best with their thin shell and tender meat), or simply in glass bowls.

SERVES 8 TO 10

1 cup large or medium tapioca pearls (about 1 7-ounce package)	200 GRAMS
2 cups whole milk	480 MILLILITERS
1 (6-ounce) can evaporated milk	180 MILLILITERS
3 cups unsweetened coconut milk	720 MILLILITERS
1½ cups granulated sugar	300 GRAMS
½ teaspoon salt	

◉ In a large mixing bowl, cover the tapioca pearls with cold water and soak for at least 8 hours or overnight, until the pearls look slightly translucent and glossy.

◉ In a large saucepan, combine the milk, evaporated milk, coconut milk, sugar, and salt. Drain the tapioca very well in a sieve, then stir it into the milk mixture. Bring to a boil over medium heat. Reduce the heat and simmer, stirring constantly, until the tapioca pearls become clear and glossy, about 10 minutes.

◉ Pour the pudding into a large nonreactive bowl, cover with plastic wrap, and refrigerate for at least 2 hours or up to 5 days. Serve cold.

Adorno Especial

Barritas de Avena con Guayaba

Oatmeal Guava Bars 1 recipe (page 57)

Spoon the pudding into bowls or parfait glasses and top each portion with a cookie.

CATALONIAN CRÈME BRÛLÉE
Crema Catalana

Traditional *crema catalana* is often flavored with orange zest and vanilla bean, but I prefer this combination of vanilla and cinnamon. Just about any type of fresh fruit—especially fresh berries—is a nice garnish. If you don't have a bakers' torch, you can put the sugar-coated custards under a preheated broiler for about 2 minutes. You want to caramelize the sugar while still keeping the custards cool.

SERVES 8

2½ **cups heavy cream**	600 MILLILITERS
1½ **cups whole milk**	360 MILLILITERS
1½ **cups granulated sugar**	300 GRAMS
2 **vanilla beans, halved lengthwise, seeds scraped out and reserved (or 3 tablespoons vanilla extract)**	
1 **cinnamon stick**	
11 **egg yolks**	

Preheat the oven to 350° F.

In a medium saucepan over high heat, bring the cream, milk, ¾ cup (150 grams) sugar, halved vanilla beans (including seeds) and cinnamon to a boil, whisking constantly. Remove from the heat and chill in the refrigerator until completely cool, about 30 minutes.

In a large bowl, beat the egg yolks on high speed with an electric mixer for about 15 minutes, until pale and thick. When you lift the beater out of the batter, it should flow from it in a smooth, even ribbon. Turn the mixer down to low, and slowly pour the cooled cream mixture into the egg yolks to combine.

Pour the custard through a fine sieve into a clean bowl, preferably one with a spout, to remove any bits of cooked egg. Pour the custard into 8 (6-ounce) ramekins (fill to about ¼ inch from the top) and place them in a water bath (see page 6). Cover the whole pan with aluminum foil.

Put the pan in the oven, set the oven temperature to 300° F, and bake for 30 minutes, or until the custards are set (a knife inserted in the center should come out clean). The center will still look a little loose, but the custards will continue cooking after they are removed from the oven. Carefully remove the baking dish from the oven, lift out the ramekins using tongs, and let them rest for at least 20 minutes. Move them to the refrigerator and chill for at least 4 hours, preferably overnight.

Just before serving, sprinkle the remaining ¾ cup (170 grams) sugar evenly over the custards to cover the entire surface. Use a bakers' torch to caramelize the sugar until crisp and golden brown. Serve immediately.

Crema Catalana

CREMA CATALANA, A CHILLED, STIRRED CUSTARD NAMED AFTER ITS NATIVE Catalonia, is Spain's answer to crème brûlée. It is often eaten on St. Joseph's Day, the Spanish equivalent of Father's Day, and therefore also known as *crema de Sant Josep*, or St. Joseph's cream. In Spain, a round, patterned flat iron is used to caramelize the sugar on top of the custard into an intricate design, but using a small bakers' torch at home will still result in a beautifully golden crust. Where flan is an unmolded custard topped with soft caramel, *crema catalana* is served in its baking vessel and has a crisp caramel top.

You can easily find small bakers' torches for sale online (try jbprince.com or surlatable.com) or at most kitchen supply stores. Any local hardware store will sell the small butane refills that produce the flame. If you've never used one of these torches before, you'll get a kick out of trying one at home, watching the short, stiff flame turn the white sugar granules into a hard caramel coating. The flat iron (sometimes called a crème brûlée salamander) is a bit harder to track down—a trip to kitchenconservatory.com is quicker and more economical than a trip to Mexico or South America, where this tool is more readily available.

KAFFIR LIME-SCENTED CATALONIAN CRÈME BRÛLÉE

Crema Catalana con Infusion de Hojas de Limón

Kaffir lime leaves (often used in southeast Asian cooking) have an intoxicating floral citrus aroma. They can be quite strong, but they are also one of those ingredients that you can easily fall in love with. I almost always have them in my kitchen to use in ceviches, soups, and even iced tea. I recommend fresh leaves for this recipe, but you can also use dried if that's what you can easily find. I love topping this dessert with a few shavings or chunks of Mexican chocolate. The combination might seem out of the ordinary, but think how perfectly chocolate goes with citrus—say, in a chocolate-covered candied citrus rind. The richness of the chocolate, the texture of the shavings against the silkiness of the cream, and the pop of citrus from the kaffir lime just work.

If you love the flavor of this *crema catalana*, how about trying it in ice cream? Once the custard is cooked, you can puree it in a blender and then freeze it in an ice cream maker. I discovered this by accident when trying to be creative with some leftovers and the result was surprisingly delicious. Baking the custard and then pureeing it (rather than just cooking the custard on the stovetop), the result is an ice cream with a stronger caramel flavor and a creamier texture. Now I make this ice cream on purpose and serve it over slices of pistachio cake (see page 96) drizzled with Dulce de Leche (see page 52).

SERVES 6

2½ cups heavy cream	600 MILLILITERS
1½ cups whole milk	360 MILLILITERS
1½ cups granulated sugar	300 GRAMS
3 medium fresh kaffir lime leaves	
11 egg yolks	
Mexican chocolate (see page 141)	

⊚ Preheat the oven to 350° F.

⊚ In a medium saucepan over high heat, bring the cream, milk, ¾ cup (150 grams) sugar, and lime leaves to a boil, whisking constantly, being careful not to burn. Remove from the heat and chill in the refrigerator until completely cool, about 30 minutes. Discard the lime leaves.

⊚ In a large bowl, beat the egg yolks on high speed with an electric mixer for about 15 minutes, until pale and thick—the ribbon stage:

When you lift the beater out of the batter, it should flow from it in a smooth, even ribbon. Turn the mixer down to low and slowly pour the cooled cream mixture into the egg yolks to combine.

◎ Pour the custard through a fine sieve into a clean bowl, preferably one with a spout, to remove any bits of cooked egg. Pour the custard into 6 (6-ounce) ramekins (fill to about ¼ inch from the top) and place them in a water bath (see page 6). Cover the whole pan with aluminum foil.

◎ Put the pan in the oven, set the oven temperature to 300° F, and bake for 30 minutes, or until the custards are set (a knife inserted in the center should come out clean). The center will still look a little loose, but the custards will continue cooking after they are removed from the oven. Carefully remove the baking dish from the oven, lift out the ramekins using tongs, and let them rest for at least 20 minutes. Move them to the refrigerator and chill for at least 4 hours, preferably overnight.

◎ Just before serving, pour the remaining sugar over the custards to cover the entire surface. Use a bakers' torch to caramelize the sugar until crisp and golden brown. Top with shavings or small chunks of the Mexican chocolate.

PURPLE CORN PUDDING
Mazamorra Morada

Mazamorra morada is one of the classic Peruvian desserts that emerged during colonial times. It combines two pre-Hispanic ingredients, purple corn and sweet potato starch, and is as much a dessert staple to Peruvians as Natilla (page 42) is to Mexicans. My Peruvian friend Jorge Adriazola taught me this recipe. Before then, all I had made with purple corn in Mexico was tortillas and *chicha morada* (see page 20), an unfermented corn-based beverage.

The purple corn doesn't impart any unique flavor to Mazamorra Morada, but it does add antioxidants, starch, and the pudding's dramatic deep purple, almost black color. The flavor of the pudding is more about the fruit and spices in the recipe rather than the corn itself. You may substitute cornstarch for the sweet potato starch, but the sweet potato starch gives the pudding a little added sweetness and a shinier texture.

I soak the dried fruit in Pisco, a distilled grape liquor named after a coastal Peruvian town and an ingredient in the frothy Pisco sour cocktail. Try to buy organic pineapple, since this recipe includes the peel.

SERVES 12

6 to 8 cinnamon sticks

1 vanilla bean, halved lengthwise, seeds scraped out and reserved (or 1 to 2 tablespoons vanilla extract)

3 whole cloves

Grated zest of 1 orange

3 whole allspice berries, crushed (or 1 pinch ground allspice)

1 pound dried ears purple corn, cut into 2-inch chunks   455 GRAMS

Peel of 1 pineapple, roughly chopped

1 cup peeled, cored, and diced pineapple   170 GRAMS

1 green apple, peeled, cored, and diced

1 pear, peeled, cored, and diced

Juice of 2 limes

¼ cup golden raisins   85 GRAMS

¼ cup diced dried apricots   45 GRAMS

¼ cup dried cherries   45 GRAMS

1 cup Pisco   240 MILLILITERS

1 cup granulated sugar   200 GRAMS

2¼ cups packed light brown sugar   455 GRAMS

1 cup sweet potato starch   115 GRAMS

Ground cinnamon

In a medium saucepan over high heat, combine 4 quarts (4 liters) water, the cinnamon sticks, vanilla bean (including seeds) or extract, cloves, orange zest, allspice, corn, and pineapple peel and bring to a boil. Reduce the heat to a simmer and continue cooking for 45 minutes, or until the water absorbs all the flavors and the liquid turns a deep purple color.

While the corn mixture is simmering, toss the pineapple, apple, and pear with the lime juice in a small nonreactive bowl and set aside. In another small nonreactive bowl, combine the raisins, apricots, and cherries with the Pisco and set aside.

Pour the corn mixture into a sieve set over a clean large saucepan and discard the solids. Drain the dried fruit, reserving the Pisco. Add the dried fruit, the fresh fruit and lime juice mixture, and the sugars to the corn liquid and simmer for 20 minutes, or until the fruit is tender.

Mix the reserved Pisco with the sweet potato starch and add it very slowly to the corn liquid. Cook, stirring constantly for 8 to 10 minutes with a wooden spoon, until the starch is cooked and the mixture is thickened. It should remain a deep purple color and take on a shiny consistency. Remove from the heat and let cool for 20 minutes. If you want to serve the pudding chilled, cover and refrigerate for 1 to 2 hours. The pudding will keep in the refrigerator for 2 days.

Serve the pudding in parfait glasses topped with whipped cream.

Adorno Especial

Arroz con Leche Espuma

My Mazamorra Morada recipe stays true to its classic form, but this rice pudding foam gives it a twist and is a nice creamy antidote to the fruity pudding. You can also make this foam into a simpler rice pudding whipped cream.

Rice Pudding Foam 1 recipe (page 245)

When spooning the pudding into parfait glasses, leave room on top for the foam. Remove the foam canister from the refrigerator, shake it vigorously, turn it upside down, and squeeze some of the foam onto the top of the pudding. Sprinkle with cinnamon.

MEXICAN-STYLE MAMEY CUSTARD

Natilla de Mamey

My mom would often treat us kids to a pint of *natilla* while we were grocery shopping with her at the open markets, or *mercados*, in Mexico. But far better was the version my mother made at home. We would eat it warm, with cinnamon sprinkled on top. Some people like to mix *dulce de leche* (page 52) or grated orange zest into their *natilla*, or as in Colombia, top it with grated *panela* (see page 13).

SERVES 10

3 cups mamey pulp, pureed in a blender until smooth

8 egg yolks

1 whole egg

1¼ cups cornstarch — 165 GRAMS

5 cups whole milk — 1200 MILLILITERS

1½ cups chopped *panela* (see page 13) (or packed brown sugar) — 300 GRAMS

1 pinch salt

1 tablespoon vanilla extract

⅓ cup butter (5⅓ tablespoons) — 75 GRAMS

⊙ In a large bowl, combine the mamey, egg yolks, egg, cornstarch, and 1 cup (250 milliliters) of the milk.

⊙ In a medium saucepan over high heat, bring the remaining 4 cups (950 milliliters) milk, the *panela*, salt, vanilla extract, and butter to a boil, whisking constantly, being careful not to burn.

⊙ Temper the mamey mixture by very slowly mixing in the hot milk mixture. Once combined, pour everything back into the saucepan and bring back to a boil over high heat, whisking or stirring with a wooden spoon constantly to prevent the custard from sticking. Lower the heat and, still whisking or stirring, simmer for about 5 minutes to cook the cornstarch and thicken the custard. Remove from the heat and let rest for 10 minutes. Spoon into serving bowls or parfait glasses and serve warm. The pudding will keep in the refrigerator for 2 days.

Crema de Amaretto

When I lived in Mexico, I would put flan custard into a glass and top it with eggnog. The combination was delicious because the flavors and textures of each element complemented the other so well; it was kind of like pouring cold cream or milk over rice pudding. The addition of creamy amaretto sauce to *natilla* is inspired by that memory of the little treat I created.

Cold Amaretto Cream 1 recipe (page 256)

When spooning the *natilla* into bowls or parfait glasses, leave room on top. Cover each portion with a generous layer of the cream. Alternatively, you can serve the *natilla* to a group in a larger glass bowl or trifle dish. Spoon it in unevenly and top with the cream. The contrasting colors make for a nice presentation.

Mamey

THE MAMEY, OR MAMEY SAPOTE, IS ACTUALLY NATIVE TO SOUTHERN MEXICO, but is now grown in Central America and even Florida and is eaten all across Latin America. At first glance, it might pass for an oval-shaped coconut, its skin being light brownish with a sandy texture (see page 214 for a photo). But when you feel it, it's more like a rough kiwi or peach, with a slight give when ripe. The fruit can grow to up to 10 inches long, and its glorious deep orange flesh has an almost savory flavor with just a touch of sweetness—think sweet potato with a touch of cherry—and an amazing silky texture not unlike that of an avocado. Putting it into a custard takes its flavor and texture to a whole new level.

Mamey is also very healthful. My grandmother told me she fed all her children mamey at least once a month because it's so good for digestion. Some believe that the flesh itself can actually heal a wound and help prevent infection.

When in season, we would always buy mamey at the *mercados*—some that were already soft and ready to eat and some that would ripen later in the week so we would have fresh mamey all week long. When I cook with mamey, I prefer to use fresh fruit, but frozen puree will work as well.

QUINOA PUDDING
Puding de Quinoa

This dessert is similar to rice pudding, but with slightly more texture and nuttiness from the quinoa. Plus, because of quinoa's incredible nutritious value, you can feel good about eating this pudding even with its other decadent ingredients. Served in parfait glasses and garnished with cinnamon sticks, this is a straightforward, easy dessert for entertaining. You can make it 2 days ahead.

SERVES 8

2 cups white quinoa	400 GRAMS
1 cup evaporated milk	240 MILLILITERS
1 cup whole milk	240 MILLILITERS
1 (14-ounce) can sweetened condensed milk	420 MILLILITERS
¼ cup granulated sugar	50 GRAMS
(if serving cold) 2 cups heavy cream	480 MILLILITERS
Ground cinnamon	

In a medium saucepan over high heat, bring the quinoa and 3 cups (720 milliliters) water to a boil. Reduce the heat and simmer, uncovered, 15 to 20 minutes, until most of the water is gone. You will see that the skin of the grain will loosen, allowing it to puff up.

With a wooden spoon, stir the evaporated milk, milk, sweetened condensed milk, and sugar into the quinoa and continue simmering for 8 to 10 minutes, until the pudding is thickened to a honey consistency. You should be able to see a line form briefly across the bottom of the pan when you pull the spoon through the pudding. If you prefer to serve this pudding warm, stop here and skip adding the whipped cream. Otherwise, remove from the heat and refrigerate until cool, 1 to 2 hours.

In the bowl of an electric mixer fitted with a whisk attachment, whip the cream until it forms soft peaks. Gently fold the whipped cream into the quinoa pudding. Transfer the pudding to a covered container and chill in the refrigerator for at least 4 hours, preferably overnight. Spoon into parfait glasses, sprinkle with cinnamon, and serve.

If you choose to serve the Quinoa Pudding warm, the ice cream will melt a bit, creating a wonderful sauce. For a quick alternative, try a store-bought cinnamon or chai-flavored ice cream.

Spiced Ice Cream 1 recipe (page 206)
8 cinnamon sticks

When spooning the pudding into bowls or parfait glasses, leave room. Top each portion with a scoop of the ice cream and a cinnamon stick.

Quinoa

THE FIRST TIME I EVER TRIED QUINOA WAS IN A SAVORY SIDE DISH. I HAD never had it in Mexico, but I had had amaranth, which I learned later is a close relative, both grains coming from a leafy plant in the spinach family. You can actually eat the leaves as well, much as you would chard or spinach.

Since quinoa comes from a plant, not a grass, it is technically a seed rather than a grain, its seedheads growing in large clusters on the ends of the plant's stalk. But regardless, today it still holds its moniker "the mother grain" because of its incredible nutritional value. (The Incas more correctly called it "the mother seed," the source of all life.) It is extremely hardy and thrives in almost every climate and soil condition throughout Latin America and elsewhere. It passes on its strength through complete protein, calcium, and natural fat. It is also gluten free, so a wonderful starch alternative for those on gluten-free diets.

These days, it's easy to find quinoa in most grocery stores. It looks like couscous and can vary in color from creamy tan to reddish brown, depending on the variety and processing methods. It tastes a bit like a nutty couscous, and also somewhat like wild rice. In some markets, you may even find it popped, like miniature popcorn, to sprinkle on foods for texture or to eat as a breakfast cereal.

Quinoa brings a surprising twist to Chocolate Banana Bread Pudding with Quinoa (page 138) and Sour Cream Ice Cream (page 203).

MANGO CATALONIAN CRÈME BRÛLÉE
Crema Catalana de Mango

This variation of *crema catalana* is a great summer dessert—it's like eating a sweet, fresh mango bathed in a crisp sugar coating. The rich mango flavor is delicious unadulterated, but if you'd like a creative garnish, try slivers of crystallized ginger and few fresh berries.

SERVES 8

2 cups fresh mango puree from about 3 large mangoes (see page 185)	480 MILLILITERS
1½ cups granulated sugar	300 GRAMS
1 cup heavy cream	240 MILLILITERS
¾ cup whole milk	180 MILLILITERS
11 egg yolks	

⊚ Preheat the oven to 350° F.

⊚ In a medium saucepan over high heat, combine the mango puree and ¾ cup (150 grams) sugar and bring to a boil. Lower the heat and simmer for about 40 minutes, or until reduced by half. The result will be a thicker mango puree. Remove from the heat and let cool.

⊚ In a clean medium saucepan over high heat, bring the cream and milk to a boil, whisking constantly, being careful not to burn. Remove from the heat and chill in the refrigerator until completely cool, about 30 minutes.

⊚ In a large bowl, beat the egg yolks on high speed with an electric mixer for about 15 minutes, until pale and thick. When you lift the beater out of the batter, it should flow from it in a smooth, even ribbon. Turn the mixer down to low, and slowly pour the cooled cream mixture into the egg yolks to combine.

⊚ Add the mango mixture and stir by hand with a metal whisk until incorporated. Pour the custard through a fine sieve into a clean bowl, preferably one with a spout, to remove any bits of cooked egg. Pour the custard into 8 (6-ounce) ramekins (fill to about ¼ inch from the top) and place them in a water bath (see page 6). Cover the whole pan with aluminum foil.

⊚ Put the pan in the oven, set the oven temperature to 300° F, and bake for 30 minutes, or until the custards are set (a knife inserted in the center should come out clean). The center will still look a little loose, but the custards will continue cooking after they are removed from the oven. Carefully remove the baking dish from the oven, lift out the ramekins using tongs, and let them rest for at least 20 minutes. Move them to the refrigerator and chill for at least 4 hours, preferably overnight.

⊚ Just before serving, pour the remaining ¾ cup (150 grams) sugar over the custards to cover the entire surface. Use a bakers' torch to caramelize the sugar until crisp and golden brown. Serve immediately.

FRIED CUSTARD
Leche Frita

Leche frita, or fried milk, is a homestyle Latin dessert made from pieces of chilled custard that are breaded and fried to a golden brown. As flavoring, you can use whatever you like: lemon or lime zest, cinnamon, or nutmeg. You can cut the chilled custard into squares or any shape you want with a cookie cutter. Just make sure the pieces are no bigger than 3 inches in diameter or they will be too difficult to fry evenly. Try serving this with Lucuma Ice Cream (page 98).

SERVES 8 (ABOUT 5 PIECES PER PERSON)

5½ cups whole milk	1320 MILLILITERS
Grated zest of 1 orange	
2 cups granulated sugar	400 GRAMS
9 egg yolks	
1½ cups cornstarch	195 GRAMS
½ cup (1 stick) unsalted butter	115 GRAMS
2 cups canola oil	480 MILLILITERS
3 cups all-purpose flour	430 GRAMS
5 whole eggs, beaten	
3 cups plain bread crumbs	455 GRAMS
1 cup granulated sugar	200 GRAMS
1 tablespoon ground cinnamon	

◎ Grease an 11-by-17-inch half sheet pan. In a medium saucepan over medium heat, combine 5 cups (1200 milliliters) of the milk, the orange zest, and sugar and bring to a boil.

◎ In a medium mixing bowl, whisk together the remaining ½ cup (120 milliliters) milk, the egg yolks, and cornstarch. Continue whisking while pouring a small amount of the hot milk mixture into the yolk mixture. This will temper the yolks and keep them from curdling. While whisking the hot cream mixture in the saucepan, gradually add the yolk mixture. Bring back to a boil and stir with a wooden spoon over medium-low heat until the custard sticks to the spoon and has a puddinglike consistency, about 8 minutes. Remove from the heat and stir in the butter until melted. Pour the custard into the prepared pan and spread evenly. Refrigerate until firm, at least 8 hours.

◎ In a large, deep saucepan, heat the oil to 350° F. In four separate small bowls, place the flour, the beaten eggs, the bread crumbs, and the sugar and cinnamon. Using a pastry wheel or a knife, cut the custard into 2½-by-1½-inch pieces. Coat each custard piece first with flour, letting the excess fall through your fingers, then the egg, then the bread crumbs, placing the coated pieces on a clean sheet pan until ready to fry.

◎ Fry the custard squares a few at a time for about 2 minutes per side, or until golden brown and crisp. Remove from the oil with a slotted spoon, drain briefly on paper towels, and dust with the cinnamon sugar. Serve immediately.

2

COOKIES AND SWEET BREADS

Galletas y Panes

In This Chapter

DULCE DE LECHE–FILLED BUTTER COOKIE SANDWICHES
Alfajores de Maizena

Alfajores have a Middle Eastern pedigree, but are extremely common all across Latin America. Although ingredients and fillings may vary, the form is always the same: two or three round, cake-like cookies sandwiching a sweet filling, such as jam or *dulce de leche*. The Colombian version, called *obleas con arequipe*, is made with larger, thinner, crispier wafers similar to a flattened waffle cone or an Italian pizzelle cookie. You'll even find *alfajores* bathed in melted dark or white chocolate. You can try this decadent version using chocolate ganache (see page 254).

I recommend dusting the *alfajores* with powdered sugar or rolling the edges in chopped toasted pecans, but you can also dust them with cocoa powder or roll the edges in toasted coconut (see page 101). They are very pretty cookies, so great as gifts or for entertaining.

MAKES 2 DOZEN COOKIES

1 cup (2 sticks) butter, softened	25 GRAMS
1⅓ cups granulated sugar	265 GRAMS
3 whole eggs	
1 egg yolk	
1 tablespoon vanilla extract	
2 cups all-purpose flour	285 GRAMS
2½ cups cornstarch	325 GRAMS
1½ teaspoons baking powder	
1 recipe Dulce de Leche (page 52)	
Confectioners' sugar or chopped toasted pecans	

◎ In a large bowl, cream together the butter and sugar. Add the eggs and egg yolk one by one, beating thoroughly after each addition, then add the vanilla extract. In a small bowl, whisk together the flour, cornstarch, and baking powder. Add the flour mixture to the butter and sugar mixture and stir with a wooden spoon until a smooth dough forms. Place the dough on a lightly floured surface, divide it in half, and wrap each half in waxed paper or plastic wrap. Chill in the refrigerator for at least 2 hours, preferably overnight. The dough can be made several days ahead and even frozen for up to 2 months.

◎ Preheat the oven to 350° F.

◎ Take one piece of dough out the refrigerator and place it on a lightly floured surface. With a rolling pin, roll out the dough to ⅛ inch thick, rotating the dough as you go and adding a light sprinkling of flour on top and underneath to prevent it from sticking to the rolling pin or work surface.

◎ Cut 2½-inch rounds with a cookie cutter and place them 1 inch apart on a nonstick baking sheet or on a sheet that is lined with parchment paper. Bake the cookies for about 10 minutes, or until they are slightly golden around the edges. Cool on wire racks. Repeat with the second piece of dough. The cookies will keep in an airtight container in a cool, dry place for about a week.

⑨ Once the cookies are cool, spread about 2 tablespoons of the Dulce de Leche on a single cookie and top it with a second cookie like a sandwich. Repeat with all the cookies. Dust with confectioners' sugar, or roll the edges of each cookie sandwich in chopped toasted pecans so they stick to the Dulce de Leche.

Dulce de Leche

WHEN THE ICE CREAM CONGLOMERATES START USING A FLAVOR IN THEIR line-up, you know it has hit mass-market popularity. And so it is in the United States with *dulce de leche*, or sweet milk. Of course, in Latin American countries, *dulce de leche* has long been a popular dessert ingredient. It takes the classic idea of caramelized sugar and adds the richness of milk, creating a thick, creamy delicacy that's downright addictive.

The first time I tried to make *dulce de leche* from scratch, it definitely wasn't perfect. I stirred it only occasionally rather than frequently and wound up with a big mess of burnt, crystallized sugar. The pot went into the garbage, and I started again. It really isn't hard; it just requires patience. You can be imaginative and add your own favorite flavorings: vanilla extract, rum, or citrus zest, for example.

Try it over ice cream, rolled between crêpes, or as a spread for waffles or even just toast to enjoy with your morning coffee. In Colombia, they make a giant sandwich cookie with *dulce de leche* spread between two crisp, tortilla-size *oblea*—similar to Italian pizzelles. You certainly won't have any trouble finding a use for *dulce de leche*—I promise. It will keep in the refrigerator for up to a month.

MAKES ABOUT 3½ CUPS

4 cups whole milk   950 MILLILITERS

4 cups granulated sugar   800 GRAMS

2 tablespoons vanilla extract

2 tablespoons light corn syrup

In a heavy, medium saucepan, combine the milk, sugar, vanilla extract, and corn syrup.

Bring the mixture to a gentle simmer and cook over very low heat, stirring frequently until slightly thickened and golden brown, about 2½ to 3 hours. The liquid will reduce to about 3½ cups. Cool overnight in the refrigerator. The *dulce de leche* can be made ahead of time and stored in the refrigerator for up to 1 month.

WALNUT COCONUT COOKIES

Galletitas de Nuez con Coco

Whenever I'm eating granola or trail mix, I find myself searching for the best bits: the nuts, coconut flakes, and chocolate chips. Pair these cookies with a bowl of home-made or store-bought chocolate ice cream and you'll have all three of these ingredients and great contrasting textures in every bite.

MAKES ABOUT 2 DOZEN COOKIES

1¼	cups (2½ sticks) butter, softened	280 GRAMS
¾	cup granulated sugar	150 GRAMS
2	egg yolks	
½	cup chopped walnuts	65 GRAMS
1½	cups all-purpose flour	210 GRAMS
½	cup unsweetened shredded coconut	40 GRAMS

◎ Preheat the oven to 350° F.

◎ In the bowl of an electric mixer fitted with the paddle attachment, cream together the butter and sugar until light and fluffy. Reduce the speed to low, add the egg yolks, and continue beating for 1 minute. Add the remaining ingredients and mix until combined.

◎ Drop tablespoons of the batter 3 inches apart onto a nonstick baking sheet or one lightly buttered or lined with parchment or a Silpat mat.

◎ Bake for 15 minutes, or until the cookies are golden brown and crisp. Let cool completely on the pan, then carefully remove the cookies with a small spatula and place them in an airtight container at room temperature until ready to use. They will keep in a cool, dry place for up to 1 week, or the dough can be frozen for up to 1 month. For easy future baking, consider pre-rolling the dough before freezing it, or shaping it into logs. Bring the dough to room temperature and cut shapes from the rolled dough with cookie cutters or cut logs into slices.

CRISP MERINGUES

Merengues Crujiente

These sweet, light meringues make the perfect contrasting textural garnish for Banana Three Milks Cake (page 84), but they're equally good simply crumbled over ice cream, or mixed with chocolate pieces or nuts and piped into "kiss shapes" before baking. Unlike more traditional meringues (*suspiros*), which are baked quickly to barely dry out the meringue, these are baked longer and completely cooked through to produce a nice crisp crunch. In humid weather, put them in an airtight container as soon as they are cool so they remain crisp.

MAKES ABOUT 3 DOZEN MERINGUES

6	(about 1½ cups) egg whites	360 MILLILITERS
1¾	cups granulated sugar	350 GRAMS
1½	cups confectioners' sugar	180 GRAMS
4½	tablespoons cake flour	

◉ Preheat the oven to 200° F.

◉ Soak the bowl and the whisk attachment of an electric mixer in warm water and dry thoroughly. This will ensure that the egg whites gain enough volume during beating. Put the egg whites and granulated sugar in the bowl and beat until stiff peaks form. Quickly and thoroughly, whisk in the confectioners' sugar and flour.

◉ To make meringue sticks, grease a baking sheet and dust it with flour, or line it with parchment paper. Transfer the meringue to a pastry bag with a ½-inch plain tip (no. 805, if you have a professional set) and pipe 3- to 4-inch strips of meringue onto the prepared baking sheet 1 inch apart. If you don't have a pastry bag, a plastic bag with the corner cut off (to create a ½-inch opening) will work just fine. (Alternatively, shape the meringues into round, cookielike shapes with the back of a spoon.)

◉ Bake for about 3 hours, or until the meringues are dry to the touch. Note that they will not change color. Let cool on the pan or on a rack. The meringues will keep in an airtight container in a cool, dry place 2 to 3 days.

CRISP COCONUT MERINGUES
Suspiros de Coco

I love the chewy texture of these meringues. Try them alongside Cherimoya Mousse (page 180) or dip them into Coffee Whipped Cream (page 235).

MAKES ABOUT 1 DOZEN MERINGUES

⅓ **cup sweetened shredded coconut**	30 GRAMS
⅓ **cup confectioners' sugar**	40 GRAMS
2 **tablespoons all-purpose flour**	
2 **egg whites**	
1 **pinch salt**	
4 **teaspoons granulated sugar**	
1 **lemon for grated zest**	

◎ Preheat the oven to 250° F.

◎ In a small bowl, combine the shredded coconut, confectioners' sugar, and flour. Set aside.

◎ In the bowl of an electric mixer fitted with a whisk attachment, beat the eggs whites and salt on high speed for 1 minute. Slowly add the granulated sugar and continue beating until stiff peaks form. With a rubber spatula, fold the dry ingredients and the lemon zest into the egg whites. Be careful not to overmix, as you will deflate the egg whites.

◎ On an ungreased nonstick baking sheet or one lined with parchment paper or a Silpat mat, place dollops of the meringue mixture 1 inch apart. With the help of a metal spatula or spoon, spread the dollops into circles about 2½ inches round by ¼ inch thick. (Alternatively, you can pipe the mixture into circles with a pastry bag or a plastic bag with the tip cut off. Create flatter disks or small mounds—whatever you prefer.)

◎ Bake for 35 minutes, or until the meringues are nice and crisp. Note that they will not change color very much; you are simply drying out the meringue. Let cool on the pan or on a rack. The meringues will keep in an airtight container in a cool, dry place 2 to 3 days.

CRISP CHOCOLATE MERINGUES

Suspiros de Chocolate

A great accompaniment to Lucuma Parfait (page 178) or just eaten out of hand.

MAKES ABOUT 1 DOZEN MERINGUES

⅓ cup confectioners' sugar	40 GRAMS
2 tablespoons all-purpose flour	
2 tablespoons unsweetened cocoa powder	
3 egg whites	
1 pinch salt	
¼ cup granulated sugar	50 GRAMS
1 tablespoon freshly squeezed lemon juice	
¼ cup halved or chopped cashews, toasted	30 GRAMS

◉ Preheat the oven to 250° F.

◉ In a small bowl, combine the confectioners' sugar, flour, and cocoa powder, and set aside.

◉ Follow the instructions for Suspiros de Coco (page 55), replacing the lemon zest with lemon juice, and dot the meringues with cashews before baking. Increase the baking time to 40 minutes.

◉ The meringues will keep in an airtight container in a cool, dry place 2 to 3 days.

OATMEAL GUAVA BARS
Barritas de Avena con Guayaba

You'll find the guava paste at most Latin American markets, or in the imported foods section of your local supermarket, but this oatmeal dough can be filled with any thicker fruit paste, marmalade, or jam—whatever fits your mood or complements the flavors of the other desserts on your table. Try filling these addictive bars with mango or passion fruit.

The crunch of the cookies works well to balance the creamy consistency and rich coconut flavor of my Coconut Tapioca Pudding (page 35). They are pretty cut into long, skinny bars. They are quick to make and hold up well in the freezer (tightly wrapped, they'll keep for up to 1 month)—a great treat to bring along as a last-minute host or hostess gift, to have around the house for a snack, or to toss into a lunch box.

MAKES 2 DOZEN BAR COOKIES

2 cups (4 sticks) butter, softened	455 GRAMS
2¾ cups packed dark brown sugar	625 GRAMS
3 cups rolled oats	285 GRAMS
3 cups all-purpose flour	430 GRAMS
1 tablespoon baking powder	
1 teaspoon salt	
2 cups guava paste	455 GRAMS

☉ Preheat the oven to 325° F.

☉ With an electric mixer on medium speed, cream the butter and sugar until light and fluffy, about 2 minutes. Reduce the speed to low and add the oats, flour, baking powder, and salt. Continue mixing until the dough pulls away from the sides of the bowl, but is still crumbly, about 5 minutes.

☉ Grease an 11-by-7-inch half sheet pan and dust with flour, or line the bottom with parchment paper. Press half of the dough firmly and evenly across the baking sheet. In a clean bowl with clean beaters, beat the guava paste on medium speed until light and smooth, about 3 minutes. (If you don't have a hand-held electric mixer or standing mixer, you can use a wooden spoon for this entire preparation; it will just take a little more muscle.)

☉ Spread the guava paste over the dough and, using your fingers to break up the remaining dough, dot the top of the cookies with the dough pieces. Bake for about 25 minutes, or until the top is golden brown. Let cool for at least 15 minutes, then cut into bars. The bars can be stored in an airtight container at room temperature for up to 2 days or in the freezer for up to 1 month.

NOUGAT CANDY
WITH ALMONDS AND CASHEWS

Turrón con Almendras y Semillas de Marañon

Often prepared around Christmastime, homemade *turrón* is a great treat for yourself and an even better gift for friends and family year round. Wrapped in confectioners' sugar-dusted waxed paper, the nougats will keep at room temperature for 2 weeks. Feel free to experiment and add anything from candied or dried fruits to chocolate chips to puffed rice.

MAKES ABOUT 4 DOZEN 2-BY-1-INCH PIECES

⅓ cup granulated sugar   65 GRAMS

1 cup honey   240 MILLILITERS

1 vanilla bean, halved lengthwise, seeds
    scraped out and reserved
    (or 1½ tablespoons vanilla extract)

1 egg white

1 pinch cream of tartar

1 cup toasted and
    coarsely chopped almonds   125 GRAMS

1 cup toasted and
    coarsely chopped cashews   125 GRAMS

About 2 cups confectioners'
    sugar   240 GRAMS

◉ In a small saucepan over medium heat, bring the granulated sugar, honey, and vanilla bean and seeds or extract to a boil. Continue cooking, without stirring, until the temperature on a candy thermometer reaches 248° F (the "soft ball" stage). If you don't have a candy thermometer, scoop a bit of the sugar mixture onto a spoon and submerge it in a bowl of ice water for a few seconds. Grab the sugar with your fingertips. You should be able to form it into a small, soft ball. Remove the vanilla bean.

◉ While the syrup is cooking, soak the bowl and the whisk attachment of an electric mixer in warm water and dry thoroughly. This will ensure that the egg whites gain enough volume during beating. Put the egg whites and cream of tartar in the bowl and beat until soft peaks form. Turn the mixer to high speed and slowly and carefully add the hot syrup to the egg white mixture. Continue beating at high speed until the meringue becomes nice and fluffy, 5 to 7 minutes, or until the bowl no longer feels hot to the touch. Fold in the nuts.

◉ Dust a work surface generously with confectioners' sugar. Pour the warm nougat on top and cover it with more confectioners' sugar. Knead it until it is fully coated with the sugar and no longer sticking to the surface or your hands, about 1 minute. Form the nougat into a large rectangle and, using a rolling pin dusted with more sugar, flatten it to ½ inch thick. Cut the nougat into pieces (I usually cut 2-by-1-inch rectangles), and transfer them to a container dusted with confectioners' sugar. Once the candy has cooled completely, cover the container and store in a cool, dry spot. The nougat will keep at room temperature for up to 2 weeks. For a nicer presentation, you can wrap the individual pieces in waxed paper or plastic wrap before storing.

Turrón

FOR CENTURIES NOW, *TURRÓN*—NOUGAT CANDY TYPICALLY MADE WITH egg whites, honey, sugar, and nuts—has been a traditional confection enjoyed in Spain, Italy (where it is known as *torrone)*, and across Latin America. The most common variation is in its texture—either hard and crunchy or soft and chewy. The traditional version in Mexico is of the softer variety and is made with a mix of peanuts and almonds, but these days you can find *turrón* made with different kinds of nuts (pistachios, cashews, and so on), candied or dried fruits, even chocolate. Feel free to play with my recipe for *turrón* and experiment.

When I was younger, *turrón* was one of my favorite sweets. On Sundays, when I would go to Mass with my family, the nuns would sell homemade *turrón* to raise money for the church. At the market, the nougat came packed five pieces to a box, each wrapped in waxed paper or plastic. At church, the candies were sold in small bags containing a mix of the different flavors: pecan, *cajeta, turrón,* and a pale-colored variety in which you could see all the pieces of nuts inside. Or you could get the nougat packed into a little handmade wooden box along with a spoon so you could eat it right away.

My favorite was the *cajeta* flavor studded with pecans. It was called Moreliana after the city of Morelia northwest of Mexico City, known as "the candy capital of Mexico." There candy-happy culture of Morelia explodes at the Mercado de Dulces, near the city's magnificent cathedral.

The last time I was in Mexico, I visited the markets of Tacubaya in Mexico City with my grandmother, who has since passed away. The nuns there still make *turrón* using traditional methods. Now, every time I enjoy these candies, I think of my grandmother.

ORANGE BUTTER COOKIES

Polvorones de Naranja

Walk into any Mexican bakery, and you will see mountains of *polvorones* in a variety of shapes and a rainbow of colors: white-vanilla, brown-chocolate, pink-strawberry, green-lime, yellow-lemon. You can use either butter or vegetable shortening to make them. I prefer butter for the superior flavor, but shortening will turn out a flakier cookie, similar to a good piecrust.

MAKES 10 COOKIES

¾ cup (1½ sticks) butter, softened	70 GRAMS
1 cup granulated sugar	200 GRAMS
1 tablespoon orange extract	
1 large orange, grated for zest	
1 egg	
1¾ cups all-purpose flour, sifted, plus more for dusting	245 GRAMS
2 tablespoons nonfat dry milk powder (or 1 tablespoon milk)	
¼ teaspoon baking soda	
1 teaspoon baking powder	

⊚ Preheat the oven to 325° F.

⊚ In the bowl of an electric mixer fitted with the paddle attachment, cream the butter and ¾ cup (150 grams) of the sugar on medium speed for about 8 minutes, until light and fluffy. Add the orange extract, orange zest, and egg and mix until incorporated. Add the flour, milk powder, baking soda, and baking powder and mix for 8 more minutes on medium speed, or until the dough is smooth.

⊚ Dust a work surface with flour. Place the dough on top and, using a rolling pin dusted with more flour, flatten to ½ inch thick. Line a baking sheet with parchment paper or use a nonstick baking sheet. Cut the dough into 2½-inch rounds with a cookie cutter and place them 1 inch apart on the baking sheet. Sprinkle the cookies with the remaining ¼ cup (50 grams) sugar and bake for 15 minutes, or until they are just slightly puffy in the center (they should not brown). Let cool. The cookies may be kept in an airtight container at room temperature for up to 3 days, or the dough may be frozen for up to 2 months.

Macadamia Nut Butter Cookies

Polvorones de Macadamia

⊚ Replace the orange extract with vanilla extract and omit the zest. Mix ¼ cup chopped macadamia nuts into the dough before rolling it out.

CHOCOLATE BUTTER COOKIES

Galletas de Mantequilla Sabor a Chocolate

Flakier and even butterier than *polvorones*, these cookies are almost more like rich chocolate pastry crust. If you want to unmold the Avocado Panna Cottas (page 176) on top of these cookies, use the ramekins you will bake the panna cottas in as a guide to cut the cookies, rather than a cookie cutter.

MAKES 10 COOKIES

¾	cup (1½ sticks) unsalted butter, softened	170 GRAMS
1	cup confectioners' sugar	120 GRAMS
1	tablespoon vanilla extract	
1	egg yolk	
1½	cups all-purpose flour, sifted, plus more for dusting	210 GRAMS
½	cup unsweetened cocoa powder	60 GRAMS

◎ Preheat the oven to 350° F.

◎ In the bowl of an electric mixer fitted with the paddle attachment, cream the butter and confectioners' sugar until light and fluffy. Add the vanilla extract and egg yolk and mix until incorporated. Add the flour and cocoa powder and mix on low speed until combined, about 5 minutes. Remove the dough from the bowl, flatten into a disk, wrap in waxed paper or plastic wrap, and refrigerate until cold, at least 30 minutes or overnight.

◎ Dust a work surface with flour. Place the dough on top and, using a rolling pin dusted with more flour, flatten to ¼ inch thick. Line a baking sheet with parchment paper or use a nonstick baking sheet. Cut the dough into 2½-inch rounds with a cookie cutter and place them 1 inch apart on the cookie sheet. Bake for about 12 minutes, or until they look dry, not glossy. Let cool. The cookies may be kept in an airtight container at room temperature for up to 3 days, or the dough may be frozen for up to 2 months.

COCONUT TUILES
Tejas de Coco

French for "tiles," tuiles are very thin, buttery, candylike crisps. Great as a garnish for creamy dessert, they are also perfect with ice cream and sorbets or nibbled with coffee or tea. These tuiles are used as a garnish for my Chilean Papaya Stuffed with Cream Cheese Mousse (page 164).

MAKES ABOUT 2 DOZEN TUILES

2 cups sweetened shredded coconut	90 GRAMS
1½ cups granulated sugar	300 GRAMS
¾ cup all-purpose flour	105 GRAMS
3 whole eggs	
6 egg whites	
¾ cup (1½ sticks) butter, melted	170 GRAMS

◉ In a large bowl, combine the coconut, sugar, and flour. With a wooden spoon or whisk, beat in the eggs and egg whites. Add the butter and stir until the batter is smooth and soft. Put the batter in a covered container in the refrigerator until cold, at least 30 minutes or up to 3 days.

◉ Preheat the oven to 350° F.

◉ Follow instructions for Chocolate Tuiles (opposite) for forming, baking, and storing the tuiles.

CHOCOLATE TUILES
Tejas de Chocolate

These tuiles are used as a garnish for my Coffee Tres Leches (page 80), or try them with Toasted Coconut Ice Cream (page 196).

MAKES ABOUT 2 DOZEN TUILES

½ cup (1 stick) plus 2 tablespoons
   butter, softened   140 GRAMS

¾ cup confectioners' sugar   90 GRAMS

½ cup dark corn syrup   120 MILLILITERS

3 egg whites

½ cup plus 2 tablespoons
   all-purpose flour   90 GRAMS

3 tablespoons unsweetened
   cocoa powder

◎ In the bowl of an electric mixer fitted with the paddle attachment, cream the butter and confectioners' sugar until light and fluffy. Add the corn syrup and beat for 1 minute. Add the egg whites and mix until just combined.

◎ In a small bowl, sift together the flour and cocoa powder. Add to the butter mixture and mix until well incorporated. Transfer the dough to a small, airtight container and refrigerate until cold, at least 30 minutes or up to 3 days.

◎ Preheat the oven to 325° F.

◎ Drop tablespoons of the batter 4 inches apart onto a nonstick baking sheet or one lightly buttered or lined with parchment or a Silpat mat. (The tuiles have such a high butter content, you shouldn't have trouble with sticking, but they are delicate, so nonstick is best.) If you want a more consistent shape, you can use a pastry bag or a plastic bag with the tip cut off to pipe the dough or spread the mounds of dough into 3-inch circles with an offset spatula.

◎ Bake for 10 minutes, or until the tuiles are golden brown and crisp. The edges will begin to pull away from the pan, but the centers will still look slightly shiny. Let cool completely on the pan, then carefully remove the tuiles with a small spatula and place them in an airtight container at room temperature until ready to serve. They will keep for up to 1 week in a cool, dry place. Humidity is the tuiles' worst enemy, so try to find a dry place and do not put them in the refrigerator. If the tuiles do seem soggy after storage, simply reheat them in the oven at 350° F for about 1 minute.

◎ If you'd like to shape the tuiles into cigars, cones, or another shape of your choice, turn the oven off, leaving the tuiles inside. Remove them one at a time and shape before setting on another baking sheet to cool. Store them just as you would the flat tuiles.

LATIN COCONUT BARS
Cocadas

In every Latin country you will find vendors along the street or in *mercados* selling traditional candies from carts. There is always a version made with coconut, often in the style of a macaroon, made chewy and sweet with a mixture of eggs, sugar, and sometimes milk or condensed milk. Just as with cookies or nougats, you will find *cocadas* in many shapes flavored with a variety of dried fruits, chocolate, zests, extracts, and spices. For instance, in Brazil, *coco queimando* is made with caramelized brown sugar and flavored with cinnamon and cloves. In Cuba, a similar sweet showcases vanilla and orange zest. In Colombia, *cocada de mani* adds peanuts, and *panelita de coco* uses *panela* instead of regular sugar. I love making these sweet, gooey, chocolate-covered *cocadas*, studded with raisins and apricots and lined with chocolate, for parties or just as a quick after-dinner sweet to have on hand.

MAKES ABOUT 24 BARS

18 ounces (about 3 cups) semisweet chocolate chips	510 GRAMS
5 cups sweetened shredded coconut	475 GRAMS
2 cups grated fresh coconut (see page 98)	150 GRAMS
5 cups granulated sugar	995 GRAMS
1½ cups raisins	270 GRAMS
1½ cups dried apricots	270 GRAMS
10 whole eggs, beaten	
6 egg yolks, beaten	
1¼ cups (2½ sticks) butter, melted	280 GRAMS

◉ Preheat the oven to 325° F.

◉ Cover the bottom of an 11-by-17-inch half sheet pan with aluminum foil, trying to keep the foil as flat and unwrinkled as possible. In the top of a double boiler over gently simmering water, melt the chocolate. Pour the chocolate into the foil-lined sheet pan and refrigerate until set, about 10 minutes.

◉ In a large bowl, stir together all of the remaining ingredients except the butter. Add the melted butter and stir until combined. Pour the mixture into the pan, over the hardened chocolate, spread evenly, and bake for 40 minutes, or until golden brown on top.

◉ Let cool at room temperature or refrigerate until set, at least 4 hours or overnight. Unmold onto a cutting board and remove the foil before cutting into squares or bars.

◉ Wrap in plastic wrap, place in an airtight container, and refrigerate for up to 2 weeks or freeze for up to 2 months.

"GOOD BREAD" (CHEWY CHEESE ROLLS)

Pan de Bono

These rolls are sweet and salty, crisp and chewy, all at the same time, with a unique spongy texture from the yuca flour. *Pan de bono*, or good bread, is a traditional Latin bread found in Venezuela, Colombia, Ecuador, and Brazil (where it is called *pan de queso*). Each country's version varies slightly, switching out an ingredient or two. This recipe is the Colombian version and uses a combination of three different flours or starches: sour yuca (*almidón agrio/polivilho azedo*), sweet yuca (*almidón dulce/polivilho doce*), and corn. Both yuca starches are sold under a number of different brands, but the Brazilian brand Yoki is one of the most widely available. If you can't find *queso fresco* you can substitute farmer's cheese or any similarly dry, salty cheese. And in a pinch you can even use one of the many *pan de bono* mixes available. Find the flour and the mixes (try the Colombiana brand) at www.mylatinfood.com.

MAKES ABOUT 32 (2-OUNCE) ROLLS

2¼	cups sour/fermented yuca flour	380 GRAMS
1¼	cups sweet yuca flour (tapioca starch)	140 GRAMS
1¼	cups cornstarch	165 GRAMS
½	cup granulated sugar	100 GRAMS
1½	teaspoons salt	
¼	cup nonfat dry milk powder	25 GRAMS
¼	cup (½ stick) butter, melted	55 GRAMS
3	eggs	
¾	cup whole milk	180 MILLILITERS
¼	cup vegetable oil	60 MILLILITERS
2	pounds *queso fresco*, grated	910 GRAMS

◎ Preheat the oven to 350° F.

◎ In the bowl of an electric mixer fitted with the paddle attachment, combine all the dry ingredients. Add the butter, eggs, milk, oil, and *queso fresco* and beat on low speed until the dough comes together, about 5 minutes.

◎ Using a 2-ounce ice cream scoop or ¼-cup measuring cup, scoop balls of dough onto a nonstick baking sheet or one lined with parchment paper. Alternatively, roll the dough into logs and divide it by hand into about 32 pieces. Once all the dough has been scooped out, roll each portion in your hands to create a smooth ball. The dough will be heavy and soft, but not as sticky as typical bread dough, so you should not need any flour to prevent it from sticking to your hands.

◎ Bake for 35 minutes, or until light golden brown. If desired, you can also place the shaped dough in the freezer and bake as needed. Allow the frozen dough to thaw in the refrigerator for at least 4 hours or up to overnight before baking.

KISSES
Besos

These *besos*, or kisses, are best for breakfast or an afternoon snack—sweet, almost scone-like breads made into little sandwiches, the two halves "kissing" each other through a thin layer of jam, the whole thing coated with butter and granulated sugar. They have become one of my favorite Mexican breads and are a fun recipe to make with my children. I hope you can do the same with your family using your favorite marmalade or jam for the filling. I love quince or apricot. You can sometimes find *besos* in bakeries, but they are most often baked at home.

MAKES ABOUT 30 PIECES OR 15 SANDWICH KISSES

For the cookies:

¾	cup (1½ sticks) butter, softened	170 GRAMS
¾	cup granulated sugar	150 GRAMS
3	eggs	
4	cups all-purpose flour	570 GRAMS
2	teaspoons active dry yeast	
1½	tablespoons baking powder	
2	tablespoons vanilla extract	

For the filling and coating:

1½	cups marmalade or jam	360 MILLILITERS
1	cup (2 sticks) butter, softened	225 GRAMS
2	cups granulated sugar	400 GRAMS

In the bowl of an electric mixer fitted with the paddle attachment, cream the butter and sugar until fluffy and pale yellow. Add the eggs one at a time, mixing until combined after each one.

In a large bowl, combine the flour, yeast, and baking powder. Add this, 1 cup water, and the vanilla extract to the butter mixture and mix on low speed until combined. Then mix on medium speed until the dough becomes smooth and soft, with a thick, batterlike texture, 15 to 20 minutes. Using a 2-ounce ice cream scoop or a ¼ cup measuring cup, scoop half spheres of dough 2 inches apart onto a nonstick baking sheet or one lined with parchment paper. Alternatively, roll the dough into logs and divide it by hand into about 30 pieces. Bake for 15 to 20 minutes, until golden brown. Let cool.

Fill and coat the cookies: Spread the bottom of one cookie with about 1 tablespoon of the marmalade or jam, then top it with another cookie. Coat the assembled *besos* with softened butter using a pastry brush or your fingers, then roll each in sugar, tapping off the excess.

RUSTIC BROWN SUGARCANE BREADS
Pan de Piloncillo Aguacatas

This traditional bread has disappeared from most bakeries in Mexico. It takes patience to make, but the butterscotch flavor of the *piloncillo* or *panela* (see page 13) and the depth imparted by the double-sponge method make it worth it. Perfect for breakfast or a snack with hot chocolate, this bread is best served warm from the oven, but it reheats well too.

MAKES 20 TO 25 ROLLS

½	cup whole milk	120 MILLILITERS
1½	teaspoons active dry yeast	
⅓	cup granulated sugar	65 GRAMS
2¾	cups all-purpose flour	395 GRAMS
1	teaspoon salt	
2	eggs	
1	cup (2 sticks) butter, softened	225 GRAMS
¼	teaspoon baking powder	
½	recipe Pan Dulce dough (page 68)	
2	cups coarsely chopped *panela*	400 GRAMS

In a medium saucepan over medium heat, heat the milk until just warm (about 98° F). In a small bowl, combine the yeast and sugar and stir in the warm milk. Let rest until the yeast is bubbly, about 5 minutes.

To make the sponge, in the bowl of an electric mixer fitted with a dough hook, combine the yeast mixture with the flour, salt, and eggs. Mix thoroughly on medium speed until the mixture releases from the sides of the bowl, about 30 minutes. Put the sponge in a clean large bowl and let it rest at room temperature for at least 1 hour, or refrigerate overnight.

Clean the bowl of the electric mixer and in it combine the sponge, butter, baking powder, and Pan Dulce dough. Mix on medium speed until well combined, about 5 minutes. Add the *panela* and mix for 1 more minute. Put the dough in a lightly greased mixing bowl, rolling it around to coat it lightly with oil. Let rise in a warm place, uncovered, for 1 hour or until doubled in size.

Punch down the dough with your fists, deflating it, and roll it into a thick log. Divide the dough into 20 to 25 pieces. Place the rolls on a greased baking sheet, then, use a rolling pin, flatten each portion into a small oval shape about 5 inches long. You will see the chunks of *panela* studding the dough. Poke the dough with the tips of your fingers, dimpling the tops of each roll. Let rise again for about 30 minutes. The dough will now look slightly lumpy.

Preheat the oven to 350° F.

Bake the rolls for 15 to 20 minutes, until golden brown. During baking, the *panela* will melt, creating a natural sugar crust on top. Serve warm or let cool.

MEXICAN-STYLE SWEET BREAD
Pan Dulce Estilo Mexicano

Step into any Mexican *panadería* and you will see countless shapes of *pan dulce*—flakey, not-too-sweet breads, most topped with the traditional sugar crust made from flour, sugar, and butter.

Growing up, my family would send my sister or me on a daily trip to the bakery to buy fresh bread, *pan dulce*, and other baked goods. Before we went, we would ask everyone what bread they wanted, and the requests seemed endless: *conchas* ("shells"), *bandarilla* (puff pastry with a carmelized top named after the flag used to tag the bulls in Spanish bullfights), *rebanada* ("big slice"), *novias* ("bride"), *bigote* ("mustache"), and so many more.

I recommend shaping *conchas* with this dough, but you can really choose any shape. You can even try adding ground cinnamon or citrus zest to the sugar crust or replacing ¼ cup of the flour in the crust recipe with unsweetened cocoa powder for a chocolate twist. Roll this dough with sugar, cinnamon, and pecans for a terrific cinnamon roll. If you intend to let the dough rise overnight, increase the sugar to 1 cup. By adding the additional sugar and allowing the dough to rest overnight, the yeast will continue to grow and it will create an even more flavorful bread.

MAKES ABOUT 15 (3-OUNCE) ROLLS

For the dough:

¾	cup whole milk	180 MILLILITERS
1	tablespoon vanilla extract	
1	tablespoon active dry yeast	
⅔	cup granulated sugar	135 GRAMS
4	cups all-purpose flour	560 GRAMS
1	teaspoon salt	
4	eggs	
1	cup (2 sticks) butter, softened	225 GRAMS

For the sugar crust:

1	cup confectioners' sugar	120 GRAMS
1	cup all-purpose flour	140 GRAMS
1	cup (2 sticks) butter, softened	225 GRAMS
1	tablespoon vanilla extract	

◎ Make the dough: In a medium saucepan over medium heat, heat the milk and vanilla extract until just warm (about 98° F). In a small bowl, combine the yeast and half of the sugar and stir in the warm milk and vanilla. Let rest for 5 minutes.

◎ In the bowl of an electric mixer fitted with the dough hook, combine the flour, salt, and remaining sugar. Add the yeast mixture and eggs and mix on low speed until the dough begins to pull away from the sides of the bowl, 20 to 30 minutes. This allows the gluten to develop and creates a light, spongy bread. Add the butter and mix until incorporated, about 5 minutes.

◎ Remove the dough from the bowl and place it in another large bowl, greased lightly with butter or oil. Lightly coat the top of the dough with butter or oil, then cover it with a kitchen towel. Let the dough rise, covered, in a warm place, for 10 minutes. Punch down the dough with your fists, deflating it, re-cover it, and let it rise until it doubles in volume, about 30 minutes. Re-cover the dough with a damp towel or plastic wrap and put it in the refrigerator for at least 30 minutes or up to overnight.

◎ Make the sugar crust: In the bowl of an electric mixer fitted with the paddle attachment, mix the confectioners' sugar, flour, butter, and vanilla extract until it becomes a smooth dough. Set aside at room temperature while you shape the dough.

◎ Using a 3-ounce ice cream scoop or a ⅓-cup measuring cup, scoop balls of dough onto a nonstick baking sheet or one lined with parchment paper. Alternatively, roll the dough into logs and divide it by hand into about 15 pieces. Once all the dough has been scooped out, roll each portion in your hands to create a smooth ball. Flatten small pieces of the sugar crust dough into disks just large enough to cover each ball of dough. Place the disks on top of each ball of dough and flatten slightly with the back of your hand. You can use a knife to make thin, shallow cuts into the top of the sugar crust dough to imitate the outside of a clam shell or make cross cuts to create a diamond pattern.

◎ Preheat the oven to 350° F.

◎ Let the shaped dough rise, uncovered, in a warm place until it almost triples in volume, about 30 minutes. Bake for 15 to 20 minutes, until the sugar crust is a dark golden brown. Transfer to a wire rack to cool. The bread can be stored in an airtight container for up to 2 days.

Pan de Muerto

PAN DE MUERTO IS STEEPED IN A NEARLY THREE-THOUSAND-YEAR-OLD
tradition dating back to the Aztec celebration of Mictecacihuatl, the goddess
of the afterlife or Lady of the Dead. This variation on *pan dulce* is shaped into
round loaves decorated with bone-shaped pieces of dough. It is one of the things
Mexican families prepare to honor their deceased loved ones for the November 2
Day of the Dead, or Día de los Muertos, holiday. In connection with the Catholic
All Saints' Day, or All Souls' Day, Mexicans across the globe celebrate Día de los
Muertos with visits to grave sites, home altars decorated to welcome the spirits of
family and friends, and celebrations including food, drink, and dancing. Similar
customs are practiced in Brazil and Spain.

I was raised with this wonderful tradition. And it took on particular impor-
tance in my childhood household after the death of my father. Every year, my
grandmother was the one to prepare our family's offerings for the Día de los
Muertos. She would decorate a small altar in our home a few days before the
holiday, adorning it with a candle for each of our deceased relatives, photographs,
colorful and aromatic *pericón* (Mexican mint marigold) and *cempasúchitl* flowers,
calaveras de azucar (sugar skulls), and *pan de muerto*, which she bought from our local
bakery. We would wait to eat the bread until after the holiday, usually enjoying it
after dinner dipped into hot chocolate or alongside rice pudding.

I still follow the Day of the Dead customs that my grandmother taught me as
a way to honor and remember my friends and family who have passed away.
And I hope it is a tradition that my children and my children's children will
continue. Today, I bake my own *pan de muerto* and flavor it with orange blossom
and rum. The bread is traditionally flavored with aniseed, but you will also
find it in bakeries scented with cinnamon or vanilla.

MAKES 2 (22-OUNCE) LOAVES OR 1 LARGER LOAF

Pan Dulce dough 1 recipe (page 68),
   using 2 teaspoons orange blossom water
   in place of vanilla extract
Vegetable oil

¼ cup dark rum	60 MILLILITERS
½ stick butter, softened	55 MILLILITERS
¼ cup granulated sugar	50 GRAMS

Remove the Pan Dulce dough from the refrigerator and divide it in half (to make 2 loaves). Take the first half of the dough and set aside about 1 cup of it to make the decorative "bones" for the top. On a floured surface, shape the larger piece into a ball. Using a small amount of oil on your hands, coat the dough lightly with oil. Split the reserved 1 cup dough into 2 pieces. Roll each piece into a log long enough to drape over the large loaf in an "X" shape. Use your fingers to make a number of indentations in the logs to imitate bone joints. In the center where the two logs meet, press your finger to create a buttonlike indentation. Again using a small amount of oil, coat the decorative dough lightly with oil. Repeat with the second half of dough to form another loaf.

Let the shaped loaves rise, uncovered, in a warm place until they double in volume, 1 to 1½ hours.

Preheat the oven to 350° F.

Bake for 25 minutes, or until the crust is dark brown. Remove from the oven and transfer to a wire rack. Immediately brush the bread with the rum, then let cool to room temperature. Once cool, brush with the butter and coat with the sugar, tapping off excess.

KINGS' CAKE
Rosca de Reyes

Kings' cake is a traditional sweet bread enjoyed during the Catholic feast day of the Epiphany or Día de Reyes, Three Kings' Day, the day the biblical three kings visited the baby Jesus bearing gifts. Rosca de Reyes represents these gifts with its decorative pastry and colorful candied fruit toppings. My recipe uses candied figs, guava paste, and candied citrus rind. Also, tucked inside the bread is a symbolic surprise—a small figurine of the baby Jesus. The belief is that whoever finds the figurine when the bread is served is blessed with good luck for the year. Americans may be most familiar with this custom through the Louisiana tradition of enjoying king cake during Mardi Gras season.

Falling on January 6, Día de Reyes is a more important holiday than Christmas in many Latin American and Mexican homes and is the day when many families exchange their holiday gifts. When my father was alive, he would bring home a huge loaf of kings' cake from our neighborhood bakery for everyone to share on the feast day. In Mexico there is a small price to pay for receiving the luck of the baby Jesus: You must cook and throw a party for your family and friends on the next feast day, Candlemas, or Dia de la Candelaria, which falls on February 2. So now that I am baking the bread myself, I try to hide as many figurines in it as possible so that everyone has to cook on February 2.

**MAKES 2 (22-OUNCE) LOAVES OR
1 LARGER LOAF**

For the decorative pastry:
¾ cup (1½ sticks)
    butter, softened   170 GRAMS
1 cup granulated sugar   200 GRAMS
1¾ cups all-purpose flour   255 GRAMS
2 eggs
2 teaspoons baking powder
1 tablespoon orange extract

For the decorations:
½ cup guava paste   120 GRAMS
½ cup candied lemon
    or lime peel   90 GRAMS
1 cup figs in syrup, halved   240 GRAMS
1 egg

For the bread:
1 recipe Pan Dulce dough (page 68)
½ cup granulated sugar   100 GRAMS
½ cup confectioners' sugar   60 GRAMS

◎ Make the decorative pastry: In the bowl of an electric mixer, cream the butter and sugar until light and fluffy. Add the flour and mix until combined. Add the eggs, baking powder, orange extract, and 1 cup water and mix until a soft, piecrustlike dough forms. Set aside at room temperature.

◎ Make the decorations: Cut the guava paste and candied citrus peels into strips about ½ inch wide by 3 inches. In a small bowl, beat the egg together with 2 tablespoons water to create an egg wash.

◎ Remove the Pan Dulce dough from the refrigerator and divide it in half (to make 2 loaves). On a lightly oiled surface, shape each portion of dough into a log about 20 inches long. With each log, form a ring of dough along the inside perimeter of a greased 11-by-8½-by-¼-inch sheet pan. Make sure to pinch the ends together tightly with your fingers so that the dough does not separate when it starts to bake. Slightly flatten the ring of dough using your hands. Let rest, uncovered, in a warm place for about 10 minutes.

◎ Remove the pastry dough from the refrigerator and roll it into a thick log about 2 inches in diameter. Cut the log into about 16 pieces. Roll each into a log, then flatten it to look like a ribbon and place the strips crosswise on the Pan Dulce dough ring, creating a striped pattern around the entire ring. In between the stripes of dough, place one strip of guava paste, one strip of candied lemon or lime peel, and one candied fig, repeating this pattern until the whole loaf is decorated.

◎ Let the bread rise in a warm place, uncovered, for at least 30 minutes, or until doubled in volume. Brush any exposed Pan Dulce dough with the egg wash, being careful not to coat the fruit decorations or the decorative pastry stripes.

◎ Preheat the oven to 350° F. Mix the sugars together and generously cover the raised bread stripes with the mixture. Use the remaining sugar mixture to sprinkle lightly over the whole loaf.

◎ Bake for 20 to 25 minutes, until dark golden brown. Let cool.

3

CAKES AND PASTRIES

Bizcochos y Pastelitos

In This Chapter

THREE MILKS CAKE
Tres Leches

COCONUT THREE MILKS CAKE
Tres Leches de Coco

COFFEE THREE MILKS CAKE WITH CHOCOLATE-KIRSCH SAUCE
Tres Leches de Café con Salsa de Chocolate y Brandy de Kirsch

PEACH THREE MILKS CAKE WITH POACHED PEACHES
Tres Leches de Melocotón con Melocotón en Almibar

BANANA THREE MILKS CAKE
Tres Leches de Banana

LATIN-STYLE FRENCH TOAST WITH MILK-CARAMEL AND FRESH CHEESE
Torrejas con Dulce de Leche y Queso Fresco

MANGO AND WHITE CHOCOLATE CHEESECAKE
Pastel de Queso Crema con Mango y Chocolate Blanco

PINEAPPLE UPSIDE-DOWN CAKE
Volteado de Piña

DRUNKEN CAKES
Borrachitos

MILK-CARAMEL CAKE ROLL
Dulce de Leche Brazo Gitano

PECAN CAKE ROLL
Brazo Gitano de Nuez

BAKED PATAGONIA WITH TROPICAL FRUIT AND BERRY SALSA
Patagonia Horneado con Salpicón de Fruta

SWEET FRIED LATIN DOUGHNUTS WITH CHOCOLATE SAUCE
Churros con Chocolate

CINNAMON TART STUFFED WITH DATES
Encanelado Relleno con Datil

APPLE EMPANADAS
Empanadas de Manzana

GOAT CHEESE AND GUAVA EMPANADAS
Empanadas de Queso de Cabra y Guayaba

COCONUT AND CREAM CHEESE EMPANADAS
Empanadas de Coco y Queso Crema

CHOCOLATE AND SAFFRON "THOUSAND LEAVES" NAPOLEON WITH APPLE COMPOTE
Mil Hojas de Chocolate y Azafran con Compota de Manzana

PUFF PASTRY
Pasta de Hojaldre

PERUVIAN SWEET POTATO AND PUMPKIN FRITTERS WITH SPICED SYRUP
Picarones con Miel de Especias

YUCA FRITTERS WITH PASSION FRUIT, BANANA, AND ORANGE BLOSSOM SYRUP
Buñuelos de Yuca con Almibar de Maracuya, Banana, y Flor de Azar

THREE MILKS CAKE
Tres Leches

This recipe stays pretty true to the classic form of *tres leches* with its vanilla cake and rum-flavored milk mixture. Make sure the cake is well chilled when served and all you'll need for garnish is whipped cream, fresh fruit, and nuts if you like. I prefer sliced strawberries, or peaches or mixed berries, and toasted pecans. This *tres leches* cake is ideal for crowds, as it's straightforward to make and can be made up to 2 days ahead of time and kept in the refrigerator. Just wait to prepare the fresh fruit and whipped cream garnishes until just before serving.

SERVES 18 TO 24

10 egg

1⅛ cups granulated sugar — 225 GRAMS

1 tablespoon vanilla extract

1⅛ cups all-purpose flour — 160 GRAMS

2 (12-ounce) cans
evaporated milk — 720 MILLILITERS

1 (14-ounce) can sweetened
condensed milk — 420 MILLILITERS

2 cups heavy cream — 480 MILLILITERS

½ cup dark rum — 120 MILLILITERS

2 recipes Whipped Cream (page 235)

Fresh fruit and toasted nuts (optional)

◎ Preheat the oven to 325° F.

◎ In the bowl of an electric mixer, beat the eggs on high speed until they are thick and light in color, about 5 minutes. While beating, gradually add the sugar and vanilla extract and continue beating for an additional 7 to 8 minutes, until the eggs have tripled in volume. Sift the flour into the egg and sugar mixture and gently fold to combine. Do not stir or beat, as this will cause the eggs to deflate and lose their volume.

◎ Grease a 13-by-9-inch baking pan, making sure to fully coat the sides, including the rim. Pour the batter into the pan; it will completely fill the pan. Bake for 40 to 50 minutes, until the cake springs back to the touch when lightly pressed. The cake will be golden, and will pull away from the sides of the pan, and a toothpick inserted in the center will come out clean. Let cool. Once cool, pierce the cake all over with a toothpick or skewer.

◎ Whisk the two milks and cream together with the rum and slowly pour over the cake. Cover and refrigerate for at least 2 hours, until the liquid is completely absorbed. The cake will keep, refrigerated, for up to 2 days.

◎ To serve, cut squares or rectangles of cake right out of the pan and garnish each with a dollop of whipped cream and, if you wish, fresh fruit and toasted nuts.

Three Milks Cake

AMONG LATIN DESSERTS SECOND ONLY TO FLAN, *TRES LECHES*, MEANING "three milks," is a classic. Its popularity continues to fuel great debate over its origin. Most historians claim that the cake is native to Nicaragua. There is even a festival in Nicaragua to see who can make the biggest *tres leches*. But the dessert also has a long history in Mexico, Puerto Rico, Guatemala, and Ecuador. I have found that we play with the flavors a bit more in Mexico, rather than sticking to the traditional version of vanilla cake soaked in rum-flavored milk.

A rich, almost puddinglike cake, *tres leches* starts with a vanilla sponge cake, which is then soaked in a combination of evaporated and condensed milks and either heavy cream or whole milk. The resulting rich, incredibly moist cake is practically foolproof. You never have to worry about a dry cake.

Tres leches is also soaked in tradition. You truly can't find a celebration in Mexico that doesn't include a *tres leches* cake. At *quince años* celebrations, when a girl turns fifteen years old, the *tres leches* is typically served after the first dance by the *quinceañera* and her friends. At weddings, the cake is served after the bride and groom make their first appearance to their guests as a couple. It is also a common ritual to pose for a family photo around the cake, signifying the sweet memories that were captured that day.

If you want to present the cake to a group, you can unmold it from the pan onto a platter and decoratively cover the top with the fruit and nuts, serving the whipped cream on the side. To transfer the cake to a platter, first place a large sheet pan over the top of the baking pan and invert the cake. Its moist consistency will make it easy to unmold. Then place your chosen platter over the bottom of the cake, and invert it again to serve, being careful not to apply too much pressure, as the cake will be somewhat delicate. After unmolding and decorating it, you may want to return the cake to the refrigerator for about 30 minutes to make sure it is well chilled before serving.

This was one dessert that my family often purchased for special occasions at our town bakery, rather than making it from scratch at home. The tiny shop had one of the best *tres leches* for miles, and because of all the milks held within the cake, it was actually sold by the kilo rather than by the slice. How can you resist a cake that's sold by the kilo?

COCONUT THREE MILKS CAKE
Tres Leches de Coco

The coconut is one of Latin America's favorite fruits. Even though it is not native to Mexico, we have adopted it as our own, especially over the last decade, when the flavors of Mexico, Central and South America, Cuba, the Dominican Republic, and Puerto Rico began to blend with the flavors of the broader Latin America including places like Jamaica, Antigua, Haiti, and Martinique to create Nuevo Latino cuisine.

Try this cake with whipped cream and a refreshing garnish of orange or lime sorbet. One tip: Choose a coconut liqueur other than Coco Lopez, which is particularly sweet and will overpower the cake in combination with the sweetened condensed milk.

SERVES 18 TO 24

10 eggs	
1⅛ cups granulated sugar	225 GRAMS
3 tablespoons coconut extract	
1⅛ cups all-purpose flour	160 GRAMS
1 (12-ounce) can evaporated milk	360 MILLILITERS
1 (14-ounce) can sweetened condensed milk	420 MILLILITERS
1 (13.5-ounce) can coconut milk	400 MILLILITERS
2 cups heavy cream	480 MILLILITERS
1 cup coconut liqueur	240 MILLILITERS
2 recipes Whipped Cream (page 235)	
Orange or lime sorbet (optional)	

◎ Preheat the oven to 325° F.

◎ In the bowl of an electric mixer, beat the eggs on high speed until they are thick and light in color, about 5 minutes. While beating, gradually add the sugar and coconut extract and continue beating for an additional 7 to 8 minutes, until the eggs have tripled in volume. Sift the flour into the egg and sugar mixture and gently fold to combine. Do not stir or beat, as this will cause the eggs to deflate and lose their volume.

◎ Grease a 13-by-9-inch baking pan, making sure to fully coat the sides, including the rim. Pour the batter into the pan; it will completely fill the pan. Bake for 40 to 50 minutes, until the cake springs back to the touch when lightly pressed. The cake will be golden, and will pull away from the sides of the pan, and a toothpick inserted in the center will come out clean. Let cool. Once cool, pierce the cake all over with a toothpick or skewer.

Whisk the three milks and cream together with the liqueur and slowly pour over the cake. Cover and refrigerate for at least 2 hours, until the liquid is completely absorbed. The cake will keep, refrigerated, for up to 2 days.

To serve, cut squares or rectangles of cake right out of the pan and garnish each with a dollop of whipped cream and, if you wish, orange or lime sorbet. Alternatively, if you want to present the cake to a group, you can unmold it from the pan (see page 77) and serve the whipped cream and sorbet on the side.

Adorno Especial

Granizado de Naranja Agria, Salsa de Litchi, Naranja Confitada, y Suspiros de Coco

Here the rich milks and coconut are set off by the acidity of sour orange and litchi. The combination works in much the same way as when that punch of pineapple flavor cuts through the coconut milk in a piña colada. Adding the contrasting crunchy, meringue makes this dessert a showstopper. But it will still be extraordinary on its own, especially during warmer months. If you wanted to pick one easy garnish, I would go for the Litchi Sauce, which can quickly be made in a pinch with canned litchis.

Candied Orange 1 recipe (page 175)
Sour Orange Granita 1 recipe (page 222)
Litchi Sauce 1 recipe (page 252)
Crisp Coconut Meringue 1 recipe (page 55)

Rather than cutting the cake in squares, cut pieces with a 2-inch round cookie cutter. Place 2 slices of Candied Orange on each plate, top with a piece of cake, add 2 tablespoons of the Sour Orange Granita, and decorate the plate with about 3 tablespoons of the Litchi Sauce. Crown the whole masterpiece with a piece of the meringue or crumble it over the top.

COFFEE THREE MILKS CAKE WITH CHOCOLATE-KIRSCH SAUCE

Tres Leches de Café con Salsa de Chocolate y Brandy de Kirsch

The layers of flavors you might find in a wine—coffee, chocolate, fruit—are also found in this dessert. For another level of complementary flavor, pair the dessert with a glass of vintage port, which offers a bright cherry note. Or try one of my favorite dessert wines from Spain, Pansal del Calas from Celler de Capcanes.

Don't skip the sauce made with chocolate and kirsch, a cherry brandy. You can use any leftovers to pour over pound cake or ice cream or stir it into your evening coffee. A good-quality store-bought cherry ice cream is another good addition if you don't have time to make ice cream from scratch.

SERVES 18 TO 24

10 eggs

1⅛ cups granulated sugar — 225 GRAMS

3 tablespoons coffee extract (or 4 tablespoons instant coffee granules)

1⅛ cups all-purpose flour — 160 GRAMS

2 (12-ounce) cans evaporated milk — 720 MILLILITERS

1 (14-ounce) can sweetened condensed milk — 420 MILLILITERS

2 cups heavy cream — 480 MILLILITERS

1 cup Tía Maria (or other coffee-flavored liqueur) — 240 MILLILITERS

1 recipe Chocolate-Kirsch Sauce (page 254)

1 recipe Cherry Ice Cream (optional) (page 204)

⊚ Preheat the oven to 325° F.

⊚ In the bowl of an electric mixer, beat the eggs on high speed until they are thick and light in color, about 5 minutes. While beating, gradually add the sugar and coffee extract and continue beating for an additional 7 to 8 minutes, until the eggs have tripled in volume. Sift the flour into the egg and sugar mixture and gently fold to combine. Do not stir or beat, as this will cause the eggs to deflate and lose their volume.

⊚ Grease a 13-by-9-inch baking pan, making sure to fully coat the sides, including the rim. Pour the batter into the pan; it will completely fill the pan. Bake for 40 to 50 minutes, until the cake springs back to the touch when lightly pressed. The cake will be golden, and will pull away from the sides of the pan, and a toothpick inserted in the center will come out clean. Let cool. Once cool, pierce the cake all over with a toothpick or skewer.

⊚ Whisk the two milks and the cream together with the Tía Maria and slowly pour over the whole cake. Cover and refrigerate for at least 2 hours, or until the liquid is completely absorbed. The cake will keep, refrigerated, for up to 2 days.

⊚ To serve, cut squares or rectangles of cake right out of the pan and serve each with the sauce and, if you like, a scoop of ice cream. Alternatively, if you want to present the cake to a group, you can unmold it from the pan (see page 77) and serve the sauce and ice cream on the side.

Adorno Especial

Crèma Helada de Cereza, Espuma de Almendra, y Tejas de Chocolate

Almond Foam 1 recipe (page 246)
Cherry Ice Cream 1 recipe (page 204)
Chocolate Tuiles 1 recipe (page 63)

Rather than cutting the cake into squares, cut pieces with a 2-inch round cookie cutter.

Drizzle each plate with the sauce, and top with a piece of cake and some foam. To the side, place a quenelle of the ice cream and garnish with a tuile.

PEACH THREE MILKS CAKE WITH POACHED PEACHES

Tres Leches de Melocotón con Melocotón en Almibar

Peaches and cream is a natural combination, and this *tres leches* just magnifies those flavors. I usually prepare this dessert in the summer, when the local peaches available in Miami are at their peak ripeness.

The poached peaches are easy enough to prepare and you can enjoy them over ice cream, waffles, or pancakes. But you can also use a good peach preserve or marmalade as an accompaniment. The creaminess of the cake paired with the delicate fruit is rich, but not cloyingly sweet or too heavy.

SERVES 18 TO 24

For the poached peaches:

5 large fresh peaches (ripe but firm), halved and pitted

½ cup freshly squeezed lime juice   120 MILLILITERS

½ cup dark rum   120 MILLILITERS

4 cinnamon sticks

1 vanilla bean, halved lengthwise, seeds scraped out and reserved (or 1½ tablespoons vanilla extract)

4 whole black peppercorns

1 whole clove

For the cake:

10 eggs

1⅛ cups granulated sugar   225 GRAMS

1 tablespoon vanilla extract

1⅛ cups all-purpose flour   160 GRAMS

2 (12-ounce) cans evaporated milk   720 MILLILITERS

1 (14-ounce) can sweetened condensed milk   420 MILLILITERS

2 cups heavy cream   480 MILLILITERS

½ cup peach liqueur   120 MILLILITERS

⊚ Make the poached peaches: In a medium saucepan, combine the peach halves with 2½ cups water and all the remaining ingredients. Bring to a boil, then reduce the heat and simmer for about 20 minutes, until the peaches are tender.

⊚ Fill a larger bowl (or even the kitchen sink) with cold water and ice cubes and gently set the saucepan in the water to cool, being careful not to get any water into it. Transfer the pan to the refrigerator and let the peaches macerate for at least 4 hours in the syrup.

⊚ Make the cake: Preheat oven to 325° F.

In the bowl of an electric mixer, beat the eggs on high speed until they are thick and light in color, about 5 minutes. While beating, gradually add the sugar and vanilla extract and continue beating for an additional 7 to 8 minutes, until the eggs have tripled in volume. Sift the flour into the egg and sugar mixture and gently fold to combine. Do not stir or beat, as this will cause the eggs to deflate and lose their volume.

Grease a 13-by-9-inch baking pan, making sure to fully coat the sides, including the rim. Pour the batter into the pan; it will completely fill the pan. Bake for 40 to 50 minutes, until the cake springs back to the touch when lightly pressed. The cake will be golden, and will pull away from the sides of the pan, and a toothpick inserted in the center will come out clean. Let cool. Once cool, pierce the cake all over with a toothpick or skewer.

Whisk the two milks and cream together with the liqueur and slowly pour over the cake. Cover and refrigerate for at least 2 hours, until the liquid is completely absorbed. The cake will keep, refrigerated, for up to 2 days.

To serve, cut squares or rectangles of cake right out of the pan and serve each with some of the poached peaches, being sure to leave the whole spices in the poaching syrup behind. Alternatively, if you want to present the cake to a group, you can unmold it from the pan (see page 77) and serve the peaches on the side.

Adorno Especial

Mousse de Chocolate Blanco y Gelatina de Amaretto

White Chocolate Mousse 1 recipe (page 239, using white rum instead of tequila)

Amaretto Gelee 1 recipe (page 249)

Rather than cutting the cake into squares, cut pieces with a 2-inch round cookie cutter.

Put a piece of the cake on each plate and top with a quenelle of the mousse. Place a poached peach half next to the cake and garnish with a few pieces of the gelee. You can also cut each peach half into thin slices and fan it out on the plate next to the round piece of cake.

Yet another option is to layer everything in a parfait glass. This is a great idea if you want to make this dessert ahead of time and store the glasses in the refrigerator. First drop in a poached peach, followed by a piece of cake, then the mousse, and garnish with the gelee.

Additionally, if you want to use the syrup from the peaches, you can strain it into a plastic container, freeze it for a couple of hours, and shave the ice for a *granizado* garnish. Or reduce the syrup to a thicker consistency and drizzle it as a sauce over any of the above presentations.

BANANA THREE MILKS CAKE

Tres Leches de Banana

When I was growing up, we'd enjoy a treat of sliced bananas with freshly grated coconut and either honey or yogurt on top. In Mexico, a common simple dessert is sliced bananas served with a bit of sweetened sour cream, sometimes dotted with strawberries. Just as creamy yogurt and sour cream taste great with bananas, so does creamy, moist *tres leches* cake. For a special presentation, I like to top each cake slice with a dollop of Italian Meringue (page 236) and serve with Prunes in Passion Fruit Syrup (page 188).

SERVES 18 TO 24

10 eggs

1⅛ cups granulated sugar   225 GRAMS

1 tablespoon vanilla extract

1⅛ cups all-purpose flour   160 GRAMS

2 (12-ounce) cans evaporated milk   720 MILLILITERS

1 (14-ounce) can sweetened condensed milk   420 MILLILITERS

2 cups heavy cream   480 MILLILITERS

1 cup banana liqueur   240 MILLILITERS

2 to 3 bananas, sliced

2 recipes Whipped Cream (page 235)

◉ Preheat the oven to 325° F.

◉ In the bowl of an electric mixer, beat the eggs on high speed until they are thick and light in color, about 5 minutes. While beating, gradually add the sugar and vanilla extract and continue beating for an additional 7 to 8 minutes, until the eggs have tripled in volume. Sift the flour into the egg and sugar mixture and gently fold to combine. Do not stir or beat, as this will cause the eggs to deflate and lose their volume.

◉ Grease a 13-by-9-inch baking pan, making sure to fully coat the sides, including the rim. Pour the batter into the pan; it will completely fill the pan. Bake for 40 to 50 minutes, until the cake springs back to the touch when lightly pressed. The cake will be golden, and will pull away from the sides of the pan, and a toothpick inserted in the center will come out clean. Let cool. Once cool, pierce the cake all over with a toothpick or skewer.

◉ Whisk the two milks and cream together with the liqueur and slowly pour over the cake. Cover and refrigerate for at least 2 hours, until the liquid is completely absorbed. The cake will keep, refrigerated, for up to 2 days.

◉ To serve, cut squares or rectangles of cake right out of the pan and serve each with some sliced bananas and a dollop of whipped cream. Alternatively, if you want to present the cake to a group, you can unmold it from the pan using the instructions for Tres Leches Adorno Especial (see page 77), decorate the top with the sliced bananas, and serve the whipped cream on the side.

LATIN-STYLE FRENCH TOAST WITH MILK-CARAMEL AND FRESH CHEESE

Torrejas con Dulce de Leche y Queso Fresco

Torrejas, or Latin-style French toast, is a perfect example of the way Latin Americans use cheese as a component in sweet preparations (see page 5). This recipe is similar to the milk-and-egg-soaked fried bread eaten for breakfast in America, but it's more of an adult version—spiked with white wine, fried until well caramelized and crunchy, and sprinkled with salty *queso fresco*. If you prefer, you can drizzle it with syrup or honey instead of the *dulce de leche* or *cajeta*.

SERVES 6

2 cups canola oil for frying	480 MILLILITERS
½ cup white wine	120 MILLILITERS
2 cups whole milk	480 MILLILITERS
2 tablespoons vanilla extract	
2 teaspoons ground cinnamon	
3 eggs	
1 loaf French or Italian bread, cut into ¾-inch slices	
¼ cup confectioners' sugar, for dusting	30 GRAMS
1 recipe Dulce de Leche (page 52) or Cajeta (page 15)	
1 cup crumbled *queso fresco*	140 GRAMS

In a large, deep saucepan, heat the oil to 350° F.

In a medium bowl, whisk together the wine, milk, vanilla extract, and cinnamon. In a separate medium bowl, beat the eggs.

Dip each bread slice first into the milk mixture, coating one side and then the other, then into the egg mixture, coating one side and then the other.

Place the coated slices, 2 or 3 at a time, immediately into the hot oil. Fry, turning, until golden brown and crisp, 1½ to 2 minutes per side. Drain on a paper towel–lined plate and finish coating and frying the remaining slices.

Serve warm, dusted with the confectioners' sugar, drizzled with Dulce de Leche, and sprinkled with *queso fresco*.

MANGO AND WHITE CHOCOLATE CHEESECAKE

Pastel de Queso Crema con Mango y Chocolate Blanco

Although cheesecake is certainly not a classic Latin dessert, the addition of mango, orange, and banana is reminiscent of Caribbean island cuisine. And cheese and fruit is a very common Latin pairing. In Mexico, we eat *queso crema* with *dulce de papaya* or *dulce de calabaza* (papaya or pumpkin in spiced syrup) or in *torrejas con queso fresco* (Latin-style French toast, page 85). In Cuba, they enjoy *queso crema* in chunks with *dulce de coco* (candied coconut) or *mermelada de mango* (mango marmalade).

I like the fact that the "crust" of this cheesecake is really just a cookie on which the cheesecake rests. Prepare the components of this dessert separately so you don't end up with that typical mushy crust baked underneath the cheesecake. If you don't have time to make the *polvorones*, you can use a store-bought butter cookie (orange-flavored ones, like those made by Elsa's Story or Anna's Swedish Thins, available at specialty food stores, would be particularly good). Or you can serve the cheesecake over roughly crushed graham crackers sautéed with a little melted butter until browned. Even with no crust component at all, the addition of sour cream gives this cheesecake a silkier, creamier, slightly lighter texture that works all on its own.

SERVES 12

4 cups mango puree	950 MILLILITERS
½ cup granulated sugar	100 GRAMS
9 ounces (about 1½ cups chips) chopped white chocolate	255 GRAMS
1½ cups sour cream	340 GRAMS
2 (8-ounce) packages cream cheese, softened	455 GRAMS
2 teaspoons vanilla extract	
1 tablespoon freshly squeezed lemon juice	
1 pinch salt	
3 eggs	
12 cookies such as polvorones (see page 60) or crushed graham crackers sautéed in butter	

⊚ Preheat the oven to 300° F.

⊚ In a small saucepan over high heat, combine the mango puree and sugar. Bring to a boil, then lower the heat and simmer for about 30 minutes, until reduced by half and a thick, honeylike consistency. It should still pour easily from a spoon. Remove from the heat.

⊚ In a double boiler set over a pan of gently simmering water, melt the white chocolate. Remove from the heat. In the bowl of an electric mixer, beat the cream cheese together with the vanilla extract, lemon juice, and salt for about 3 minutes, until soft and creamy. Lower the speed and add the eggs one at a time, beating until incorporated. Add the melted white chocolate, sour cream, and 1 cup of the mango reduction.

◎ Divide the cheesecake mixture among 12 lightly buttered muffin tins, ramekins, or mini springform pans (about 4½ ounces each), filling them to ⅛ inch from the top. Cover with buttered aluminum foil, buttered side down so that it doesn't stick to the tops of the cakes. Place the muffin tins in a large baking dish or on a sheet pan to avoid spills. Bake for 40 minutes, or until the cheesecakes are just set. The centers will look a little loose, but will set up as they cool. Remove the cheesecakes from the oven and let rest at room temperature for at least 20 minutes. Leave covered and chill in the refrigerator for at least 4 hours, or overnight.

◎ Alternatively, you can make one large cheesecake in an 8-inch springform pan: Bake for about 1 hour, or until the top is firm except for the very center, uncovering it after the first 30 minutes of baking. Turn off the heat and let the cake rest in the hot oven for another 20 minutes to finish baking. This will help keep the top from browning or cracking.

◎ If using muffin tins or ramekins, invert them onto a sheet pan and tap the bottoms with a butter knife to help unmold. You may also very quickly submerge the tins or ramekins in hot water, being careful not to get water onto the cakes; this will slightly soften the cheesecakes, making them easier to unmold. If using springform pans, simply release the cakes from the pans. Place a cookie or some sautéed crushed graham crackers on each plate. Place a slice or an unmolded individual cheesecake right side up on top of the cookie or crackers and garnish with the remaining mango reduction.

Adorno Especial

Polvorones de Naranja y Salsa de Chocolate

4 fresh bananas
Orange Butter Cookies 1 recipe (page 60)
Chocolate Sauce 1 recipe (page 253)
12 fresh strawberries

When ready to serve, peel and slice the bananas into ⅛-inch-thick slices. Form a circle with several sliced bananas in the center of each plate and place a cookie on top. Place an unmolded cheesecake on top of the cookie, drizzle with the mango reduction, and garnish with dots of sauce and strawberries.

PINEAPPLE UPSIDE-DOWN CAKE

Volteado de Piña

The concept of the upside-down cake is an ingenious one: a cake whose ultimate topping begins as a base of butter, sugar, and fresh fruit that is baked to a wonderful caramelized garnish and glaze all in the same pan as the batter. This baking method works with many fruits, but pineapple is the one that made the upside-down cake famous—the apple in the French tarte tatin perhaps placing at a close second.

Serve plain or with a good-quality store-bought vanilla ice cream.

SERVES 12

¼ cup chopped walnuts	30 GRAMS
¾ cup chopped *panela* (see page 13)	
(or packed brown sugar)	150 GRAMS
¼ cup butter	55 GRAMS
⅜ cup dark rum	90 MILLILITERS
1 medium pineapple, peeled and cored	
6 whole eggs	
6 egg yolks	
¾ cup granulated sugar	150 GRAMS
1 tablespoon vanilla extract	
1 teaspoon ground cardamom	
1½ cups all-purpose flour, sifted	210 GRAMS
1 cup whole milk	240 MILLILITERS
¼ cup (½ stick) butter, melted	55 GRAMS

Preheat the oven to 350° F.

In a large sauté pan over medium heat, combine the walnuts, *panela*, butter, and rum and cook, stirring occasionally, until the *panela* is dissolved, about 3 minutes. Cut the pineapple into ¼-inch-thick slices and cook in the sugar mixture for about 4 minutes on each side. The pineapple will become slightly more translucent and may brown slightly, but be careful not to overcook.

In the bowl of an electric mixer, beat the eggs and yolks until they are thick and light in color, about 5 minutes. White beating, gradually add the sugar, vanilla extract, and cardamom and continue beating for an additional 10 minutes, or until the eggs have tripled in volume. Sift the flour into the egg and sugar mixture, a little at a time, and gently fold together, alternating with the milk and melted butter. Do not stir or beat, as this will cause the eggs to deflate and lose their volume.

Grease a 10-inch springform pan or a 13-by-9-inch baking pan. Arrange the caramelized pineapple circles on the bottom, pouring in all the caramelized juices and nuts from the pan, then pour in the cake batter.

◎ Bake for about 50 minutes, until the cake springs back to the touch when lightly pressed. The cake will be golden, and will pull away from the sides of the pan, and a toothpick inserted in the center will come out clean. Let cool for about 20 minutes (to allow the caramel bottom to harden enough so that it remains intact, but not enough that it sticks to the pan), then invert the warm cake onto a round serving platter. If the cake cools too long and won't unmold easily, simply set the bottom in hot water to loosen, being careful not to get any water onto the cake. Once unmolded, the cake can be placed in an airtight container and kept at room temperature for up to 1 day.

Adorno Especial

Helado de Queso

Cheese Ice Cream 1 recipe (page 200)
Chopped fresh basil or tarragon

If you're entertaining and want an even more impressive presentation, divide the caramelized pineapple mixture among 12 buttered muffin tins or ramekins. You may have to break the pineapple rounds into smaller pieces to make them fit. Place the muffin tins or ramekins in a large baking dish or on a sheet pan to avoid spills and fill about ¾ full with batter.

Bake for about 35 minutes. Remove from the oven and let cool for about 20 minutes. The ramekins can be inverted onto individual plates, while the tins should be inverted onto a jellyroll pan or other large platter with sides (to catch the caramelized juices). Use a spatula to transfer the individual cakes to each plate, drizzling on any remaining caramel from the platter.

Top each slice or individual cake with a scoop of ice cream and some basil or tarragon.

DRUNKEN CAKES
Borrachitos

Borrachito, meaning "drunken," is the nickname of this traditionally rum-soaked cake—in essence, the Latin version of the *baba au rhum* or French *savarin*. In Cuba, this cake is called *panetela borracha*, and rather than a yeast bread the base is a vanilla cake. In Mexico, you'll find *borrachitos* in every *panaderia*, the small cylindrical cakes lined up in deep pans soaking in their sweet syrup flavored with cinnamon, orange zest, and rum or tequila.

I flavor my syrup with fresh ginger and use cachaça (of caipirinha fame), a distilled Brazilian alcohol made from sugarcane juice, instead of rum. Pronounced "ka-SHA-sa," it has a lighter, cleaner flavor than rum that lets the other ingredients really stand out. Cachaça is sometimes called by the more generic name *aguardiente* meaning "firewater." Many Latin countries have their own version of *aguardiente*, some made from sugarcane and others made from fermented fruits or grains. But you can feel free to experiment with your favorite liquor—try Calvados and serve with sautéed apples, or Poire Williams and fresh or sautéed pears, or tequila and lemon ice cream.

Traditionally, these little cakes are made in baba molds, individual baking vessels that look like tall, steep-sided muffin tins. But you can also use regular 2-ounce mini muffin tins or mini aluminum foil cups. Regular muffin tins or cups will be too large.

SERVES 12

For the cakes:

4	teaspoons active dry yeast	
¼	cup warm water	60 MILLILITERS
1½	tablespoons granulated sugar	
1	cup all-purpose flour	140 GRAMS
½	teaspoon salt	
3	whole eggs	
1	egg yolks	
½	cup (1 stick) butter, softened	115 GRAMS

For the syrup:

2	cups sugar	400 GRAMS
¼	cup peeled and thinly sliced fresh ginger	55 GRAMS
1	cup cachaça	240 MILLILITERS

⊙ Make the cakes: In a small bowl, mix the yeast with the water and 1 tablespoon of the sugar and let proof for about 5 minutes. When the yeast starts to bubble, combine it with the flour, salt, eggs and yolks, and remaining ½ tablespoon of sugar in a large mixing bowl. Turn the dough out onto a flat surface and knead for about 15 minutes to develop the gluten in the dough and bring it to an elastic, pliable consistency. Knead in the butter for about 3 more minutes.

⊙ Preheat the oven to at 350° F.

⊙ Divide the dough equally among 12 buttered baba molds, each about 2¼ inches high by 2½ inches in diameter, cover with a towel, and let rise in a warm place for 15 to 20 minutes, until it has doubled in volume. Do not put the dough in the oven to rise, as it will dry out the top of the dough. Bake for 18 minutes, or until deep golden brown on top.

⊙ Unmold the breads onto wire racks and let cool.

⊙ Make the syrup: In a medium saucepan over medium heat, bring 4 cups (960 milliliters) water, the sugar, and ginger to a boil. Lower the heat and simmer for 5 minutes. Remove from the heat and stir in the cachaça. You may either leave in the ginger pieces for a more robust flavor, or remove them before soaking the breads.

⊙ Put the breads in a storage container or baking dish that will fit them in a single layer and cover them with the warm syrup, turning them to coat. For the best flavor, let them soak in the syrup for at least 30 minutes before serving. They can be stored in the syrup and refrigerated for up to 2 days, or frozen, without the syrup, for up to 2 months.

Adorno Especial

Crema de Manzanilla y Nieve de Guayaba

Traditionally, *baba au rhum* is served with whipped cream, while the Latin *borrachitos* are served plain. I like a version somewhere in between, so I created a cream sauce from one of my favorite teas, somewhat similar to a custard sauce you might see served with a dessert soufflé. The sorbet adds a nice refreshing touch to the powerful flavors of this rich dessert.

Chamomile Cream 1 recipe (page 258)
Guava Sorbet 1 recipe (page 219)
Fresh berries

To serve, cover each plate with a few tablespoons of the sauce, place a *borrachito* on top, and garnish with a scoop of sorbet and some berries.

MILK-CARAMEL CAKE ROLL

Dulce de Leche Brazo Gitano

This type of cake is one of the first desserts I remember my grandmother making when I was a child. She used to do all the beating by hand, and every time I make this dessert I think of her, whipping the egg whites into stiff peaks while my sisters and I stood by, peering wide-eyed over the kitchen table. These days I take the "easy" way out and use an electric mixer, wondering if she would approve.

Brazo gitano, meaning "gypsy's arm," is a delicate Spanish sponge cake typically filled with pastry cream, mousse, or jam. In Chile and Ecuador, it is known as *brazo de reina* (queen's arm) and in Puerto Rico as *pionono* (jelly roll). The recipe for the sponge cake is very similar to a French *génoise* cake, but without the butter—making it lighter in texture and easier to shape into a jellyroll. I love using Dulce de Leche (page 52) for the filling, but this cake is also delicious simply filled with strawberry preserves, as my grandmother used to do. Vanilla or caramel ice cream is a nice addition on the side. And although I prefer the whipped cream plain in this preparation, consider adding your favorite extract (almond, orange, vanilla) or spice (cinnamon, nutmeg) before beating.

The *brazo gitano* is best when made with a fresh cake. However, if necessary, you can make the cake ahead of time and store it in the freezer, wrapped very well in plastic, for up to 2 months and bring to room temperature before assembling.

SERVES 10 TO 12

8 eggs, separated	
½ cup granulated sugar	100 GRAMS
2¼ teaspoons vanilla extract	
1 teaspoon almond extract	
¼ cup all-purpose flour	35 GRAMS

Confectioners' sugar for turning out the cake
About 1 cup Dulce de Leche (page 52)
1 recipe Whipped Cream (page 235)

⊚ Preheat the oven to 350° F. Grease a 12-by-17-inch half sheet pan (jellyroll pan) and either dust it with flour or line the bottom with parchment paper.

⊚ In the bowl of an electric mixer, beat the egg yolks, sugar, and extracts until pale and thick. Soak a separate bowl and the whisk attachment of an electric mixer in warm water and dry thoroughly. This will ensure that the egg whites gain enough volume during heating. Beat the egg whites until stiff peaks form. Fold the beaten egg whites and the flour into the egg yolk mixture. Do not overmix.

◎ Pour the batter into the prepared pan, spread evenly, and bake for 10 minutes, or until the cake springs back to the touch when lightly pressed. The cake will be golden, and will pull away from the sides of the pan, and a toothpick inserted in the center will come out clean. Let cool.

◎ Sprinkle a clean kitchen towel with confectioners' sugar and invert the cake onto the towel. Peel off the parchment paper, if used, and if necessary trim the edges of the cake so that they are straight and even. Carefully invert the cake onto a wire rack to cool. This cake is quite forgiving and will withstand handling without falling apart.

◎ Spread the top of the cake with a thin, even layer of the Dulce de Leche. Gently roll the cake, from one of the short sides to the other, using the kitchen towel as a guide and keeping the roll tight. Place it seam-side down on a serving plate. Don't worry about small cracks and crumbs; the whipped cream will cover any missteps.

◎ Place several large dollops of whipped cream on the top of the cake and spread evenly with a spatula, covering the cake on all sides. Make a decorative wave pattern in the whipped cream

icing with a fork, if you like. Refrigerate for at least 2 hours, or up to 2 days. Slice crosswise to serve.

Adorno Especial

Ceviche de Mango, Guanabana Granizado y Helado de Dulce de Leche

Mango Ceviche 1 recipe (page 184)
Soursop Granita 1 recipe (page 224)
Milk-Caramel Ice Cream 1 recipe (page 195)

Arrange a layer of ceviche on each plate, slightly overlapping the slices of fruit in various directions. Next, place a mound of 2 to 3 tablespoons of the granita in the center of the ceviche. On top, carefully place the slice of cake. Finally, top with a small scoop or quenelle of the ice cream. Or skip the garnishes and just serve with the *dulce de leche* ice cream.

If you are serving to a group, you can present the whole cake roll decoratively surrounded by the mango ceviche with the ice cream on the side.

PECAN CAKE ROLL

Brazo Gitano de Nuez Relleno de Mousse de Chocolate

This is yet another variation of the popular *brazo gitano* cake roll. Slices of *brazo gitano*–type cake rolls can be found for sale in bakeries across Latin America with any number of fillings and toppings and some slight variations on the cake itself. Since it makes a particularly impressive presentation for serving to groups, it is often made for celebrations during the holiday season.

The light, nutty texture of the cake and the creamy mousse is a perfect combination and much easier to make than its beautiful appearance would suggest. Plus, the sponge cake alone or even the fully assembled cake roll can be frozen for up to 2 months, so you can prepare it ahead of time.

As an alternative to the whipped cream icing, you can simply dust the cake with unsweetened cocoa powder.

SERVES 10 TO 12

8 eggs, separated

2 cups packed light
   brown sugar   455 GRAMS

1 cup cake flour, sifted   140 GRAMS

2 teaspoons baking powder

1 teaspoon salt

3 tablespoons vanilla extract

3 cups finely minced pecans   320 GRAMS

1 recipe Chocolate Mocha Mousse (page
   238), with Kahlúa instead of espresso

1 recipe Whipped Cream (page 235)

◎ Preheat the oven to 350° F. Grease a 12-by-17-inch half sheet pan (jellyroll pan) and either dust it with flour or line the bottom with parchment paper.

◎ In the bowl of an electric mixer, beat the egg yolks, brown sugar, and cake flour until pale and thick, about 5 minutes. Add the baking powder and salt and beat 1 more minute, then add the vanilla extract. Soak a separate bowl and the whisk attachment of an electric mixer in warm water and dry thoroughly. This will ensure that the egg whites gain enough volume during heating. Beat the egg whites until stiff peaks form. Fold the beaten egg whites and the pecans into the egg yolk mixture. Do not overmix.

◎ Pour the batter into the prepared pan, spread evenly, and bake for 9 minutes, or until the cake springs back to the touch when lightly pressed.

The cake will be golden, and will pull away from the sides of the pan, and a toothpick inserted in the center will come out clean. Let cool. Do not refrigerate or the cake will collapse.

◎ Follow the instructions for the Milk-Caramel Cake Roll (page 92) for assembling and icing the cake roll, filling it here with mousse rather than caramel.

◎ Remove from the heat and let rest for 10 minutes. Spoon into serving bowls or parfait glasses and serve warm. (Alternatively, chill it and serve cold; it will keep, covered and re-frigerated, for a day or two. Longer than that, and the pudding will become dry and lose its creamy texture.)

Adorno Especial

*Crema de Canela y
Reduccion de Café*

These special garnishes add classic "cup of coffee" flavors to this dessert. If you only have time to make one, opt for the creamy cinnamon sauce.

Cinnamon Cream 1 recipe (page 257)
Coffee Reduction 1 recipe (page 259)

Pour a puddle of the cream on each plate, drizzle with the reduction, and top with a slice of cake.

BAKED PATAGONIA WITH TROPICAL FRUIT AND BERRY SALSA

Patagonia Horneado con Salpicón de Fruta

This dessert was named to honor Argentina and to capture a little bit of the beauty of Patagonia. Patagonia occupies nearly a quarter of Argentina, as well as parts of Chile, and its name was derived from Patagones, what the sixteenth-century Spanish explorers called the native Tehuelche Indians of the region. Most important, the name of this dessert has a good dose of humor.

The traditional baked Alaska dessert is an impressive combination of layers of sponge cake and ice cream, blanketed with peaks of meringue and quickly baked to a golden brown. Rather miraculously, the meringue layer insulates the ice cream and prevents it from melting.

One of the first books I read on cakes and pastries during my time as an apprentice in New York had a beautiful picture of baked Alaska. When I first created this dish, I wanted to take that idea and inject it with Latin flair. So I gave the cake a pistachio base, used Dulce de Leche Ice Cream, and served the whole masterpiece with a fresh fruit *salpicón*. The French term *salpicón* refers to a mixture of fresh fruit or savory ingredients mixed with syrup, cream, or a complementary sauce. This preparation with tropical fruit and berries is very typical in Colombia. It is a beautiful accompaniment to my version of baked Alaska, but it's just as refreshing served over a simple dish of vanilla ice cream or used to top yogurt, waffles, or cheesecake.

SERVES 12

½ cup plus 2 tablespoons pistachio flour	90 GRAMS
½ cup confectioners' sugar	60 GRAMS
5 whole eggs	
2 tablespoons butter, melted	
3 tablespoons all-purpose flour	
3 egg whites	
¼ cup granulated sugar	50 GRAMS
1 medium mango, finely diced	
1 papaya, diced	170 GRAMS

1 cup diced pineapple	170 GRAMS
2 cups blueberries	340 GRAMS
2 cups raspberries	340 GRAMS
½ cup Simple Syrup (page 237)	120 MILLILITERS
1 cup guava puree	240 MILLILITERS
½ cup passion fruit puree	120 MILLILITERS
1 recipe Milk-Caramel Ice Cream (page 195)	
1 recipe Italian Meringue (see page 236)	

◎ Preheat the oven to 350° F. Grease a 12-by-17-inch half sheet pan (jellyroll pan) and either dust it with flour or line the bottom with parchment paper.

◎ In an electric mixer, combine the pistachio flour, confectioners' sugar, and whole eggs and beat on high speed (or whisk by hand) for about 15 minutes, until pale and thick—to the ribbon stage: When you lift a beater out of the batter, it should flow from it in a smooth, even ribbon. Transfer the mixture to a large mixing bowl and add the melted butter. Sift the flour into a small bowl and gently fold it into the batter.

◎ With an electric mixer beat the egg whites and granulated sugar until soft peaks form. Fold the egg white mixture into the batter, about one third at a time.

◎ Pour the batter into the prepared pan, spreading it out evenly. Bake for 15 minutes, or until a toothpick inserted in the center comes out clean. The cake will not rise significantly.

◎ Put all the fruit in a large mixing bowl. Add the syrup and fruit purees and gently toss to combine. Put in the refrigerator until ready to serve. (The salsa can be made up to 2 days in advance.)

◎ Cut 2-inch rounds of the pistachio cake with a cookie cutter and place them on a sheet pan. Top each round with a medium-size scoop of ice cream and place in the freezer until reset. Working quickly, remove each dessert one at a time from the freezer and cover each completely with a ¾-inch layer of meringue (you will use a little more than half of the recipe). Be sure there are no gaps or air spaces, and return to the freezer for at least 1 hour or up to 12 hours. Prior to adding the meringue, the cake and ice cream rounds can be frozen for up to two months.

◎ Preheat the oven to 400° F. Bake the cakes for 5 to 6 minutes, until the meringue is lightly browned. Serve at once with the fruit salsa.

◎ If you don't want to use the oven and happen to have a small butane kitchen torch (you can find them in stores such as Williams-Sonoma or Crate and Barrel), I prefer that option for browning the meringue, as it will keep the ice cream slightly more set.

Cracking a Coconut

SEVERAL OF MY DESSERT RECIPES CALL FOR FRESHLY GRATED COCONUT. You can get away with using bagged, sweetened shredded coconut from the grocery store for the Coconut Rice Pudding (page 53), but I wouldn't recommend it for the Coconut and Cream Cheese Empanadas (page 118). Fresh is best for both, as you really taste the true coconut flavor. I also love a snack or breakfast of sliced bananas with freshly grated coconut and either honey or yogurt on top. If you need to use bagged coconut for the Walnut Coconut Cookies (page 53) or Fried Ice Cream (page 230), look for unsweetened shredded coconut (such as Bob's Red Mill and King Arthur brands, which are fairly easy to find).

If you've never cracked a fresh coconut before, it can be a little daunting at first. But it's really fairly simple and one of those fun kitchen projects that can impress friends, especially your kids. Look for mature coconuts with brown, fibrous husks, rather than young, green coconuts, which are mostly used for the coconut water they hold rather than their flesh or the meat of the coconut.

Hold the coconut in an unbreakable bowl (to catch the coconut milk, which is delicious over ice and a great tonic for the body) and, using a heavy meat mallet or even a regular hammer, firmly tap the side of the coconut until it cracks in half (consider the end with the eyes the top and the opposite end the bottom). You can chip out the coconut by hand, using a butter knife, but it is slow and time-consuming to separate the flesh from the shell. A surprising and efficient method is to place the coconut half skin-side down directly over a medium flame on a gas stove. The skin should darken but not burn or catch fire. The skin will tighten and shrink, causing the flesh to loosen and separate from the shell. Be careful not to leave it over the flame too long, or the coconut flesh will roast—about 5 to 7 minutes will do the trick, although the exact time will depend on the thickness of the shell. Turn off the flame and remove the coconut shells from the stovetop with an oven mitt or a pair of tongs, being careful not to touch them with your hands. Place them in the sink and run under cold water until cool to the touch. The coconut flesh should come out easily in a few large pieces. The flesh will still have a thin, brown skin attached to it. Use a pairing knife or potato peeler to remove this before grating the coconut on a hand grater.

MILK-CARAMEL CAKE ROLL (*page 92*)
with Mango Ceviche (page 184)

99

**CHOCOLATE AND SAFFRON
"THOUSAND LEAVES" NAPOLEON
WITH APPLE COMPOTE** *(page 120)*

DRUNKEN CAKES *(page 90)*
with Chamomile Cream (page 258)
and Guava Sorbet (page 219)

COOKIES *From left:*

LATIN COCONUT BARS
(page 64)

DULCE DE LECHE-FILLED BUTTER COOKIE SANDWICHES *(page 50)*

OATMEAL GUAVA BARS *(page 57)*

CRISP CHOCOLATE MERINGUES *(page 56)*

APPLE EMPANADAS *(page 112)*

CINNAMON TART
STUFFED WITH DATES
(page 110)

**PERUVIAN SWEET POTATO AND PUMPKIN
FRITTERS WITH SPICED SYRUP** *(page 124)*

Churros

IT SEEMS THAT JUST ABOUT EVERY ETHNIC CUISINE HAS ITS OWN VERSION of sweet, fried dough: *struffoli* from Italy, *loukoumades* from Greece, *beignets* from France. So it's no surprise that Latin America has a few of its own: *picarones, buñuelos, churros.* *Churros* are piped into fat, round strips, as opposed to the spherical, more doughnutlike *buñuelos* or loosely shaped *picarones,* and are one of the most traditional and most popular desserts in Latin America. They are usually eaten with thick, hot chocolate for breakfast, sort of like a Latin fondue, as an afternoon snack, or as a dessert after dinner. Any of these types of fried dough are common street food, especially during holidays or other local celebrations or festivals.

Growing up in Mexico, I enjoyed similar types of fried dough. Mostly those made with all-purpose flour, more like a sweet bread dough, flattened like a thick tortilla and fried until crunchy. Or simply fried flour tortillas dusted with sugar and cinnamon or doused with sweet syrup. We also called these *buñuelos,* but they were similar to *sopaipillas,* the fried little pillows of dough popular in the American Southwest.

In the United States, you'll find *churros* served everywhere, from four-star restaurants and local cafés and delis, to donut shops, street carts, and subway stations—hollowed out and filled with whipped cream or jam or simply dusted with sugar and cinnamon. When I was growing up in Mexico, we'd wait until about six in the evening, when the sun started to go down, and we'd all go outside to this particular street corner where the *churros* man would be frying dough until everyone had their fill. We were lucky to live near the town square so we could get our *churros* fresh after dinner. You could also buy *churros* in the bakeries, but nothing compared to *churros* fresh out of the fryer dusted with powdered sugar and cinnamon.

SWEET FRIED LATIN DOUGHNUTS WITH CHOCOLATE SAUCE

Churros con Chocolate

It's hard to improve on a dessert of traditional *churros* with chocolate sauce. Here I've added a twist with the addition of cloves and South America's native allspice berries. Both give the sauce a nice spice that plays off the sweet richness of the chocolate. This combination of sweetness and spice is deeply rooted in Latin American cuisine. I'd recommend splurging on a very-good-quality bittersweet chocolate—you'll definitely taste the difference. Try Valrhona or Callebaut if you can't find El Rey, my favorite Venezuelan chocolate. Try leftover sauce as a decadent hot chocolate drink, as a dipping sauce for fresh fruit, or poured over ice cream. For dramatic effect, you can try piping the *churros* into longer strips and serving them upright in a short glass or deep ramekin.

MAKES 12 TO 15 (4-INCH) CHURROS; SERVES 6

For the chocolate sauce:

- 3 tablespoons cornstarch
- 1 (14-ounce) can sweetened condensed
    milk   420 MILLILITERS
- 3 (12-ounce) cans evaporated milk   1 LITER
- 20 whole allspice berries
- 4 whole cloves
- 1 vanilla bean, halved lengthwise, seeds
    scraped out and reserved (or 3
    tablespoons vanilla extract)
- 3 (2.8-ounce) bars bittersweet chocolate
    (El Rey "Mijao" 61%), chopped

For the churros:

- ⅓ cup butter   75 GRAMS
- 4 teaspoons salt
- ⅓ cup rum   80 MILLILITERS
- 4 cups all-purpose flour   570 GRAMS
- About 2 cups sugar   400 GRAMS
- About 1 tablespoon ground cinnamon
- 2 quarts vegetable oil for frying   2 LITERS

◎ Make the chocolate sauce: Dissolve the cornstarch in ¼ cup (60 milliliters) cold water and set aside.

◎ Place the milks in a medium saucepan and bring to a simmer over low heat, stirring constantly. Add the allspice, cloves, and vanilla bean (including seeds) or extract. Reduce the heat to the lowest setting and continue to heat for about 20 minutes. Strain through a fine sieve into a clean saucepan. Discard the allspice, cloves, and vanilla bean pod.

◎ Bring the mixture back to a simmer over medium heat, add the chocolate, and stir to incorporate. When chocolate has melted, whisk in the cornstarch mixture in a slow, steady stream. Continue cooking for 4 to 6 minutes, stirring occasionally, until the sauce has thickened. Remove from the heat while you are making the churros and reheat just before serving. (The sauce can be made in advance and stored in the refrigerator for up to 5 days. When cool, it will form a skin on top, but that will melt away when reheated.)

◎ Make the *churros*: In a 3-quart saucepan, bring 4 cups (960 milliliters) water, butter, salt, and rum to a rolling boil. Stirring vigorously, gradually add the flour. Reduce the heat and continue to stir until the dough pulls away from the sides of the pan and forms a ball, about 1 minute. Let cool for 1 to 2 minutes before frying.

◎ (The dough can be prepared in advance and stored in the refrigerator in an airtight container for up to 2 days; let the dough rest at room temperature for about 15 minutes before frying. Unfortunately, this dough does not hold up in the freezer.)

◎ Combine the sugar and cinnamon in a large shallow bowl and set aside. Heat the oil in a large, heavy saucepan to 360° F.

◎ Spoon the dough into a pastry bag fitted with a large star tip (no. 829, if you have a professional set). If you don't have a pastry bag, a plastic bag with the corner cut off (to create a ½-inch opening) will work fine, though you won't end up with the classic ridged exterior on the *churros* (which holds the sauce better).

◎ Squeeze three or four 4-inch strips of dough—snipping them to that length with kitchen shears—into the hot oil and fry until golden brown, about 2 minutes per side. As they are finished, remove the churros with a slotted spoon and drain them well on paper towels. Repeat with the remaining dough.

◎ When the *churros* are cool enough to handle, but still warm, roll them in the cinnamon-sugar mixture and set them on a platter. Serve with the warm sauce. The sauce will remain at a good consistency for dipping even as it cools, but you may want to stir it periodically to avoid the top drying out.

CINNAMON TART STUFFED WITH DATES

Encanelado Relleno con Datil

Encanelado translates roughly to "cinnamon-y," and this dessert has an intense cinnamon flavor enrobing sweet, slightly savory dates. But I have also made this dessert with mango, quince, and guava fillings and the cinnamon flavor works equally well with each. This recipe was inspired by Peruvian *encanelado*, which has a more cakelike exterior and is traditionally stuffed with pastry cream. A second inspiration came from the Spanish Basque cake—a rich butter cake traditionally flavored with orange zest or vanilla and stuffed with almond paste. Try this with the Tamarind Ice Cream (see page 202). Be sure to mix the dough for this recipe by hand rather than using an electric mixer, or it will become too airy and will overflow the pan.

SERVES 8

For the filling:

1 cup passion fruit puree or juice	240 MILLILITERS
¼ cup granulated sugar	50 GRAMS
2 cups pitted dates	310 GRAMS

For the dough:

1½ cups (3 sticks) butter, softened	340 GRAMS
1 cup granulated sugar	200 GRAMS
1 teaspoon salt	
Grated zest of 2 lemons	
1 whole egg	
2 egg yolks	
2 cups all-purpose flour	285 GRAMS
¼ cup ground cinnamon	30 GRAMS

⊚ Make the filling: In a small saucepan, combine the passion fruit puree, sugar, and dates and bring to a boil. Reduce the heat and simmer for 15 minutes. Remove from the heat and let cool. Put in a blender or food processor and puree until smooth. (The filling will keep, tightly covered in the refrigerator, for 2 weeks or can be frozen for up to 3 months.)

⊚ Make the dough: In a medium mixing bowl, cream together the butter and sugar by hand. Stir in the salt and lemon zest. Add the egg and yolks and stir until well incorporated. Stir in the flour. The dough will be thick, just slightly looser than traditional pie dough.

⊚ Grease an oblong tart pan about 14 by 4½ inches by 1¼ inches.

⊚ Put the dough in a pastry bag fitted with a plain tip or a plastic bag with the corner cut off and pipe about half of the dough into the prepared pan to cover the bottom evenly. Pipe a strip of dough along the inside perimeter of the pan, creating a sort of ridge that can be filled with the date puree. You should have slightly less than half the dough left.

◎ Put the filling in a plastic bag with the corner cut off and pipe the puree into the center of the unbaked tart, or simply spoon it into the center of the tart and spread it evenly with a spatula, staying within the ridge of dough around the perimeter of the pan. Finally, cover the filling with a piped layer of the dough. It should be just slightly higher than the top of the pan. Using an offset spatula, smooth the top layer of the dough, making it even with the top of the pan. Cover and chill in the refrigerator for at least 30 minutes, or up to 2 days.

(The tart can also be frozen at this point for up to 1 month and thawed in the refrigerator before baking.)

◎ Preheat the oven to 375º F. Uncover the tart and set it on a sheet pan either greased or lined with parchment paper. Put the tart in the oven, reduce the oven temperature to 350º F, and bake for about 30 minutes, until golden brown. Let cool for 15 minutes. While still warm, unmold onto a platter. If not serving immediately, let cool completely, then store, tightly covered, at room temperature for up to 2 days.

◎ The tart can be served warm or at room temperature. Dust heavily with the cinnamon and slice crosswise.

Tamarind

NATIVE TO INDIA, TAMARIND CROPS UP ACROSS LATIN AMERICA IN everything from snacks to candies to beverages. I grew up on icepops and *granizados* flavored with tamarind syrup. In the *mercados*, there were fruit-roll-up-like versions of tamarind candy, and tamarind paste was sold in large, compact squares, a smaller version of which was eaten out of hand as a sweet-salty snack. In the Caribbean, little balls of tamarind paste are mixed with sugar, salt, and pepper, coated with granulated sugar, and enjoyed like pieces of fudge. See Aguas Frescas (page 191) for instructions on how to make Agua de Tamarindo.

Tamarind's long, dry, brown pods, (see photo, page 214), similar in shape to a fava bean pod, hold a fibrous brown flesh wound around kidney-shaped seeds. The allure of tamarind is its unique sweet-sour flavor, somewhat like a cross between apricots and dates but with the added tang of citrus. Tamarind is fairly easy to find in ethnic markets these days. You might find it easier to work with the already skinned pulp, often sold in bags or pressed into slabs, still containing the seeds or not, depending on the market. Soften the mass in hot water and press through a sieve to remove the fibers and seeds.

APPLE EMPANADAS
Empanadas de Manzana

There's no dessert more American than apple pie. And wrapping a souped-up apple pie filling in flaky empanada dough is one of the best marriages I can think of between American and Latin pastries. Plus, these empanadas, like most, travel extremely well when you need to bring a dessert to a party or pack something sweet in a lunchbox or for a picnic.

Just as with *pâte sucrée* or piecrust, not overmixing the dough is the secret. Mix it until it just barely holds together, but is not completely homogenous. If you try breaking off a small piece of dough, it should break off easily rather than pulling or stretching. If the latter happens, it means you have overworked the dough, the gluten has become too developed, and your empanada crust will be tough rather than light and flaky. The addition of some cake flour also helps lighten the dough and turn out a flaky crust, especially with baked empanadas.

If you choose to fry these empanadas rather than bake them, you need to add oil to the dough. For oven-baked empanadas, use only butter so that they don't become greasy.

MAKES 16 EMPANADAS

For the dough:

1½ cups all-purpose flour — 210 GRAMS

½ cup cake flour — 70 GRAMS

½ cup plus 2 tablespoons granulated sugar — 125 GRAMS

1 tablespoon baking powder

1 cup (2 sticks) butter, chilled, cut into small cubes, and then re-chilled — 225 GRAMS

½ cup heavy cream, chilled — 120 MILLILITERS

For the filling:

4 medium green apples

1 pinch saffron

1 vanilla bean, halved lengthwise, seeds scraped out and reserved (or 1½ tablespoons vanilla extract)

¼ cup dark rum — 60 MILLILITERS

½ cup brown sugar — 115 GRAMS

1 tablespoon cornstarch

To finish the empanadas:

2 whole eggs

¼ cup chopped walnuts — 30 GRAMS

◎ Make the dough: In a medium mixing bowl, combine the flours, sugar, and baking powder. Cut in the butter with a pastry blender or your fingers until it resembles coarse meal (alternatively, use a stand mixer with a paddle attachment for this step only; the remaining mixing must be done by hand). Add the cream and toss with your hands just until the mixture comes together, being careful not to overwork the dough. Divide the dough into 2 equal pieces, flatten each into a rough square, and refrigerate, wrapped in plastic wrap, for at least 1 hour.

◎ Make the filling: Peel, core, and dice the apples. In a medium saucepan over medium heat, combine the apples, saffron, halved vanilla bean (including seeds) or extract, rum, and brown sugar and cook for about 15 minutes, until the apples are tender. In a small cup or mixing bowl, combine the cornstarch and 2 tablespoons water and stir into the apple mixture. Simmer for 5 more minutes, then remove from the heat. Refrigerate until cool.

◎ Finish the empanadas: Preheat the oven to 350° F.

◎ In a small mixing bowl, whisk the eggs together with 2 tablespoons cold water.

◎ Place one square of the cold dough on a floured surface. Roll the dough out with a rolling pin to about ⅛ inch thick. Cut the dough into 3½-inch circles with a cookie cutter. If you want to roll out the scraps to form a few more circles, lightly press the remaining dough into another flattened square and refrigerate again before rolling it out a second time. Try to work the dough as little as possible so it doesn't become tough. After rolling it out 3 times, discard any remaining dough.

◎ Keeping the circles of dough refrigerated while you work, place about 2 tablespoons of apple filling in the center of one circle of dough. Using a small pastry brush or the tips of your fingers, brush the inside edges of the dough with a bit of the egg wash and carefully fold over the filling into a semicircle. Gently crimp down the edges with the tines of a fork to seal, or pinch into small creases with your fingers. Repeat with the remaining dough and filling. (Unbaked empanadas will keep for about 2 months in the freezer; defrost them in the refrigerator, then bring them to room temperature before baking.)

◎ Place the empanadas on a nonstick baking sheet or one lined with parchment paper or a Silpat mat. Alternatively, use a nonstick sheet pan or grease the pan very lightly with butter. Brush the tops with the egg wash and sprinkle with walnuts. Bake for 18 minutes, or until golden brown. Let cool for 10 minutes before serving. They are best freshly baked, but baked empandas can be stored in an airtight container for up to 2 days.

Empanadas

EMPANADAS, DERIVED FROM THE SPANISH VERB *EMPANAR*, MEANING "TO coat or bake in bread or pastry," are pastry turnovers stuffed with either sweet or savory fillings. In Uruguay and Mexico, sweet fillings, such as fruit, *dulce de leche*, cheese, or a combination of these, are the norm. In places like Argentina, it is more common to find savory empanadas filled with ham and cheese or *picadillo*, a ground beef and tomato filling sometimes studded with olives or capers.

Just as most American mothers and grandmothers have a "secret" piecrust recipe, most Latin American mothers and grandmothers swear by their methods for turning out the perfect empanada dough. It is also quite common to simply buy empanadas from street vendors or bakeries. When I was growing up my family did sometimes make empanadas at home, but our neighbor made the ones I remember most vividly. She would make empanadas and doughnuts from scratch in her home kitchen and sell them minutes after they came out of the hot oil. On Thursday evenings, just as the sun would start to set, she would arrange them in a little palm basket and sell them right on the street. She would make enough for the whole block, and she very rarely had to walk any farther away to sell out of her supply. She made apple empanadas and empanadas filled with *cajeta*, goat's milk caramel, but my favorites by far were her slightly untraditional rice pudding–filled empanadas. They remain the best empanadas I've ever had.

These days, I must give credit for "my" empanada dough to Mamá or Abuela (grandmother) Luz, whom I met during one of my first restaurant jobs in the United States. Then in her late sixties, the Empanada Queen, as we called her, would stand tirelessly for hours expertly mixing empanada dough—a skill she had learned in her native Ecuador—and nimbly shaping what seemed like hundreds of empandas a day. She taught me how to make the perfect empanada, but she also taught me a very important lesson—that it is the combination of homestyle cooking methods and professional techniques, neither one on their own, that turn out the best food.

At that time, I was most familiar with savory empanadas that were fried, and I was inspired to create a sweet dessert empanada that was baked instead. My baked Apple Empanadas (page 112), Goat Cheese and Guava Empanadas (page 116), and Coconut and Cream Cheese Empanadas (page 118) are the result. Feel free to experiment with your favorite fillings.

If you prefer your empanadas fried, use this dough recipe. It works equally well for both sweet and savory fillings. The addition of arepa flour, a pre-cooked corn flour, will make the empanadas a bit crisper. But if you can't find it, just use a total of 2½ cups of all-purpose flour.

2 cups all-purpose flour	285 GRAMS
½ cup arepa flour	70 GRAMS
1 tablespoon kosher salt	
¼ cup (½ stick) butter, melted	60 MILLILITERS
¼ cup vegetable oil	60 MILLILITERS
1 tablespoon freshly squeezed lime juice or white vinegar (from about 1 lime)	
2 quarts vegetable oil for frying	2 LITERS

MAKE THE DOUGH:

For the dough, in a medium mixing bowl, combine both flours and the salt. Add the butter, oil, 2 cups (480 milliliters) water, and lime juice or vinegar and incorporate with your hands just until the mixture comes together, being careful not to overwork the dough. Divide the dough into two equal pieces, flatten each into a rough square, and refrigerate, wrapped in plastic wrap, for at least one hour before filling and forming the empanadas.

Create a filling of your choice, and see Apple Empanadas (page 112) for instructions on forming and filling the empanadas.

FRY THE EMPANADAS:

When ready to serve, heat the oil in a large, heavy-bottomed saucepan to 350° F. Fry the empanadas in batches of 6 to 8 until golden brown, about 1½ minutes per side. Remove from the oil with a slotted spoon and drain briefly on paper towels. Serve immediately.

GOAT CHEESE AND GUAVA EMPANADAS

Empanadas de Queso de Cabra y Guayaba

It is very common in Latin countries like Cuba, Colombia, Venezuela, and Ecuador to eat *queso fresco* or *queso blanco* with guava. In Cuban markets, you'll sometimes find guava paste with a slice of *queso fresco* on top sold as a *bocadillo* or tapas. And one of my favorite, simple desserts is chunks of poached guava in sweet syrup sprinkled with salty *queso fresco*. These guava-cheese combos are similar to the Spanish pairing of manchego with quince paste or *membrillo*. I love that this empanada incorporates all my favorite cheese platter components: rich cheese, sweet fruit, flaky dough taking the place of bread, and crunchy nuts. If you like your desserts to lean toward the savory side, this one's for you. Pistachio or walnut ice cream is also a great accompaniment.

MAKES 16 EMPANADAS

1 recipe Empanada Dough (page 112)

For the filling:

8 ounces goat cheese — 225 GRAMS

1 tablespoon all-purpose flour

1 cup guava paste — 225 GRAMS

To finish the empanadas:

2 eggs

¼ cup chopped pistachios — 30 GRAMS

◉ Chill the dough in the refrigerator, as in the recipe on page 113.

◉ Make the filling: In a small mixing bowl, use a fork to blend the goat cheese and flour.

◉ Finish the empanadas: Preheat the oven to 350° F.

◉ In a small mixing bowl, whisk the eggs together with 2 tablespoons cold water.

◉ Place one square of the cold dough on a floured surface. Roll the dough out with a rolling pin to about ⅛ inch thick. Cut the dough into 3½-inch circles with a cookie cutter. If you want to roll out the scraps to form a few more circles, lightly press the remaining dough into another flattened square and refrigerate again before rolling it out a second time. Try to work the dough as little as possible so it doesn't become tough. After rolling it out 3 times, discard any remaining dough.

⑨ Keeping the circles of dough refrigerated while you work, place 1 tablespoon of guava paste and 1 tablespoon of the goat cheese mixture in the center of one circle of dough. Using a small pastry brush or the tips of your fingers, brush the inside edges of the dough with a bit of the egg wash and carefully fold over the filling into a semicircle. Gently crimp down the edges with the tines of a fork to seal, or pinch into small creases with your fingers. Repeat with the remaining dough and filling. (Unbaked empanadas will keep for about 2 months in the freezer; defrost them in the refrigerator, then bring them to room temperature before baking.)

⑨ Place the empanadas on a nonstick baking sheet or one lined with parchment paper or a Silpat mat. Alternatively, use a nonstick sheet pan or grease the pan very lightly with butter. Brush the tops with the egg wash and sprinkle with pistachios. Bake for 18 minutes, or until golden brown. Let cool for 10 minutes before serving. They are best freshly baked, but baked empandas can be stored in an airtight container for up to 2 days.

COCONUT AND CREAM CHEESE EMPANADAS

Empanadas de Coco y Queso Crema

Dulce de coco, or candied coconut, and queso crema or cream cheese is a very common pairing in Cuba. It is yet another one of those sweet-savory combinations that tastes amazing.

I know it can seem daunting to crack and grate fresh coconut (see page 98). But you won't be disappointed with the results. If you absolutely need a shortcut and don't want to make the coconut filling from scratch, the Goya brand sells a canned grated coconut in syrup, which you can use as a substitute. Just be careful to drain it extremely well, as the moisture can end up making your empanadas soggy. If you make the filling from scratch, you have the added benefit of experimenting by adding other flavorings, such as orange or lemon zest or cinnamon. I wouldn't recommend using bagged shredded coconut here.

If you have kids, empanadas (especially ones that involve breaking open a fresh coconut, which can be impressive to young eyes) are a great kitchen project for the whole family.

MAKES 16 EMPANADAS

1 recipe Empanada Dough (see page 112)

For the filling:

2 cups freshly grated coconut	150 GRAMS
1½ cups granulated sugar	300 GRAMS
2 tablespoons freshly squeezed lime juice	
1 pound cream cheese	

To finish the empanadas:

2 eggs	
½ cup granulated sugar	100 GRAMS

⊚ Chill the dough in the refrigerator, as in the recipe on page 113.

⊚ Make the filling: In a medium saucepan over high heat, combine the coconut, sugar, 1½ cups water, and the lime juice and bring to a boil. Lower the heat and simmer, stirring frequently to keep the coconut from sticking to the bottom of the pan, for about 20 minutes, until the mixture reaches a honeylike consistency. Let cool at room temperature or in the refrigerator.

⊚ Finish the empanadas: Preheat the oven to 350° F.

⊚ In a small mixing bowl, whisk the eggs together with 2 tablespoons cold water.

⑨ Place one square of the cold dough on a floured surface. Roll the dough out with a rolling pin to about ⅛ inch thick. Cut the dough into 3½-inch circles with a cookie cutter. If you want to roll out the scraps to form a few more circles, lightly press the remaining dough into another flattened square and refrigerate again before rolling it out a second time. Try to work the dough as little as possible so it doesn't become tough. After rolling it out 3 times, discard any remaining dough.

⑨ Keeping the circles of dough refrigerated while you work, place about 1 tablespoon of the coconut mixture and 1 tablespoon of cream cheese in the center of one circle of dough. Using a small pastry brush or the tips of your fingers, brush the inside edges of the dough with a bit of the egg wash and carefully fold over the filling into a semicircle. Gently crimp down the edges with the tines of a fork to seal, or pinch into small creases with your fingers. Repeat with the remaining dough and filling. (Unbaked empanadas will keep for about 2 months in the freezer; defrost them in the refrigerator, then bring them to room temperature before baking.)

⑨ Place the empanadas on a nonstick baking sheet or one lined with parchment paper or a Silpat mat. Alternatively, use a nonstick sheet pan or grease the pan very lightly with butter. Brush the tops with the egg wash and sprinkle with sugar. Bake for 18 minutes, or until golden brown. Let cool for 10 minutes before serving. They are best freshly baked, but baked empanadas can be stored in an airtight container for up to 2 days.

CHOCOLATE AND SAFFRON "THOUSAND LEAVES" NAPOLEON WITH APPLE COMPOTE

Mil Hojas de Chocolate y Azafran con Compota de Manzana

Growing up, I was always one of the first to wake up and join my grandmother in the kitchen, particularly because it guaranteed me first pick of the sweet breads set out for breakfast. Every so often, my grandmother would treat me with *mil hojas* from a well-known bakery in Mexico City named El Globo ("the balloon"), which layered the pastry with *cajeta*, goat's milk caramel, and pastry cream. What a way to start the day. Here, I've paired saffron's distinct flavor with the sweet tartness of apple, a fairly common combination in Spain. The addition of chocolate makes the treat even more addictive. You can also try layering the pastry with Dulce de Leche (page 52) and thin slices of *queso fresco* or Brie and serve garnished with sliced *tamarillos* in syrup (see page 189).

If you choose to buy puff pastry, you will need 3 pieces for the 3 layers of the napoleon, each one measuring about 8 inches by 3 inches. Follow the package instructions for baking. Dufour is the brand I recommend.

SERVES 6

For the pastry cream:

4 cups whole milk   950 MILLILITERS

1 cup granulated sugar   200 GRAMS

1 generous pinch saffron threads

5 egg yolks

½ cup cornstarch   65 GRAMS

¼ cup (½ stick) butter

9 ounces bittersweet chocolate, chopped   255 GRAMS

For the apple compote:

1 cup packed brown sugar   225 GRAMS

1 vanilla bean, halved lengthwise, seeds scraped out and reserved (or 1½ tablespoons vanilla extract)

¼ cup Pisco or rum   60 MILLILITERS

1 teaspoon salt

6 green apples, peeled, cored, and diced

¼ cup (½ stick) butter

To finish the pastries:

1 recipe Puff Pastry (page 122)

¼ cup unsweetened cocoa powder   30 GRAMS

Toasted walnuts or confectioners' sugar

Make the pastry cream: In a medium saucepan over medium heat, bring 3½ cups of the milk, the sugar, and saffron to a boil. Reduce the heat and simmer, stirring, until the sugar dissolves.

In a medium mixing bowl, whisk together the egg yolks, cornstarch, and remaining ½ cup milk, making sure there are no lumps of cornstarch. Continue whisking while pouring a small amount of the hot milk mixture into the yolk mixture. This will temper the yolks and keep them from curdling. While whisking the hot milk mixture, gradually add the rest of the yolk mixture. Return to a boil, reduce the heat to medium-low, and simmer for about 8 minutes, stirring constantly with a wooden spoon to prevent the custard from sticking to the bottom of the pan, until the cornstarch is fully cooked. Remove from the heat and stir in the butter and chocolate until melted. Transfer to a clean container and cover with plastic wrap to prevent a skin from forming. Refrigerate for at least 3 hours, or up to 2 days.

Make the apple compote: In a large saucepan over medium-high heat, combine 1 cup (240 milliliters) water, the sugar, halved vanilla bean (including seeds) or extract, Pisco, and salt and bring to a boil. Boil gently until the sugar is dissolved and the mixture thickens slightly, about 5 minutes. Add the apples and return to a boil. Lower the heat and simmer, stirring occasionally, until the apples are very tender and the mixture thickens, about 20 minutes. Remove from the heat, remove the vanilla bean pod, and stir in the butter until melted. Let cool to room temperature.

Finish the napoleons: Place one piece of the baked puff pastry on a work surface. Using an offset spatula, spread half of the pastry cream evenly over the top. Top with a layer of the apple compote. Add another layer of pastry, the remaining custard, more compote, and a final layer of pastry. With a clean kitchen towel, gently press down on the top layer of pastry to tighten up the layers. Dust the top with cocoa powder and cut with a serrated knife into 6 individual portions. Place one portion on each plate. Garnish with any remaining apple compote and sprinkle with toasted walnuts or confectioners' sugar. Serve immediately.

PUFF PASTRY

Pasta de Hojaldre

Mil hojas, or as the French say *mille-feuille*, meaning "thousand leaves," is made by layering flaky puff pastry with a variety of fillings. Although it is quite a classic and popular dessert in Latin America, it is usually only the more prestigious bakeries that actually make it from scratch, since it takes some skill and a fair amount of time. In Miami, I've found *mil hojas* in many Latin bakeries—Argentinean, Chilean, Ecuadorian, Venezuelan. In Cuban bakeries, it is known as *señoritas*. If you're short on time, you can purchase puff pastry dough for *mil hojas* from your local bakery or the frozen section of most supermarkets. It's a great dessert staple to stock in your freezer. With a simple filling, you can very quickly turn out an impressive dessert.

Making your own puff pastry is one of those kitchen projects, like baking bread from scratch, that everyone should try at least once. And with a little practice, you can master the technique. Puff pastry's flaky goodness is made from hundreds of layers of butter and dough. It's a fairly straightforward rolling and folding process that miraculously produces the layers. You'll need a good flat work surface, preferably in a cool room, on which to flour and roll out the dough.

MAKES 3 (8-BY-3-INCH) BAKED LAYERS

2½ pounds butter, chilled, cut into small
    cubes, and then re-chilled   **1135 GRAMS**

 4 cups all-purpose flour, plus additional
    for the work surface   **570 GRAMS**

 1 tablespoon salt

2½ cups very cold water   **590 MILLILITERS**

 2 tablespoons distilled white vinegar

◎ On a flat work surface, cut ½ pound of the cold butter into the flour and salt with a pastry blender or your fingers until it forms tiny beads that resemble coarse meal; this should take 2 to 3 minutes. Make a hole in the middle of the mound of flour and butter, pour the water and vinegar into the hole, and begin pulling the flour mixture into the liquid until a dough starts to form. Continue kneading the dough until it becomes smooth, 10 to 15 minutes. Form it into a ball, score the top with an "X" about 1-inch deep, cover it in plastic wrap, and let it rest for about 10 minutes.

Dust the work surface with flour and form the remaining 2 pounds of cubed butter into a 6-inch square, about 2 inches high. Wrap in plastic wrap and chill in the refrigerator.

Again, dust the work surface with flour. Remove the dough from the plastic wrap and grabbing each of the four corners made by the scored "X," open them up one at a time to form a rough rectangular shape with the dough. Using a rolling pin, roll out the dough, away from the center toward the corners and edges, to form a 12-inch square. The center of the dough square should remain slightly raised. Remove the butter from the refrigerator and unwrap it. Place it in the center of the dough square and fold the corners over the butter, stretching the corners of the dough gently to reach the opposite edge, and being careful not to tear the dough. This will cause the dough to overlap and completely cover the butter. Dust the work surface with flour and turn the butter and dough package over so that it is seam-side down.

Roll out the dough, away from the center toward the corners, to a 1-inch-thick rectangle about 6 by 24 inches, dusting lightly with flour to keep it from sticking to the work surface or the rolling pin. It's a good idea to use a pastry brush to brush away excess flour so that the dough doesn't dry out. Now there is one layer of butter in between two layers of dough.

Beginning with one of the short ends, fold the rectangle into thirds (pamphlet style), being sure that all the edges meet (every area of the rectangle now will have 9 layers, actually 3 layers of dough-butter-dough). Cover with plastic wrap and refrigerate for 30 minutes.

Remove the dough from the refrigerator, unwrap it, and repeat the rolling and folding process: Roll out the dough, away from the center toward the corners, into a 1-inch-thick rectangle about 6 by 24 inches, dusting lightly with flour and brushing away excess with a pastry brush. Beginning with one of the short ends, fold the rectangle into thirds (pamphlet style), being sure that all the edges meet. You will now have 27 layers, or 3 layers of your previous 9-layer dough. Cover with plastic wrap and refrigerate for 10 to 20 minutes.

Repeat this rolling and folding process 4 more times.

After the dough rests in the refrigerator for the last time, roll it out to a ¼-inch-thick rectangle about 9 by 24 inches. Cut the rectangle into thirds, forming three 3 by 8-inch pieces. (You can wrap the dough pieces tightly in plastic wrap and store them in the freezer for up to 3 months; defrost in the refrigerator for at least 2 hours before baking.)

To bake the puff pastry, preheat the oven to 375° F. Line an 11-by-14-inch sheet pan with parchment paper and set in 2 of the rectangles of puff pastry (the third piece will need to be baked separately). Using a fork or toothpick, poke holes in the dough about every 3 to 4 inches to prevent it from puffing up in the center. Cover with plastic wrap and refrigerate for 10 to 20 minutes.

Remove the puff pastry from the refrigerator and bake for 25 to 30 minutes, until crisp and golden brown. Remove from the oven and let cool for at least 10 minutes. Set aside, uncovered, at room temperature until use.

PERUVIAN SWEET POTATO AND PUMPKIN FRITTERS WITH SPICED SYRUP

Picarones con Miel de Especias

The first time I tried *picarones* was in a small Peruvian restaurant in Queens, New York. They were delightful and reminded me of Mexican *buñuelos* but with a slightly different flavor and texture. The *picarones* were doused with a flavorful syrup made from *chancaca* or *panela*, a candylike brick of sugar made from boiled sugarcane juice, and scented with cinnamon, star anise, and pineapple.

Picarones are one of the most classic Peruvian desserts, consumed every day in *mercados* and restaurants alike. While *buñuelos* are made with a yuca-based dough, *picarones* are made with a combination of *zapallo* (pumpkin) and *camote dulce* (sweet potato), giving them their characteristic crisp exterior, soft interior, and naturally sweet flavor. Today, you can even buy prepared mixes for *picarones*, just as you might a store-bought cake mix. But there's no substitute for fresh *picarones* right out of the fryer topped with a big splash of *chancaca* syrup.

SERVES 6 TO 10
(2 OR 3 FRITTERS PER PERSON)

For the batter:

1 cup peeled and diced sweet potato	255 GRAMS
1 cup peeled and diced fresh pumpkin	255 GRAMS
2 star anise pieces	
1 cinnamon stick	
2 whole cloves	
1¼ cups all-purpose flour	175 GRAMS
2 tablespoons granulated sugar	
1 pinch salt	
1½ tablespoons active dry yeast	
2 teaspoons vanilla extract	

For the syrup:

1 pound chopped *panela* (or 2 cups packed brown sugar)	455 GRAMS
1 vanilla bean, halved lengthwise, seeds scraped out and reserved (or 1½ tablespoons vanilla extract)	
1 whole dried ancho chile	
4 cinnamon sticks	
2 whole cloves	
2 star anise pieces	
2 quarts vegetable oil for frying	2 LITERS

Make the batter: In a medium saucepan over high heat, bring 4 cups (960 milliliters) water, the sweet potato, pumpkin, star anise, cinnamon sticks, and cloves to a boil. Lower the heat and simmer until the sweet potato and pumpkin are fork tender, about 15 minutes. Drain, reserving the cooking liquid and discarding the star anise and cinnamon sticks, and mash.

In a large mixing bowl, combine the flour, sugar, salt, and yeast. Add the vanilla extract and the warm potato and pumpkin mixture with enough of the cooking liquid to form a loose dough. Mix for an additional 5 minutes, then let rise, covered with a towel in a warm place, for about 15 minutes, until doubled in volume. If not using the dough immediately, cover it with plastic wrap and store it in the refrigerator for up to 2 hours. Bring to room temperature before frying.

Make the syrup: In a small saucepan over high heat, bring the *panela*, halved vanilla bean (including seeds) or extract, chile, cinnamon sticks, cloves, star anise, and 4 cups (960 milliliters) water to a boil. Lower the heat and cook until the mixture is reduced by half, creating a thick, flavorful syrup.

Fry the *picarones*: Heat the oil in a large, heavy saucepan to 350° F. For a more homestyle fritter, simply drop tablespoonfuls of the dough into the fryer. Alternatively, quickly shape the dough into doughnut shapes using your fingertips, being careful not to overwork the dough; dip your fingertips in water to avoid sticking. Fry in batches of 6 to 8 pieces until deep golden brown and puffy, about 4 minutes. Remove from the oil with a slotted spoon and drain briefly on paper towels. Although you can serve picarones at room temperature, I prefer them served warm fresh from the oil.

To serve, arrange the *picarones* on a platter and drizzle generously with the syrup, serving the remaining syrup on the side.

YUCA FRITTERS WITH PASSION FRUIT, BANANA, AND ORANGE BLOSSOM SYRUP

Buñuelos de Yuca con Almibar de Maracuya, Banana, y Flor de Azar

It wasn't until I moved to Miami that I first tried yuca in a dessert. In a small bakery in the Calle Ocho neighborhood a few blocks from my apartment, they sold small plastic containers filled with several yuca *buñuelos* soaking in a bit of simple sweet syrup. Since then I have also tried them with syrup flavored with anisseed or cinnamon. You can find them at almost every Latin bakery in Miami.

In Cuba, they also make *buñuelos* with *malanga* (similar to yuca, but with a different texture) or sweet potato, but I prefer the ones made with yuca. The starch content of yuca is higher than *malanga* or sweet potato, so the yuca *buñuelos* get crisper on the outside, while staying moist on the inside. They have a great texture and chew and with the fresh fruit syrup, make a delicious, classic, and simple dessert. If you make the dough in advance and store it in the freezer, you can have fresh *buñuelos* in a flash; defrost the dough overnight in the refrigerator before frying.

You can find orange blossom water in most specialty markets where they sell other baking extracts and in Middle Eastern food shops.

MAKES ABOUT 20 FRITTERS

1 **pound yuca**	455 GRAMS
½ **cup granulated sugar**	100 GRAMS
⅜ **cup all-purpose flour**	55 GRAMS
1 **egg**	
2 **teaspoons salt**	
2 **teaspoons ground cinnamon**	
1 **cup Simple Syrup**	
(page 237)	240 MILLILITERS
3 **fresh passion fruit**	
3 **medium ripe bananas**	
1 **teaspoon orange blossom water**	
2 **quarts vegetable oil for frying**	2 LITERS

Peel the yuca and cut into 3-inch-long chunks. Before cooking, score an "X" on each flat, cut end of each piece. Put in a medium saucepan, just cover with water, and bring to a boil over high heat. Boil for 10 to 15 minutes, until the yuca is just tender on the outside but not fully cooked. To test it, take out a piece of yuca and cut it in half. It should be translucent on the outside but still opaque white in the middle. Drain the yuca and put it in a large bowl. Using a potato masher, mash it together with the sugar until fairly smooth. Add the flour, egg, salt, and cinnamon and mix with a wooden spoon or your hands until combined.

The dough should be smooth and soft but not too sticky. With a 1-ounce ice cream scoop or a tablespoon, scoop portions of dough into your hands and roll into balls. Place on a baking sheet until ready to fry. (The uncooked *buñuelos* can be stored in the freezer for up to 1 month. Freeze the balls on baking sheets, then put the frozen balls into one container. Defrost overnight in the refrigerator before frying.)

◎ Put the syrup in a small mixing bowl. Cut the passion fruit in half, scoop out the fleshy pulp, and mix it with the syrup. Peel the bananas, slice or dice them, and add them to the syrup mixture. Stir in the orange blossom water.

◎ Heat the oil in a large, heavy saucepan to 350° F. Very carefully place the *buñuelos*, a few at a time, in the hot oil and cook for 4 to 5 minutes, until dark golden brown. Remove from the oil and place on a paper towel to drain. They can be served warm or at room temperature, but are of course best fresh from frying. Do not refrigerate them once they are cooked. Cover them with a clean, dry kitchen towel, not plastic wrap, to keep them warm.

◎ When ready to serve, place the warm *buñuelos* on a serving plate, forming a pyramid shape, and drizzle with the fruit syrup.

Yuca

YUCA, OR CASSAVA OR MANIOC, IS A FIBROUS ROOT VEGETABLE WITH ROUGH, dark-brown skin and white or yellowish flesh. It looks like a darker, more elongated version of a sweet potato or yam and can be upward of 10 to 12 inches long. Native to South America, yuca is an important staple carbohydrate in Latin America, as well as Africa and China.

Yuca is categorized as either sweet or bitter. Both varieties must be processed or cooked before they are edible. Bitter yuca is exclusively made into flour, while sweet yuca (simply not bitter) is found both as flour and in its fresh form.

In savory preparations, yuca is used much like potatoes—boiled and mashed, fried like French fries or potato chips, or cooked along with other vegetables in soups or stews. Tapioca is made from treated and dried yuca, as in the tapioca pearls used to make my Coconut Tapioca Pudding (page 35) or the sweet and sour tapioca/yuca flours in my addictive Pan de Bono Rolls (chewy cheese rolls, page 65). Boiled, mashed yuca is what gives my fried Buñuelos their great texture.

4

CHOCOLATE DESSERTS

Postres de Chocolate

In This Chapter

~⌒~

LIQUID CHOCOLATE CROQUETTES
Croquetas de Chocolate Líquido

CHOCOLATE CIGARS
Puros de Chocolate

CHOCOLATE CRÊPES WITH MILK-CARAMEL
Crepas de Chocolate Rellenas con Dulce de Leche

VENEZUELAN CHOCOLATE AND HAZELNUT BOMBE
Bomba de Chocolate Venezolano y Avellanas

CHOCOLATE BANANA BREAD PUDDING WITH QUINOA
Puding Andino de Chocolate y Banana con Quinoa

CHOCOLATE THREE MILKS CAKE
Tres Leches de Chocolate

VENEZUELAN CHOCOLATE BROWNIES WITH WALNUTS
Bizcocho de Chocolate Venezolano con Nueves

MASA-THICKENED HOT CHOCOLATE
Champurrado/Atole de Chocolate

CHOCOLATE FLAN
Flan de Chocolate

CHOCOLATE DOMINO CAKE
El Domino

THE "IMPOSSIBLE" CAKE
Pastel Imposible

LIQUID CHOCOLATE CROQUETTES
Croquetas de Chocolate Liquido

It's impossible not to love these crunchy fried croquettes filled with melted chocolate—two classic dessert vices rolled into one. But as you can imagine, it's not exactly easy to fry chocolate. I tried bread crumbs, then shredded coconut, but neither held up in the fryer. I ultimately reached for a box of corn flakes, and eureka. Mix ¼ cup of shredded coconut into the corn flakes if you still want a touch of that flavor.

For a casual dessert, serve the croquettes on a platter dusted with confectioners' sugar. Three 2.8-ounce bars of chocolate will give you enough for this recipe, plus a few squares to taste while you're cooking. And once again, El Rey is my chocolate of choice, but any good-quality dark chocolate, such as Valrhona or Callebaut, will work.

MAKES ABOUT 24 CROQUETTES; SERVES 6 TO 8

For the batter:

3 (2.8-ounce) bars bittersweet chocolate (El Rey "Bucare" 58.5%)	
½ cup (1 stick) butter	115 GRAMS
½ cup granulated sugar	100 GRAMS
3 eggs	
2 tablespoons dark rum	
3 tablespoons all-purpose flour	

For the coating:

1 cup all-purpose flour	140 GRAMS
2 eggs, beaten	
2 cups finely crushed corn flakes	160 GRAMS

To finish the croquettes:

2 quarts vegetable oil	2 LITERS
Confectioners' sugar for dusting	

Make the batter: In the top of a double boiler set over gently simmering water, melt the chocolate and butter. Pour the chocolate mixture into a large bowl, add the sugar and the eggs one at a time, and whisk until combined. Whisk in the rum and flour and cool in the refrigerator for at least 3 hours, or until the mixture is firm.

Place a small amount of the chocolate mixture in a pastry bag fitted with a ½-inch plain tip (no. 808 if you have a professional set) and pipe 2½-inch strips of chocolate onto a baking sheet lined with parchment paper. If you don't have a pastry bag, a plastic bag with the corner cut off (to create a ½-inch opening) will work just fine. Place the chocolate strips in the freezer for about 30 minutes.

Make the coating: Put the flour, eggs, and corn flakes in three separate bowls. Dip the cold piped chocolate pieces in the flour, then the eggs, then the corn flakes, and put them back on the baking sheet. I find it easiest to prepare all the croquettes at once, popping them back into the refrigerator to keep them cool before frying. They will also keep in the refrigerator up to 2 days—no longer, as the corn flakes get soggy. If you need to prepare them further in advance, freeze them, then let them thaw at room temperature for about 1 hour before frying.

◎ Finish the croquettes: Heat the oil in a deep, heavy saucepan to 350° F.

◎ Carefully put 4 or 5 croquettes at a time into the hot oil and fry them, turning, until they are golden brown on all sides (1 to 1½ minutes).

Remove the croquettes from the oil with a slotted spoon and drain on paper towels. Repeat until all the croquettes are fried. Dust with confectioners' sugar and serve immediately.

Adorno Especial

Crème Anglaise

1 recipe Crème Anglaise (page 255)

For a more formal touch, place 3 or 4 croquettes on each plate and garnish with a scoop of ice cream or serve in a pool of crème anglaise.

CHOCOLATE CIGARS

Puros de Chocolate

In tribute to Miami's Cuban community and their affection for hand-rolled cigars, I created this dark chocolate cigar whose "special occasion" presentation has always left a buzz of excitement in its wake. A long, slender slice of cake surrounded by rich chocolate mousse, coated in melted chocolate, and served with an edible matchbook and a mock cup of espresso filled with mocha ice cream and Litchi Foam, it makes people smile not only because of its humor, but also because of its taste.

These individual cigar-shaped cakes are equally delicious plated with fresh whipped cream or a good-quality store-bought ice cream. If you don't want to form the cigar shapes, you can make it even simpler by serving the components in a parfait glass, layering the cake, mousse, and ice cream. The key is to enjoy the combination of flavors and just have fun with it.

MAKES ABOUT 34 CIGARS; SERVES 16 OR MORE (1 TO 2 CIGARS PER PERSON)

For the cake:

¼	cup all-purpose flour	35 GRAMS
½	cup almond flour	70 GRAMS
½	cup (1 stick) butter, softened	115 GRAMS
½	cup granulated sugar	100 GRAMS
7	egg yolks	
5	ounces bittersweet chocolate chopped and melted	140 GRAMS
7	egg whites	

To finish the cigars:

1 recipe Chocolate Mousse with Rum (page 242)

1 pound bittersweet chocolate, chopped — 455 GRAMS

1 cup unsweetened cocoa powder — 110 GRAMS

½ tablespoon ground cinnamon

1 recipe Whipped Cream (page 235)

Make the cake: Preheat the oven to 350° F. Grease an 11-by-8½- inch quarter sheet pan and line the bottom with parchment paper.

Sift the flour and whisk it together with the almond flour. In the bowl of an electric mixer fitted with the paddle attachment, cream the butter and sugar on medium speed for about 3 minutes, until light and fluffy. Add the egg yolks one at a time and mix until well incorporated. Add the flours and mix for about 1 minute. Blend in the melted chocolate and transfer the batter to a mixing bowl.

In a separate bowl, beat the egg whites until they form stiff peaks. Gently fold the beaten egg whites into the chocolate batter, then pour it into the prepared pan. Spread the top evenly with a spatula. Bake for 12 minutes, or until the cake springs back to the touch or a toothpick inserted in the center comes out clean. Let cool for at least 2 hours at room temperature plus 1 additional hour in the refrigerator before assembling the cigars.

◎ Finish the cigars: Cut the cake in half lengthwise and then cut each half crosswise into ½-inch slices, each 5½ inches long. To form the cigars, lay out a 10-inch length of plastic wrap on a flat work surface and place one of the cake strips in the center. Using about 4 tablespoons of the mousse, place small dollops along each strip of cake and at both ends. Carefully roll up the plastic wrap around the cake and filling and twist the ends tightly to close. Using a long metal spatula or just your hands, gently squeeze and mold the mousse around the cake to form a cigar shape. Repeat with the remaining pieces of cake. Put the cigars back on the sheet pan and freeze for at least 2 hours.

◎ When ready to assemble the cigars, melt the chocolate in a double boiler set over gently simmering water. Again lay out a 10-inch length of plastic wrap on a flat work surface. Unwrap a cigar from the freezer and set it aside. With a pastry brush, spread some of the melted chocolate over the plastic wrap, forming a rectangular shape large enough to wrap around the cigar. Place the cigar on top of the chocolate and roll up the plastic wrap, covering the cigar with the melted chocolate. Twist the ends tightly to close. Return the chocolate-coated cigar to the freezer and repeat with the remaining cigars. Cover the sheet pan tightly with plastic wrap (this will keep any other flavors from seeping into the absorbent chocolate mixture from your freezer) and freeze for at least 8 hours.

◎ When ready to serve, combine the cocoa powder and cinnamon on a large plate. Take the cigars from the freezer and roll each one in the cocoa mixture. Serve with whipped cream.

Adorno Especial

Helado de Mocha y Espuma de Litchi

White Chocolate Mocha Ice Cream 1 recipe (page 199)
Litchi Foam 1 recipe (page 244)
Unsweetened cocoa powder
Confectioners' sugar

Place a scoop of the ice cream in an espresso cup. Remove the foam canister from the refrigerator, shake it vigorously, turn it upside down, and squeeze some of the foam onto the top of the ice cream. Dust each plate with cocoa powder and confectioners' sugar. Place the cigar in the center and serve the cup on the side.

CHOCOLATE CRÊPES WITH MILK-CARAMEL

Crepas de Chocolate Rellenas con Dulce de Leche

Often the countries that come to mind when thinking of crêpes are France or Belgium. But crêpes are also extremely popular in Spain. Here, delicate chocolate crêpes are filled with creamy *dulce de leche*.

If you want to save time, a store-bought ice cream and good-quality chocolate sauce will finish things off. But really you can serve these crêpes all by themselves filled with anything you choose: ice cream by itself, your favorite fresh fruit, or *cajeta*, (Goat's Milk Caramel, page 15), instead of *dulce de leche*. I also love them simply filled with whipped cream and berries.

SERVES 8 TO 10 (ABOUT 3 CRÊPES PER PERSON)

1¾ cups all-purpose flour   255 GRAMS

¼ cup unsweetened cocoa powder   30 GRAMS

2 tablespoons granulated sugar

1 pinch salt

2 cups whole milk   480 MILLILITERS

4 whole eggs

4 egg yolks

½ cup (1 stick) butter, melted   120 GRAMS

2 tablespoons vanilla extract

1 recipe Dulce de Leche (page 52)

⊚ Blend all the ingredients except the Dulce de Leche in a food processor until smooth. Let rest for 5 minutes.

⊚ Heat an 8-inch nonstick crêpe pan over medium heat, then ladle ¼ cup of the batter into the center of the pan and quickly rotate the pan in a circular motion until the batter coats the bottom evenly. Cook for about 35 seconds, until just set around the edges but still shiny in the center. Using a spatula, lift up one edge of the crêpe. Grab the edge gently with your fingers and flip it over. (The crêpe is too delicate to flip in the air.) Cook the second side for about 10 seconds.

⊚ Set the cooked crêpe aside on a large platter and repeat with the remaining batter. When complete, stack the crêpes one at a time on a fresh plate to make sure they aren't sticking together. Do not put waxed paper or anything else in between the crêpes, as they will sweat and become soggy. (Crêpes do not freeze well, but can be made in advance and kept covered and refrigerated for up to 4 days.)

⊚ When ready to serve, spread each crêpe with a few tablespoons of the Dulce de Leche. Fold the crêpes in half like tacos, roll them like flautas, or fold them twice into trangle-like shapes. Serve immediately.

Adorno Especial

Helado de Vanilla, Salpicón de Lulo y Fresas, y Salsa de Chocolate

Vanilla Bean Ice Cream 1 recipe (page 197)

Lulo and Berry Salsa 1 recipe (page 187)

Chocolate Sauce 1 recipe (page 253)

Serve filled crêpes with a scoop of ice cream and top with the salsa. Drizzle with sauce.

VENEZUELAN CHOCOLATE AND HAZELNUT BOMBE

Bomba de Chocolate Venezolano y Avellanas

The full preparation of this over-the-top version of chocolate cake does take some time, but it's worth it for true chocolate lovers or when celebrating a special occasion. If you need to simplify things, you can garnish the finished *bombe* with a good-quality store-bought dessert sauce and ice cream. Or pair it with a tall glass of milk—it'll still be heavenly. I use Venezuelan chocolate because it is my favorite, especially the El Rey brand, which you can find at specialty food shops or online, but any very good dark chocolate, such as Valrhona or Callebaut, will work.

The *bombe* is best when made with a fresh cake. However, you can make the cake ahead of time and store it in the freezer, wrapped very well in plastic, for up to 2 months.

SERVES 8 TO 10

½ cup plus 2 tablespoons
   almond flour   90 GRAMS
½ cup confectioners' sugar   60 GRAMS
5 whole eggs
2 tablespoons butter, melted
2 tablespoons all-purpose flour
1 tablespoon unsweetened cocoa powder
3 egg whites
¼ cup granulated sugar   50 GRAMS
1 recipe Chocolate Mousse with Hazelnuts
   (page 240)
1 recipe Chocolate Ganache (page 254)

◎ Preheat the oven to 350° F. Grease a 12-by-17-inch half sheet pan (jelly roll pan) and either dust it with flour or line the bottom with parchment paper.

◎ In the bowl of an electric mixer, combine the almond flour, confectioners' sugar, and whole eggs and beat on high speed (or by hand with a whisk) for about 15 minutes, until pale and thick—the ribbon stage: When you lift a beater out of the batter, it should flow from it in a smooth, even ribbon. Transfer the mixture to a large mixing bowl and stir in the butter. Sift the flour and cocoa powder together into a small bowl, then gently fold the mixture into the batter.

◎ Soak the bowl and the whisk attachment of the mixer in warm water and dry thoroughly. This will ensure that the egg whites gain enough volume during beating. Beat the egg whites and granulated sugar until soft peaks form. Fold the egg whites into the batter, about one third at a time.

◉ Pour the batter into the prepared pan, spreading it out evenly. Bake it for 15 minutes, or until a toothpick inserted in the center comes out clean. The cake will not rise significantly during baking. Let cool.

◉ Arrange a wire cooling rack over a sheet pan. Cut rounds of the cooled chocolate cake with a cookie cutter and place them on the rack, spaced evenly apart. The rounds should be about the same size as the top of whatever vessel you used for the mousse (half spheres, ramekins, or cupcake tins), as the individual mousses will ultimately sit on top of the rounds of cake.

◉ Remove the mousse-filled half spheres, ramekins, or cupcake tins from the freezer and unmold them by warming them slightly on the outside with your hands. If you used cupcake tins and liners, just lift each mousse out of its tin and peel off the paper.

◉ Place an unmolded mousse on top of each piece of cake. Pour a thin layer of ganache over each *bombe* until completely covered. Pour a second layer of ganache over each *bombe*. (If doing the Adorno Especial, reserve some for garnish.) Refrigerate until ready to serve. The *bombes* will keep in the refrigerator for up to 2 days and should be stored in a container deeper than their height, so as not to disturb the icing.

Adorno Especial

Salsa de Caramelo y Helado de Avellanas

Caramel Sauce 1 recipe (page 258)
Hazelnut Ice Cream 1 recipe (page 202)

Decorate each plate with the sauce and the reserved ganache. Place a *bombe* in the center of each place, on top of the sauces, and finish with a small scoop or quenelle of ice cream.

CHOCOLATE BANANA BREAD PUDDING WITH QUINOA

Puding Andino de Chocolate y Banana con Quinoa

In Peru, quinoa—what some call "the mother grain" or "supergrain" for its amazing nutritional value—is one of the most typical savory side dishes. I had been looking for something to add crunch and texture to my bread pudding, and quinoa came to mind. It made sense, since, much like rice, quinoa is also sometimes used in puddings.

If you're not typically a fan of bread pudding, try this recipe. It is surprisingly light. And with its notes of chocolate, banana, and caramel set off by the unexpected tang of the Sour Cream Ice Cream, you'll be an instant convert.

I recommend using a soft-crusted bread, like a softer Italian loaf or brioche, for this recipe.

SERVES 12

For the custard:

4 cups heavy cream	950 MILLILITERS
1 cup whole milk	240 MILLILITERS
2 tablespoons vanilla extract	
1 pound chopped bittersweet chocolate (El Rey "Mijao" 61%)	455 GRAMS
7 eggs	
1 cup granulated sugar	200 GRAMS
½ cup packed brown sugar	115 GRAMS
1 (1-pound loaf) bread, including crust, sliced (not cubed)	455 GRAMS

For the quinoa:

1 cup white quinoa	200 GRAMS
1 teaspoon ground cinnamon	
2 whole allspice berries	
½ teaspoon ground cardamom	
¼ cup dark rum	60 MILLILITERS

For the bananas:

¼ cup (½ stick) butter	50 GRAMS
½ cup granulated sugar	100 GRAMS
½ tablespoon ground cinnamon	
5 ripe but firm bananas, sliced into ¼-inch-thick rounds	

⊚ Butter a 3-inch-deep, straight-sided 9-inch round cake pan or a 9-by-13-inch baking pan.

⊚ Make the custard: In a medium saucepan over medium-high heat, bring the cream, milk, and vanilla extract to a boil. Remove from the heat, add the chocolate, and stir until melted.

⊚ In a large bowl, whisk the eggs together. Continue whisking while pouring a small amount of the hot cream mixture into the eggs. This will temper the eggs and keep them from curdling. While whisking the cream mixture in the saucepan, gradually add the rest of the eggs. Return to medium-low heat and stir with a wooden spoon until the custard coats the back of the spoon, being careful not to boil, about 4 minutes. Strain the custard through a fine sieve into an extra-large bowl (that will also hold the bread and the quinoa) to remove any bits of cooked egg. Fold in the bread until all the slices are well coated with the custard. Set aside.

⊚ Make the quinoa: In a fine sieve, rinse the quinoa under running water. In a medium saucepan over medium-high heat, bring 2 cups (480 milliliters) water, the quinoa, and spices to a boil. Lower the heat and simmer, stirring occasionally, until all the water has been absorbed, about 15 minutes. Add the rum and cook for 2 more minutes. Remove from the heat, remove and discard the allspice, and fold the cooked quinoa into the bread mixture. Set aside.

⊚ Preheat the oven to 325° F.

⊚ Make the bananas: In a medium sauté pan over medium heat, melt the butter. Add the sugar and cinnamon and stir until the sugar is dissolved, about 3 minutes. Add the bananas and cook for 3 minutes. Fold the sautéed bananas into the bread and quinoa mixture.

⊚ Pour the bread pudding mixture into the prepared pan and bake for 35 minutes, or until set (not loose) and golden brown on top. The pudding should jiggle a bit when you move the pan, but it should not look at all soupy. Let cool for 15 minutes. Cut the pudding into squares or just scoop out more rustic portions with a large spoon. Serve warm.

Adorno Especial

Salsa de Caramelo y Helado de Crema Nata

Caramel Sauce 1 recipe (page 259)
Sour Cream Ice Cream 1 recipe (page 203)

Place one portion of warm bread pudding on each plate, drizzle with sauce, and garnish with a scoop of ice cream.

CHOCOLATE THREE MILKS CAKE
Tres Leches de Chocolate

Here I doctor the traditional recipe with a little cocoa powder to produce a delicate chocolate génoiselike cake, then bathe the whole thing with a decadent milk mixture flavored with chocolate liquor and melted bittersweet chocolate. I serve this *tres leches* warm, so it has the personality of a bread pudding. I like to cut the cake into 2-inch rounds and serve drizzled with Caramel Sauce (page 258) and topped with Tangerine and Saffron Sorbet (page 220). Alternatively, a scoop of vanilla ice cream will work wonders.

SERVES 18 TO 24

10	eggs	
1	cup granulated sugar	200 GRAMS
1	cup all-purpose flour	140 GRAMS
¼	cup unsweetened cocoa powder	30 GRAMS
2	(12-ounce) cans evaporated milk	360 MILLILITERS
1	(14-ounce) can sweetened condensed milk	420 MILLILITERS
2	cups heavy cream	480 MILLILITERS
12	ounces chopped bittersweet chocolate (El Rey "Mijao" 61%)	340 GRAMS
½	cup dark chocolate liqueur (crème de cacao)	120 MILLILITERS

◉ Preheat the oven to 325° F.

◉ In the bowl of an electric mixer, beat the eggs until they are thick and light in color, about 5 minutes. While beating, gradually add the sugar and continue beating for an additional 7 to 8 minutes, until the eggs have tripled in volume. Sift the flour and cocoa powder into the egg and sugar mixture and fold to combine.

Do not stir or beat, as this will cause the eggs to deflate and lose their volume.

◉ Grease a 13-by-9-inch baking pan, making sure to fully coat the sides, including the rim. Pour the batter into the pan and bake for 40 to 50 minutes, until the cake springs back to the touch. The cake will pull away from the sides of the pan, and a toothpick inserted in the center will come out clean. Let cool. Once cool, pierce the cake all over with a toothpick or skewer.

◉ In a large saucepan over medium-high heat, bring the milks and cream to a boil. Remove from the heat and stir in the chocolate until melted. Stir in the liqueur. Slowly pour the mixture over the cake. Cover and refrigerate for at least 2 hours, or until the liquid is completely absorbed. The cake will keep, refrigerated, for up to 2 days.

◉ When ready to serve, preheat the oven to 325° F. Heat the cake for about 2 minutes, just until warm. To serve, scoop out rustic portions with a large spoon.

VENEZUELAN CHOCOLATE BROWNIES WITH WALNUTS

Bizcocho de Chocolate Venezolano con Nueves

El Rey chocolate from Venezuela and Ibarra chocolate from Mexico infuse this classic American dessert with a touch of Latin flavor. El Rey is the highest quality chocolate in Latin America, and the quality of the cocoa beans really set it apart from typical European chocolates. The chopped chunks of Ibarra chocolate tablets, typically used to make hot chocolate, add more chocolate flavor and a dose of cinnamon. The 10 eggs in this recipe give these brownies an incredibly moist, chewy, fudgelike texture. If you prefer a firmer, slightly drier brownie, bake them a bit longer. For something extra special, top the brownies with a scoop of Caramelized Banana Ice Cream (page 201).

MAKES ABOUT 18 BROWNIES

1½ pounds chopped bittersweet chocolate (El Rey "Mijao" 61%)	680 GRAMS
1 pound butter	455 GRAMS
10 eggs	
3 cups granulated sugar	600 GRAMS
1 cup all-purpose flour	140 GRAMS
2 cups walnut halves	170 GRAMS
1 cup chopped Ibarra chocolate tablets	
¼ cup vanilla or coffee extract	60 ML
Confectioners' sugar	

⊚ Preheat the oven to 350° F.

⊚ Butter a 13-by-9-inch baking pan and dust it with flour.

⊚ In the top of a double boiler set over gently simmering water, melt the bittersweet chocolate and butter. Remove from heat and transfer to a mixing bowl.

⊚ Gradually stir in the eggs, sugar, and flour. The batter will be shiny and very thick. Stir in the walnuts and chocolate tablets.

⊚ Pour the batter into the prepared pan and bake for 15 minutes, or until a toothpick inserted in the center comes out clean, the brownies look set, and the center is matte, not shiny. Let cool for about 10 minutes, then cut and serve the brownies warm, dusted with confectioners' sugar.

MASA-THICKENED HOT CHOCOLATE
Champurrado/Atole de Chocolate

CHAMPURRADO IS THE CHOCOLATE VERSION OF *ATOLE* OR *ATOLL*, A WARM beverage made with water, masa, and *panela* (an unrefined brown sugar) and flavored with everything from vanilla and cinnamon to fresh fruit and, of course, chocolate. *Atole* is enjoyed any time of day, is readily sold by street vendors, and is a traditional drink on the Mexican holiday Day of the Dead, a day of remembrance for friends and family who have passed away.

When I was growing up, we mostly enjoyed chocolate *atole* much as Americans might enjoy coffee or tea after dinner. My grandmother used to bribe me with an after-dinner treat so I would sit and visit with her in the kitchen while she stirred the *atole*. That was the trick, she said, the constant stirring. First, she would put milk and cinnamon sticks on the stove to boil. Then she would take some masa dough, the same dough we used for tortillas, and break it up in a small bowl with a little bit of milk. She'd add that, along with chocolate— usually Ibarra brand—and sometimes chopped pecans, to the hot milk on the stovetop. That's when the stirring started. She would stir until the mixture started simmering again, then she would stir some more while the masa dissolved and thickened the milk. The masa dough was used in the same way Americans might use cornstarch to thicken sauces or stews.

Give this recipe a try and you will never go back to "regular" hot chocolate.

MAKES ABOUT 6 CUPS

4½ cups whole milk   1070 ML
  1 cup granulated sugar or chopped
    panela (see page 13)   200 GRAMS
  1 tablespoon vanilla extract
  2 cinnamon sticks
½ cup *masa harina* (instant corn masa
    flour, preferably maseca brand) 70 GRAMS
  2 tablespoons cornstarch
Semisweet or bittersweet chocolate
    (about 1⅓ cups chips)   225 GRAMS

In a medium saucepan over medium-high heat, bring 4 cups of the milk and the sugar, vanilla extract, and cinnamon sticks to a boil. Lower the heat. Using a whisk, combine the remaining ½ cup milk with the *masa harina* and cornstarch and slowly add it to the pot, stirring constantly. Slowly bring the mixture back up to a boil, continuing to stir. Cook, stirring constantly, for about 5 minutes, until thickened. Remove from the heat and stir in the chocolate until melted. Serve immediately.

CHOCOLATE FLAN
Flan de Chocolate

When you purchase chocolate flan from a bakery, it's often made with cocoa powder. Here I use melted chocolate to give the flan a richer chocolate flavor. I like to pair this flan with Yellow Corn Foam (page 247) and Chocolate Sauce (page 253), for a new interpretation of the classic Latin combination of corn and chocolate, as in *champurrado* (see opposite).

SERVES 8

1	recipe Caramel for Flan (page 234)	
1½	cups evaporated milk	360 MILLILITERS
2½	cups whole milk	600 MILLILITERS
¼	cup granulated sugar	50 GRAMS
1	vanilla bean halved lengthwise, seeds scraped out and reserved (or 1 tablespoon vanilla extract)	
1	pinch salt	
12	ounces chopped bittersweet chocolate (El Rey "Bucare" 58.5%)	340 GRAMS
5	eggs	

Pour the cooled caramel into the bottoms of 8 (6-ounce) ramekins and set aside.

In a medium saucepan over medium-high heat, bring the milks, sugar, vanilla bean (including seeds) or extract, and salt to a boil. Remove from the heat, add the chocolate, and stir until melted. Chill the mixture in the refrigerator until completely cool, about 30 minutes.

Preheat the oven to 300° F.

In a medium bowl, beat the eggs together. Stir them into the cooled chocolate mixture. Pour the custard through a fine sieve into a clean bowl, preferably one with a spout. Straining will remove any skin that may have formed on the chocolate mixture. Pour the custard into the caramel-filled ramekins (fill to about ¼ inch from the top) and put them in a deep baking pan.

To make a water bath, fill the baking pan with water to reach one quarter of the way up the sides of the ramekins. Cover the whole pan with aluminum foil. Bake for 30 minutes, or until the custards are set (a knife inserted in the center should come out clean). The center will still look a little loose, but the custards will continue cooking after they are removed from the oven. Carefully remove the baking dish from the oven, lift out the ramekins using tongs, and let them rest for at least 20 minutes. Move them to the refrigerator and chill for at least 4 hours, preferably overnight.

When ready to serve, invert a ramekin onto each serving plate and gently tap the bottom with the end of a butter knife to help unmold.

CHOCOLATE DOMINO CAKE
El Domino

In Cuba and the Dominican Republic, the game of dominos is incredibly popular, so I wanted to create a dessert presentation that mimicked domino tiles. To make these miniature layer cakes truly look like domino tiles, you will need a 3-inch-tall metal frame that fits just inside a 12-by-17-inch half sheet pan.

SERVES 9 TO 14 (1 SLICE OR 2 OR 3 DOMINO PIECES PER PERSON)

1 cup (2 sticks) butter, chilled, cut into cubes	225 GRAMS
3 cups granulated sugar	600 GRAMS
1 tablespoon ground cinnamon	
3 cups all-purpose flour	430 GRAMS
2½ cups whole milk	600 MILLILITERS
1 cup unsweetened cocoa powder, plus more for dusting	110 GRAMS
1 tablespoon baking powder	
1 pinch salt	
½ teaspoon baking soda	
4 eggs	
1 tablespoon vanilla extract	
1 cup Crème de cacao, Tia Maria, or Kahlúa	240 MILLILITERS
1 recipe Chocolate Mocha Mousse (page 238)	
1 recipe Chocolate Ganache (page 254)	
15 ounces chopped white chocolate (about 2½ cups chips)	430 GRAMS

⊚ Preheat the oven to 325° F.

⊚ Grease 2 (12- by-17-inch) half sheet pans (jelly roll pans) and either dust them with flour or line the bottoms with parchment paper.

⊚ In the bowl of an electric mixer fitted with the paddle attachment, cream the butter, sugar, and cinnamon on medium speed for about 3 minutes, until light and fluffy. Add the flour and mix until combined. The texture will be sandy with lumps of flour and butter.

⊚ In a small saucepan over medium heat, bring the milk to a slow simmer. Remove from the heat and whisk in the cocoa powder, baking powder, and salt until there are no lumps. Turn the mixer containing the butter-flour mixture back on low speed and very slowly add the warm milk mixture. In a small mixing bowl, whisk ½ cup (120 milliliters) cold water and the baking soda together and add it to the batter. Add the eggs and vanilla extract and mix on medium speed for about 3 minutes, until the batter is smooth and shiny with no lumps.

⊚ Pour the batter into the prepared pans and bake for 18 minutes, or until the cakes spring back to the touch or a toothpick comes out clean. Let cool for at least 2 hours. (The cake can be frozen for up to 1 month.)

◎ Using a pastry brush, brush one cake layer with half of the liqueur. Press a 3-inch-tall, 12-by-17-inch frame down into the half sheet pan, fitting it snugly between the outside edge of the cake and the lip of the pan; this will keep the mousse filling from seeping out from in between the layers of cake. Using an offset spatula, spread the mousse in a 1-inch-thick layer evenly over the top of the cake. Unmold the second cake layer directly on top of the mousse, fitting it into the frame. Peel the parchment off the bottom of the second cake layer. Brush it with the remaining liqueur. Cover and refrigerate for at least 1 hour or up to 8 hours, or freeze for up to 1 month.

◎ Remove the cake from the refrigerator and pour 4 cups of the ganache over the top, creating a ⅛-inch-thick layer held within the frame. Working quickly, swirl the pan until the ganache covers the cake fully and evenly. Refrigerate again for about 3 hours, until the ganache is set, being careful not to touch the ganache so that it remains a smooth, glossy surface.

◎ Remove the cake from the refrigerator. To remove the frame, dip a portion of a clean kitchen towel in hot water, ring it out, and carefully rub the sides of the frame, being careful not to get any water onto the ganache. This will loosen the frame from the cake. Pull straight up on the frame to remove it. You will now have even layers of cake, mousse, cake, and ganache in the half sheet pan.

◎ Dip a long serrated bread knife in hot water to warm the blade. Dry off the knife and cut the layer cake in half lengthwise. Dip and dry the

knife again, then cut the 2 halves in half again lengthwise so that you are left with 4 long strips of layer cake. Dip and dry the knife again. Gently press the back of the knife into the middle of each strip of layer cake and pull it down the strip, making a lengthwise line that will ultimately be the seam of each domino tile.

◎ In the top of a double boiler set over gently simmering water, melt the white chocolate. Let cool slightly and using a disposable pastry bag fitted with a small plain tip, a plastic bag with the corner just barely snipped off, or a cone of parchment paper, pipe a line of white chocolate onto each of the 4 lengthwise seams in the ganache. (I find it easier to keep the line straight and steady if I concentrate on moving my hips and body as a whole rather than moving my arms as I pipe the chocolate.)

◎ To cut the domino tiles, dip the knife in hot water again and dry. Make each cut in one smooth motion, pulling the knife out of the base of the cake rather than up through the ganache again. This will keep the ganache neat and clean. Cut each strip in half widthwise, then make 2 more cuts on either side of that to form 6 equal domino-shaped tiles, each with a white seam down the middle. You will now have 24 domino tiles.

◎ Using the same pastry bag and tip filled with white chocolate, pipe dots onto each one of the cakes to mimic the look of domino tiles. If you are going to serve 2 pieces per serving, make certain to have matching pairs so that the tiles can be plated just like a matching pair in a real game of dominos.

◎ Dust each plate with cocoa powder. Place two or three pieces of cake over the cocoa.

Chocolate

CHOCOLATE IS ONE OF THE MOST BELOVED INGREDIENTS OF THE LATIN American kitchen, not only for sweet preparations, but also for savory. Take moles, the traditional Mexican sauces often served with poultry in which chocolate adds depth and richness to a puree of onions, garlic, chiles, various nuts and seeds, tomatoes, and sometimes cinnamon. On the sweet side, this chapter is full of my favorite examples of chocolate desserts, from simple brownies made with cinnamon-scented Ibarra-brand chocolate, to chocolate flan and *tres leches*, to more imaginative pastries like my Chocolate and Hazelnut Bombe (page 136). Even with all these creative interpretations, one of my favorite ways to enjoy chocolate is simply drinking a frothy cup of Champurrado (page 142).

Chocolate was in fact first enjoyed in its drinking form as early as 1100 B.C. The Aztec king Montezuma allegedly drank fifty goblets-full a day because chocolate was believed to be an aphrodisiac. Of course, this wasn't the sweet hot chocolate of today. True to its original Aztec name, *xocolatl*, or "bitter water," it was a spicy, reddish-hued concoction made with ground cocoa beans, achiote, toasted corn, and chiles. In Chiapas, the southernmost state in Mexico, they still prepare drinking chocolate using traditional methods, grinding cocoa beans by hand in a *metate*, along with vanilla and honey, then adding hot water or milk.

One of my happiest childhood memories is drinking chocolate milkshakes with my dad. His "rule" was to enjoy one every single day. Not a bad habit, in my opinion, and one that certainly foreshadowed my career in pastries. I would often share one with him before he left for work in the morning. On Sundays, his day off, he would sometimes send me to the store down the street to buy a package of his favorite Express chocolate. I can still see the image of a little train on the packets.

The Venezuelan chocolate brand I often recommend is El Rey. The company started producing chocolate in 1929 and, instead of blending beans from different growing regions as some manufacturers do to mask the lackluster flavor of inferior beans, El Rey produces single-variety, regional chocolate made exclusively with Venezuelan beans. Any good-quality chocolate will work in my recipes, and there are certainly other brands that pursue regionally focused production.

THE "IMPOSSIBLE" CAKE
Pastel Imposible

The name of this traditional Mexican celebratory cake comes from its miraculous transformation in the oven. Its layers of chocolate cake and flan virtually flip while baking.

SERVES 10

7 eggs	
1 (14-ounce) can sweetened condensed milk	420 MILLILITERS
1 cup heavy cream	240 MILLILITERS
1 tablespoon vanilla extract	
3 ounces chopped bittersweet chocolate	85 GRAMS
1¼ cups whole milk	300 MILLILITERS
1½ cups (3 sticks) butter, softened	340 GRAMS
1¾ cups granulated sugar	350 GRAMS
1½ tablespoons baking powder	
2½ cups all-purpose flour	355 GRAMS
2 cups Cajeta (page 15)	455 GRAMS

For the flan, combine 4 of the the eggs, the sweetened condensed milk, cream, and vanilla in a food processor or blender until smooth.

For the cake, put the chocolate in a medium bowl. In a small saucepan over medium-high heat, bring ½ cup of the milk to a boil. Pour the hot milk over the chocolate and stir until melted. In the bowl of an electric mixer fitted with the paddle attachment, cream the butter and sugar on medium speed for about 3 minutes, until light and fluffy. Add the remaining 3 eggs one at a time and mix until well incorporated.

Mix in the chocolate mixture. Whisk the baking powder together with the flour and add the mixture to the batter in two batches, alternating with the remaining ¾ cup milk. Mix for 2 more minutes.

Preheat the oven to 325° F. Butter a 3-quart Bundt pan or a 3½-quart angel food cake pan and dust it with flour.

Pour the *cajeta* into the bottom of the prepared pan and spread it out. Pour in the chocolate batter and tap the pan on a work surface to spread the batter out evenly to the edges. Very slowly, top that with the flan mixture.

Set the cake pan in a deep baking dish. To make a water bath, fill the baking dish with water to reach one third of the way up the side of the pan. Bake for 1 hour, or until a toothpick inserted in the center comes out clean. Let cool for 30 minutes. While still slightly warm, place a serving plate on top of the cake pan and very carefully flip it over. Let the pan rest upside down like this for 5 minutes to allow the Cajeta to release from the pan. You can gently shake the pan and plate together to help unmold the cake, but be cautious, as the flan is very delicate and you don't want to break it. Remove the pan and chill the cake in the refrigerator for at last 30 minutes or up to 2 days.

5

FRUIT DESSERTS

Postres de Fruta

In This Chapter

PAPAYA SOUP
Sopa de Papaya

My inspiration for fruit soups comes mostly from the extremely popular *aguas frescas* of Latin America (see page 191), typically made with pureed fruit, water, and sugar, served over ice, and enjoyed through a thick straw. In Latin countries, *aguas frescas* are made with the whole fruit—pith, pulp, and all—so they tend to be thicker and richer than American fruit juices and translate well from a glass to a bowl.

Fruit soups are full of flavor, refreshing, and simple to make, lending themselves to easy experimentation. Get inspired by the fresh fruits you find in your local market and don't be afraid to throw together unusual combinations—one of my favorites growing up was pineapple and parsley. This papaya soup with vanilla is beautiful for the summer and a very healthy alternative to a traditional dessert at the end of a meal. To dress up this dessert, top each serving with a scoop of Mango Ginger Sorbet (page 220) and garnish with fennel flowers if available.

SERVES 6

1 football-sized or 2 baseball-sized papayas

1 cup Simple Syrup (page 237)   240 ML

2 tablespoons (from about 1 lime) freshly squeezed lime juice

1 vanilla bean, halved lengthwise, seeds scraped out and reserved (or 1 ½ tablespoons vanilla extract)

To peel the papaya, cut off both ends. Stand the fruit up on a cutting board and run the knife down the sides to remove the skin. Cut it in half lengthwise and, using a spoon, scoop out the seeds from each half. Dice the flesh; you should have 4 cups (680 grams).

In a blender, puree the diced fruit with the syrup, lime juice, and vanilla bean seeds or extract until smooth. Transfer to a container, cover, and refrigerate until cold.

Choose pretty soup bowls or glasses for serving this soup and refrigerate them for at least 30 minutes before filling them. Serve chilled.

Papaya

I GREW UP EATING THIS COMMON MEXICAN FRUIT QUITE OFTEN. SIMPLY sliced and sprinkled with fresh lime juice and a little bit of chile powder and salt, it is heavenly. My mom would prepare it this way as an after-school snack and have it out on the table, surrounded by forks, when we came home at the end of the day. *Mercados* also sell papaya like this, the doctored slices piled into a paper cone. My family would also eat diced papaya for breakfast, topped with fresh lime juice, oats, and honey.

When I went to the *mercado* with my mom or grandmother, we would often stop to get a papaya *batido* (fruit smoothie) before we shopped. When buying fresh papayas, we would tell the vendors when we planned to eat the fruit, and they would pick out the perfect ones. They always ripened exactly as planned.

Fresh papayas are easy to find these days, even in average American grocery stores. Like pumpkins, their size can vary widely, but most you will find here will be the size of a football and weigh a couple pounds. The most common variety is a large, elongated fruit, with smooth green skin that starts to turn yellow as it ripens, with a bright salmon-colored interior. The center is filled with a long cluster of shiny, round, black seeds that are edible but have an intense spicy taste. When ripe, papayas taste like a refreshing yet mild combo of pineapple, melon, and peach, with a very silky texture.

Throughout Latin America, you will find ripe papaya in everything from marmalades and mousses, to ice creams and sorbets, and even served with cheeses. Unripe, green papaya is used in candies, jarred in syrup, or served as street food diced with pineapple and jicama, doused with freshly squeezed lime juice, and sprinkled with chile powder and salt.

The easiest way to eat a papaya is to slice it in half lengthwise, remove the seeds, and just scoop out the flesh with a spoon. Or try filling it with a little orange juice, yogurt, and honey. And one of the best fruit combinations is papaya and banana.

Besides being delicious, papaya has many other benefits. The flesh is known to calm the stomach. The seeds can be dried and ground to use like pepper. Even the skin can be used as a tenderizer: Simply wrap the skin around a piece of meat and refrigerate for a few hours to allow the fruit enzymes to break down the meat protein.

PEACH SOUP

Sopa de Melocotón

Part of the inspiration for this sophisticated fruit soup is the popular Peruvian and Chilean cocktail the Pisco sour, made with the regional *aguardiente* called Pisco, lemon or lime juice, egg whites, simple syrup, and a dash of bitters. For a special presentation, you could make a granita from the reserved peach-poaching liquid (for the technique, see page 225). Then top each serving of soup with a scoop of Mamey Ice Cream (page 194) and a bit of the granita.

SERVES 6

5	medium peaches (ripe but firm)
1	vanilla bean, halved lengthwise, seeds scraped out and reserved (or 1½ tablespoons vanilla extract)
¼	cup freshly squeezed lemon juice — 60 MILLILITERS
½	cup Pisco — 120 MILLILITERS
2	cups granulated sugar — 400 GRAMS
½	stalk lemongrass
2	cinnamon sticks
	Zest of 1 lemon

With a paring knife, score the peaches in half lengthwise, cutting just through the skin. In a large saucepan over medium heat, bring the peaches, 4 cups water (960 milliliters), and all the remaining ingredients to a boil. Lower the heat and simmer for 30 to 40 minutes, until the peaches are fork tender. Remove from the heat and refrigerate until cool, about 1 hour.

Peel and pit the peaches. In a food processor or blender, puree the peaches until smooth. Strain the poaching liquid through a fine sieve and add half of the liquid (about 1½ cups) to the peaches. Blend until incorporated. Set the remaining liquid aside if you plan to make the granita (see note above). Transfer the peach puree to a bowl, cover, and refrigerate until cold, at least 1 hour or up to 2 days. The puree can also be frozen for up to 1 month and thawed in the refrigerator before serving. Serve chilled.

GUAVA SOUP WITH CHAMOMILE SABAYON

Sopa de Guayaba con Crema de Manzanilla

Just as in my Peach Soup with Mamey Ice Cream, I love the way a creamy ice cream or sauce elevates a simple fruit puree into a true dessert soup. The flavor of chamomile tea in the sabayon is a nice surprise in this refreshing, healthful dessert.

SERVES 6

For the soup:

4 cups guava puree	950 MILLILITERS
½ cup granulated sugar	100 GRAMS

For the sabayon:

2 cups heavy cream	480 MILLILITERS
5 chamomile tea bags	
(paper tags/string removed if necessary)	
8 egg yolks	
¼ cup granulated sugar	50 GRAMS
2 tablespoons dry white wine	
Mixed berries	

◉ Make the soup: In a small saucepan over medium heat, bring the guava puree, 1 cup (240 milliliters) water, and the sugar to a boil. Reduce the heat and simmer, stirring occasionally, until the sugar is dissolved, 2 to 3 minutes. Remove from the heat, transfer to a bowl, cover, and refrigerate until cold, at least 2 hours, or up to 3 days.

◉ Make the sabayon: In a clean small saucepan over medium-high heat, bring the cream and tea bags to a boil. Reduce the heat and simmer for 5 minutes to steep. Discard the bags.

◉ In the top of a double boiler over gently simmering water, whisk together the egg yolks and sugar. Continue whisking until the yolks are pale and thick, about 5 minutes. Whisk in the wine, then add the tea-cream mixture slowly, a little bit at a time, whisking constantly. Continue whisking the sabayon for 3 to 5 more minutes, until it is light, creamy, and fluffy. Remove from the heat, transfer to a bowl, cover, and refrigerate until cold, at least 1 hour, or up to 2 days.

◉ Pour the soup into 6 bowls or parfait glasses and top with a spoonful of the sabayon. Garnish with berries.

CARAMELIZED PINEAPPLE
Piña Caramelizada

Y ou can't get much better than the taste of a perfectly fresh pineapple. Except, of course, if you caramelize it with sweet *panela* and honey, add a touch of vanilla and orange juice, and top it off with the kick of tequila. I would recommend *tequila reposado*, the first level of aged tequila, for its combination of both oak and agave flavors, but any tequila will work. As with any of my desserts using pineapple, save the skin and core and use it to make a batch of *chicha de piña*, pineapple punch (page 20), or an agua fresca (page 191). Serve the caramelized pineapple with vanilla ice cream or Yogurt Ice Cream (page 207), as well as, for a special presentation, a garnish of Cucumber Green Apple Granita (page 222) and thin slices of Manchego cheese.

SERVES 8 TO 10

1 large pineapple

1 cup chopped *panela* (see page 13)
(or packed brown sugar)　　　200 GRAMS

½ cup tequila　　　120 MILLILITERS

2 tablespoons honey

1 tablespoon vanilla extract

½ cup freshly squeezed
orange juice　　　120 MILLILITERS

To peel the pineapple, cut off both ends. Stand the fruit up on a cutting board and run the knife down the sides to remove the skin, being careful to remove all the eyes. Cut the fruit crosswise into ¾-inch slices and, using a small, round cookie cutter, remove the hard core from each slice. You should have about 10 slices.

In a large saucepan over high heat, bring the remaining ingredients to a boil and stir until the *panela* is dissolved and the mixture thickens to a heavy syrup, about 8 minutes. Cook the pineapple slices, a few at a time, in the syrup until they are browned and caramelized, about 2 minutes per side. Serve warm.

**VENEZUELAN CHOCOLATE AND
HAZELNUT BOMBE** *(page 136)*
with Caramel Sauce (page 259)

**CHOCOLATE CRÊPES WITH
MILK-CARAMEL** *(page 134)*
*with Vanilla Bean Ice Cream (page 197)
and Chocolate Sauce (page 253)*

**NOUGAT CANDY WITH
ALMONDS AND CASHEWS** *(page 58)*

SWEET BREADS
Clockwise from top center:

"GOOD BREAD" (CHEWY CHEESE ROLLS)
(page 65)

MEXICAN-STYLE SWEET BREAD
(page 68)

KISSES
(page 66)

RUSTIC BROWN SUGARCANE BREADS
(page 67)

PAPAYA SOUP *(page 150)*
with Mango Ginger Sorbet
(page 220) and fennel flowers

161

**LIQUID CHOCOLATE
CROQUETTES** *(page 130)*

**CHOCOLATE
DOMINO CAKE** *(page 144)*

162

COLOMBIAN FRUIT SALAD

Salpicón Estilo Colombiano

When I lived in New York, there was a Colombian woman who would sell fruit *salpicón* and *obleas con arequipe* (wafer-cookie sandwiches spread with *dulce de leche*) from a small cart parked right at Eighty-Second Street and Roosevelt Avenue next to the stairs of the number 7 train in Queens. That was the first time I had Colombian-style *salpicón*, and I've been a fan ever since. You can try this recipe with any of your favorite fruits. I've tasted great versions made with a variety of melons mixed with watermelon juice and Colombian apple soda to give the salad some effervescence. You can also puree the fruit, rather than dicing it, and serve it over vanilla ice cream more like a sauce, or drink it like a smoothie. To dress it up, I like to top it with a scoop of Coconut Sorbet (page 210) and add a Coconut Tuile (page 62). Whatever you decide, this is a refreshingly healthy dessert that is still very satisfying, especially on a hot day.

SERVES 8

4 cups freshly squeezed
   orange juice   950 MILLILITERS

¼ cup honey   60 MILLILITERS

2 tablespoons finely chopped fresh mint

2 cups diced ripe bananas   340 GRAMS

2 cups diced golden pineapple 340 GRAMS

2 cups diced ripe papaya   340 GRAMS

1 cup halved seedless red grapes 170 GRAMS

1 cup halved seedless green grapes

1 cup heavy cream   240 MILLILITERS

¼ cup sweetened condensed milk

                          60 MILLILITERS

◎ In a medium bowl, whisk together the orange juice, honey, and mint and toss with the fruits. Cover and refrigerate for at least 1 hour.

◎ In the bowl of an electric mixer fitted with the whisk attachment, whip the cream and sweetened condensed milk until stiff peaks form. Spoon the salad into chilled serving bowls and top with the whipped cream.

CHILEAN PAPAYA STUFFED WITH CREAM CHEESE MOUSSE

Papaya Chilena Rellena de Crema Esponjada de Queso

Jarred Chilean papaya is one of my favorite fruits to enjoy with cheese. Unlike the bright salmon-colored flesh of the most common papayas found fresh in the United States, the Chilean golden, mountain, or desert papaya (called *carica*) is a beautiful yellow color that tastes like a cross between a pear and an apple. Three to four inches long, the Chilean papaya lends itself to being stuffed. I've tried a variety of fillings, from raspberry mousse to key lime custard, but I've always liked the creamy, smooth cheese mousse filling the best. If you can't find jarred papaya in your local Latin market, try www.cilantrotrading.com. Buy an extra jar for chopping into salads or eating with ice cream. Alternatively, the cream cheese mousse makes a great dessert on its own, served with any pureed fruit of your choice.

SERVES 6

1½ (¼-ounce) envelopes unflavored gelatin powder	
2 tablespoons grand Marnier	
1 pound cream cheese, softened	455 GRAMS
½ cup (1 stick) butter, softened	115 GRAMS
7 eggs (whites and yolks separated)	
2 tablespoons freshly squeezed lemon juice	
1 cup granulated sugar	200 GRAMS
1¼ cups heavy cream	300 MILLILITERS
1 (35-ounce) jar Chilean papayas	1000 GRAMS

◉ In a small bowl, sprinkle the gelatin over the Grand Marnier and 2 tablespoons water and let stand for 5 minutes.

◉ In a food processor, blend the cream cheese, butter, egg yolks, and lemon juice until smooth. Transfer to a medium bowl.

◉ In the top of a double boiler over gently simmering water, melt the gelatin mixture, then whisk it into the cheese mixture.

◉ In the bowl of an electric mixer fitted with the whisk attachment, beat the egg whites until they just start to form very soft peaks, then add the sugar and continue to beat until soft peaks form. Fold into the cheese mixture.

◉ Clean the electric mixer well and, using the whisk attachment again, beat the cream until soft peaks form. Fold into the cheese mixture, being careful not to overmix or the mousse will deflate. Transfer to a plastic container, cover, and refrigerate until set, at least 2 hours. (Do not freeze. The mousse will keep in the refrigerator for up to 3 days.)

⑨ To assemble, drain the papayas and, using a pastry bag fitted with a large plain tip, a plastic bag with the tip cut off, or a spoon, stuff each papaya with about 4 tablespoons of the cheese mousse. Serve immediately.

Adorno Especial

Cigarritos de Coco y Salsa de Frambuesa

I like to add the crunch and nuttiness of a coconut tuile cigar and a sweet-tart raspberry sauce to these stuffed papayas.

2 cups fresh raspberries 340 GRAMS
½ cup Simple Syrup
    (page 237) 120 MILLILITERS
Coconut Tuiles 1 recipe (page 62), shaped
    into cigars

Put the raspberries and syrup in a food processor and puree until smooth, about 30 seconds. Pass the mixture through a fine sieve to remove the seeds and refrigerate until ready to serve. The sauce will keep in the refrigerator for up to 2 days.

Place a stuffed papaya in the center of each plate, drizzle with sauce, and garnish with a tuile cigar or two.

PASSION FRUIT TART
Tartaleta de Maracuya

These passion fruit custard-filled tarts are beautiful and easy to make. When I serve this recipe in a restaurant or more formal setting, I prepare it in a deconstructed style. I pipe the Italian meringue onto each plate, brown it briefly with a small bakers' torch, then add a quenelle of the passion fruit custard topped with crumbled pieces of the baked butter cookie dough (sometimes enhanced with crushed toasted almonds). For garnish, I add a scoop of Vanilla Bean Ice Cream (page 197) mixed with more cookie crumbs and a Coconut Tuile (page 62) for a dose of drama and crunch. This more traditional home preparation is no less delicious.

MAKES 6 TO 8 INDIVIDUAL TARTS
OR 1 11-INCH ROUND TART

1 recipe Butter Cookie dough (page 60), chilled in one piece	
1 cup passion fruit puree	240 ML
¼ cup granulated sugar	50 GRAMS
1 cup sweetened condensed milk	240 MILLILITERS
3 whole eggs	
3 egg yolks	
1 cup (2 sticks) butter, cut into chunks	225 GRAMS

On a lightly floured surface, roll the dough out to ¼ inch thick. If using individual tart pans, use one pan as a guide and cut circular pieces of dough about ½ inch outside the edge of the pan. Press the crusts into the tart pans so that the crusts cover the bottom and the ridged sides of the pans. Trim the dough so that it does not overlap the lip of the pan (as you might do with a pie crust). If using 1 large pan, follow the same instructions for forming the crust and use the rolling pin to lift the dough into the pan. Refrigerate for at least 30 minutes.

Preheat the oven to 350° F.

Prick the crust several times with a fork or toothpick to prevent it from bubbling up and bake until dark golden brown, about 15 minutes for the individual tarts and 20 minutes for the large tart. For the large tart, you can place a piece of parchment paper or a coffee filter in the center of the crust and weight it with rice or dried beans before baking. (I prefer to bake my crusts longer than many chefs, to a dark golden brown, so that they remain crisp after the addition of the filling.) Let cool slightly. Unbaked tart shells will keep for up to 2 months in the freezer.

◉ In a medium bowl, stir together the passion fruit puree, sugar, sweetened condensed milk, and eggs and transfer the mixture to the top of a double boiler over gently simmering water. Heat, whisking occasionally to prevent lumps from forming, until the mixture reaches a thick custardlike consistency, 35 to 40 minutes. Remove from the heat and let cool for about 10 minutes. Stir in the butter until melted. (The filling can be made ahead and refrigerated for up to 3 days.)

◉ Unmold the tart shells, then fill each shell with the passion fruit custard and refrigerate until set, about 2 hours. Filled tarts will keep for up to 2 days in the refrigerator.

Adorno Especial

Crema Batida

With the addition of meringue, this tart becomes a Latin take on lemon meringue pie.

Whipped Cream or Italian Meringue
1 recipe of either (page 235 or 236)
2 bananas, cut into rounds

The tarts can be served with Whipped Cream or dots of Italian Meringue and sliced banana. If using meringue, brown the tops using a small bakers' torch, similar to the process for Crema Catalana (page 36).

Passion Fruit

NATIVE TO BRAZIL, THE SMALL, EGG-SHAPED PASSION FRUIT IS AN UGLY little thing that hides a glorious interior—a futuristic-looking mass of crunchy, edible seeds wrapped in a yellowish, jellylike flesh. If you're not familiar with the fruit, it's easy to mistake ripe passion fruit for spoiled. The most common variety that you'll find in the States has a thick, leathery, dark-purple skin that becomes wrinkled when ripe. If you buy fruit with tight, smooth skin, let it sit out on your counter until the prunelike wrinkles appear.

In contrast to the modest exterior of the fruit, the blossoms of the flowering passion fruit vine are quite beautiful and have long been thought of as a holy flower named by Spanish missionaries to represent the passion of Christ in their preaching.

Passion fruit has an intoxicating aroma, and its concentrated, sweet-tart flavor, somewhat like a cross between pineapple and guava, adds a vibrant acidic punch to many desserts. For 1 cup of passion fruit puree, you'll need 6 to 7 pieces of fruit, which these days are fairly easy to find, even in traditional grocery stores. Or you can purchase frozen puree. The crunch of the passion fruit seeds also adds texture as well as flavor to composed desserts like my Passion Fruit with Cherimoya Granita (page 227) and Walnut Coconut Cookies (page 53). Try adding a few spoonfuls to fruit salad or blend some into a caipirinha.

Guanábana

GUANÁBANA, OR SOURSOP, IS A LARGE, OVAL, OR HEART-SHAPED TROPICAL fruit in the custard apple family, sometimes weighing as much as 10 pounds. The last time I visited Chiapas with my mother and grandmother, we saw enormous *guanábanas* the size of footballs. The soursop's slightly menacing name and appearance—yellow-green leathery skin dotted with small, pliable "spines"—gives way to a soft, white flesh that is incredibly aromatic. The flavor is somewhat like a cross between a pineapple and a mango, yet it is a completely unique, sweet-tart combination. All over Mexico, the Caribbean, and Central and South America, the popular *guanábana* is found in many forms: fresh, frozen, canned, as a fruit juice or syrup, in ice creams, and even in carbonated soft drinks.

I grew up eating this fruit, much as American children might eat an apple or a banana, and I just love it. I was always the first one of my family to get up in the morning, along with my grandmother, and she would often make me a *guanábanas batido* or *licuado* for breakfast. *Batidos* are like the milk version of *aguas frescas*, similar to an American smoothie, usually blending milk, fresh fruit, and ice. If you can find fresh *guanábana*, you will want to give this *batido* a try for breakfast, as a snack, or as a refreshing drink while you're working in the kitchen. The segmented pulp should be pulled from the rind and the few shiny black, almond-sized seeds removed before eating. Growing up, we would save the seeds to play with or glue them to paper to create artwork. You can use evaporated milk for a slightly richer version of this shake, called *guanábanas*.

Fresh *guanábanas* will keep in your refrigerator for several days. Don't be alarmed if the skin becomes blackened—the inside flesh often remains unspoiled even when the exterior looks otherwise.

SOURSOP MOUSSE
Mousse de Guanábana

The soursop's distinctive, slightly fermented aroma and unique flavor is best used in simple dessert preparations, such as milkshakes (try blended with vanilla ice cream), ice pops, or mousses. On its own, *guanábana* is very smooth and when blended it becomes very light and airy, making it perfect for this simple and elegant mousse, in which the unique flavor and velvety texture of the fruit are preserved and enhanced. Sliced strawberries or mixed berries are a nice garnish.

If you have the chance to travel to southern Mexico, to Chiapas or the Yucatán, you may see *guanábana* trees on the side of the road, fallen fruit split open on the ground, but outside of Mexico fresh *guanábana* can be difficult to find, so don't hesitate to use frozen pulp.

If working with fresh fruit, cut the *guanábana* in half and remove the seeds. Scoop out the flesh and process it in a blender until you have a fairly smooth puree. You may want to follow this same process with thawed frozen fruit to reach a similarly smooth consistency.

SERVES 6 TO 8

2 (¼-ounce) envelopes unflavored gelatin powder

2 cups *guanábana* pulp (from about 1 *guanábana*)   480 MILLILITERS

½ recipe Italian Meringue (page 236)

1 cup heavy cream   240 MILLILITERS

½ cup sweetened condensed milk   120 MILLILITERS

◎ Sprinkle the gelatin over 2 tablespoons (30 milliliters) water and let stand for 5 minutes.

◎ Put the *guanábana* pulp in a medium bowl and set aside.

◎ In a small saucepan over low heat, warm up 2 tablespoons (30 milliliters) water for 1 to 2 minutes. Remove from the heat and immediately add the gelatin mixture and stir until dissolved. Whisk the gelatin mixture into the *guanábana* pulp, then slowly fold the puree into the meringue.

◎ In the bowl of an electric mixer fitted with the whisk attachment, whip the cream until soft peaks form. Gently fold the cream and sweetened condensed milk into the *guanábana* and meringue mixture. Transfer the mousse to parfait glasses and chill in the refrigerator for at least 4 hours, preferably overnight. Serve cold.

SOURSOP SMOOTHIE
Batido de Guanábana

SERVES 4

3	cups chopped fresh *guanábana*	540 GRAMS
3	cups milk	720 MILLILITERS
½	cup evaporated milk	120 MILLILITERS
1	cup ice	
½	cup granulated sugar	100 GRAMS
1	tablespoon vanilla extract	

◉ Combine all the ingredients in a blender and blend for about 2 minutes. Serve in a tall glass. Alternatively, replace the evaporated milk and sugar with ½ cup sweetened condensed milk

PASSION FRUIT SOUFFLÉ

Soufflé de Maracuya

Baking your own soufflé is one of those home-cook milestones akin to baking bread. While chilled or frozen soufflés are pretty foolproof, baked soufflés can be finicky. But I've found that with a very good recipe (like this one), anyone can turn out a beautiful baked soufflé at home. Although soufflés are classically French, adding passion fruit gives this one a Latin twist.

SERVES 8

1¼ cups granulated sugar, plus more for the molds	250 GRAMS
1 cup passion fruit puree	240 MILLILITERS
2 cups whole milk	480 MILLILITERS
8 eggs, separated	
1 tablespoon vanilla extract	
⅜ cup all-purpose flour	55 GRAMS
2 tablespoons butter, plus more for the molds	

◉ Generously butter 8 (6-ounce) soufflé molds or ramekins and dust with sugar, tapping out the excess. Put the molds on a sheet pan.

◉ Preheat the oven to 400° F.

◉ In small saucepan over medium heat, cook the passion fruit puree and ½ cup of the sugar until slightly thickened, about 15 minutes. Let cool to room temperature.

◉ In a medium saucepan over medium-high heat, bring the milk and ½ cup of the sugar to a boil. Reduce the heat to low. In a small bowl, whisk together the egg yolks, remaining ¼ cup sugar, the vanilla extract, and flour. Continue whisking while pouring a small amount of the hot milk mixture into the yolk mixture. This will temper the yolks and keep them from curdling. While whisking the hot milk mixture in the saucepan, gradually add the tempered yolk mixture. Stir with a wooden spoon over medium-low heat until the custard coats the back of the spoon, being careful not to boil, about 3 minutes. Remove from the heat, add the butter, and set aside to cool. Transfer to a large bowl and fold in the passion fruit mixture.

◎ In the bowl of an electric mixer fitted with the whisk attachment, beat the egg whites until soft peaks form. Fold one third of the egg whites into the passion fruit mixture, then, gently but thoroughly, fold the mixture into the remaining whites.

◎ Spoon the batter into the prepared molds, filling almost to the top, and lightly run the tip of a knife around the inside rim to create a "moat." This will keep the batter from sticking to the edge of the molds and will allow them to rise properly. Put the sheet pan on the middle rack of the oven and bake until the soufflés have risen above the rims of the molds and are golden brown, about 25 minutes. Serve immediately.

Adorno Especial

Salsa de Chocolate y Salsa de Vainilla

Traditionally, soufflés are served with some kind of sauce, so I've suggested two here: a rich chocolate sauce and a crème anglaise. If you just have time to make one, go for chocolate; it is wonderful with passion fruit.

Chocolate Sauce 1 recipe (page 253)
Vanilla Crème Anglaise 1 recipe (page 255)

Serve the soufflés with the Chocolate Sauce and Crème Anglaise on the side.

BANANA FRITTERS

Bananas Fritas

You can serve these fritters as a dessert, but my family and I like them equally well as a sweet breakfast or brunch treat.

SERVES 8 TO 10

2	cups all-purpose flour	285 GRAMS
¼	teaspoon freshly grated nutmeg	
1	teaspoon ground cinnamon	
¾	cup whole milk	180 MILLILITERS
1½	teaspoons active dry yeast	
4	tablespoons granulated sugar	
1	tablespoon vanilla extract	
1	egg	
5	ripe bananas, diced	
2	quarts vegetable oil for frying	2 LITERS
	Confectioners' sugar, or half cinnamon, half granulated sugar	

◎ In a medium bowl, combine the flour, nutmeg, and cinnamon.

◎ In a small saucepan over medium-low heat, slightly warm the milk. It should not be too hot to the touch, or it will be too hot for the yeast. Add the yeast and granulated sugar and stir until dissolved.

◎ Pour the milk mixture into the flour mixture, along with the vanilla extract and egg, and with your hands or a wooden spoon mix until combined. Fold in the bananas and let rise in a warm place, covered with a kitchen towel, for about 15 minutes, until the dough has doubled in volume. If not using immediately, cover and refrigerate for no more than 2 hours. Bring to room temperature before frying.

◎ Heat the oil in a deep, heavy saucepan to 350° F. In batches, drop tablespoonfuls of the dough into the oil, cooking 6 or 7 per batch. Fry until golden brown and puffy, 4 to 5 minutes. Remove from the oil with a slotted spoon and drain briefly on paper towels. Serve warm, sprinkled with confectioners' sugar or cinnamon sugar.

Adorno Especial

Salsa de Maracuya y Fresa

1 pint fresh strawberries 400 GRAMS

1 cup passion fruit puree (or the flesh from about 2 passion fruits) 240 MILLILITERS

1 cup granulated sugar 200 GRAMS

Puree the strawberries, passion fruit puree or fresh pulp, and sugar in a blender until smooth. Refrigerate until needed, up to 3 days, or freeze for up to 2 months. Serve as a dipping sauce with the fritters.

CANDIED ORANGE
Naranja Confitada

Choose organic oranges, since this recipe includes the peel. Florida navels will work well.

MAKES ABOUT 5 CUPS

2 medium oranges

2 cups granulated sugar   400 GRAMS

2 tablespoons light corn syrup

4 whole allspice berries

2 whole cloves

1 cinnamon stick

◎ Slice the oranges horizontally into ⅛-inch-thick rounds. In a small saucepan over medium heat, combine the oranges with 2 cups (480 milliliters) water and the remaining ingredients and bring to a gentle boil. (Be cautious, as a rapid boil can break up the orange slices.) Reduce the heat and simmer for about 35 minutes, until the liquid reaches a thick, honeylike consistency. Be careful not to over-reduce, or the mixture will become more of a marmalade and it will be difficult to separate the orange slices. Remove from the heat and let cool.

◎ The candied orange can be made in advance and stored in an airtight container in the refrigerator for up to 1 month.

◎ You can also use this recipe to make a delicious marmalade. Just boil the mixture for about 10 more minutes (45 minutes total), watching carefully to make sure it doesn't burn, until you get a nice, thick syrup. Let cool, remove the whole spices, and blend in a food processor or blender to desired consistency. It will also keep well in the refrigerator for about 1 month.

AVOCADO PANNA COTTA

Panna Cotta de Aguacate

Many people don't realize that avocados are actually a fruit, not a vegetable. Although avocados are typically used in savory dishes in the United States, they crop up in many sweet preparations in Latin America and across the globe. In Xochimilco, Mexico, at an annual ice cream and sorbet festival, residents and visitors come up with really shocking flavor combinations that taste surprisingly delicious. Flavors like shrimp, snake (yes, snake ice cream!), cactus, corn, mango, and chile powder. Although slightly less outrageous, one of the best flavors I tasted at this festival was a lemon-avocado sorbet. The lemon added a delicious tangy flavor but also preserved the bright green color of the avocado. The sorbet, as well as avocado's naturally creamy texture, is what inspired this panna cotta.

SERVES 6

2 (¼-ounce) envelopes unflavored gelatin powder

2½ cups whole milk   600 MILLILITERS

2 cups heavy cream   480 MILLILITERS

¾ cup granulated sugar   150 GRAMS

Grated zest of 1 lemon

1 vanilla bean, halved lengthwise, seeds scraped out and reserved (or 1½ tablespoons vanilla extract)

½ cup ripe avocado pulp (from about 1 Hass avocado)   120 GRAMS

◎ Sprinkle the gelatin over ½ cup (120 milliliters) of the milk and let stand for 5 minutes.

◎ In a medium saucepan over medium heat, bring the remaining 2 cups (480 milliliters) milk, the cream, sugar, lemon zest, and vanilla bean (including seeds) or extract to a boil. Boil for 1 minute, then remove from the heat. Add the gelatin mixture and whisk until dissolved. Strain though a fine sieve into a large, clean bowl (preferably one with a spout) to remove the vanilla bean and any bits of zest or gelatin. Cool in an ice bath (see page 195), stirring occasionally to prevent the mixture from setting, but still allowing it to thicken, 10 to 12 minutes.

◎ In a blender or food processor, puree the avocado pulp until smooth. Add half of the cream mixture and puree again until smooth. Add the avocado mixture to the remaining cream mixture and whisk to combine. Pour into 6 (6-ounce) ramekins or tea or coffee cups. Refrigerate, uncovered, until set, at least 2 hours. The panna cottas will keep in the refrigerator for 3 days. Serve cold in the ramekins or cups.

Adorno Especial

Galleta de Chocolate con Salpicón de Tamarillo y Banana

The chocolate cookie and fruit salsa are nice additions, but the panna cotta is both silky rich and light and refreshing all on its own.

2 ripe bananas

2 tamarillos in syrup (jarred or made fresh, (see page 189), stems removed

¼ cup Simple Syrup (page 237)

60 MILLILITERS

Chocolate Butter Cookies 1 recipe (page 61)

Dice the bananas and tamarillos. In a small bowl, mix the diced fruit with the syrup and use immediately or refrigerate for up to 24 hours.

Serve ramekins or cups of panna cotta topped with a spoonful of salsa and a butter cookie. Alternatively, briefly immerse the base of each ramekin or cup in hot water to help unmold (you may need to slide a hot knife around the inside of the ramekin or cup to loosen). Place one butter cookie in the center of each plate, top with the unmolded panna cotta, and surround with a few spoonfuls of the salsa.

Tomates de Arbol

ALTHOUGH TAMARILLOS ARE FOUND IN MEXICO, THEY NEED HIGH altitudes to grow, and so they are more prevalent in southern Mexico close to the Guatamalan border. They are more prevalent in Colombia. The flavor of a tamarillo is probably closest to passion fruit, but it also has notes of strawberry and pineapple with a more savory, tomato-like aftertaste. The fruit's appearance reminds me a bit of a plum tomato: an oblong, round fruit with smooth reddish purple or yellow-orange skin surrounding a soft yellowish interior flesh with pockets of dark edible seeds. Native to the Andes mountains, tamarillos grow on trees, in clusters on a tree much like cherries. And although they are cultivated in many Latin American countries, the main source of export to the United States today is New Zealand. In fact it was a marketing mind in New Zealand that came up with the name *tamarillo* (certainly sexier than *tree tomato*)—a cross between *tomato* and *amarillo*, the Spanish word for "yellow."

LUCUMA PARFAIT

Lucuma Parfait

Lucuma, or *lucmo* or eggfruit as it is sometimes called (because of the cooked egg yolk–like texture of the pulp), is native to Peru, where it is popular as an ice cream or milkshake flavor. The smooth, yellow-green skin gives way to a dry, fibrous, yellow flesh that isn't appealing to all, but when pureed and prepared with cream and cinnamon, as here, transforms into an addictive combination of butterscotch and sweet potato. Extremely common in Peru, lucuma remains fairly rare even in other Latin American countries. Be careful that you are buying pureed lucuma fruit and not the actual lucuma ice cream, as tubs of the ice cream are sometimes simply labeled "lucuma."

If frozen lucuma is unavailable, lucuma powder (also called lucuma flour) can be substituted. Use 1 cup (115 grams) lucuma powder and increase the heavy cream by ½ cup (120 milliliters).

SERVES 10

2 cups lucuma puree   480 MILLILITERS

½ tablespoon vanilla extract

¼ teaspoon ground cinnamon

2 cups heavy cream   480 MILLILITERS

¼ cup granulated sugar   50 GRAMS

4 egg yolks

2 (¼-ounce) envelopes unflavored gelatin powder

൭ In a blender or food processor, puree the lucuma, vanilla extract, and cinnamon until smooth. Transfer to a large bowl, preferably one with a spout.

൭ Sprinkle the gelatin over 2 tablespoons (30 milliliters) of cold water and let stand for 5 minutes.

൭ In a large saucepan over medium heat, bring the cream and sugar to a boil. If using lucuma powder, add it now, to allow it to dissolve. Reduce the heat and stir until the sugar (and lucuma powder, if using) is completely dissolved. Remove from the heat and let rest for 5 minutes.

൭ In a medium bowl, whisk the egg yolks together. Continue whisking while pouring a small amount of the hot cream mixture into the yolks. This will temper the yolks and keep them from curdling. While whisking the remaining hot cream mixture in the saucepan, gradually add the tempered yolks and then the gelatin.

◎ Set aside and whisk occasionally to make sure the mixture remains smooth as it begins to set. Once the mixture starts to set and becomes slightly jiggly, about 10 minutes, pour it into a blender or food processor and puree on high speed for about 5 minutes, until it's doubled in volume and begins to look like whipped cream. Fold the whipped custard into the lucuma mixture, being careful not to overmix.

◎ If you intend to serve unmolded individual parfaits, pour the custard into 10 (2½-inch) ring molds or muffin tins lined with paper baking cups. Cover and freeze for at least 4 hours, or overnight. Well wrapped and in an airtight container, the parfaits will keep frozen for 2 months. Alternatively, you can cover the whole batch of custard and scoop out portions when ready to serve.

Adorno Especial

Suspiros de Chocolate y Reduccion de Café

Crisp Chocolate Meringues
  1 recipe (page 56)

Coffee Reduction
  1 recipe (page 259)

To serve, place a meringue in the center of each plate and top with either an unmolded individual parfait or a scoop of the parfait. Drizzle with the reduction.

CHERIMOYA MOUSSE
Mousse de Cherimoya

The cherimoya's cultivation here in the United States is very small, and since it's a delicate fruit it doesn't ship well from overseas and is difficult to find fresh in the States. You can, however, find frozen pulp that will still impart this light mousse with addictive flavor—like a supersweet combination of pineapple, strawberry, and apple. Look for brands like Goya or La Fe. If you ever spot a fresh one, buy it immediately. If it's not ripe, leave it on your counter wrapped in a paper bag or newspaper for a day or two. When ready, it should give to the touch like a ripe peach. If working with fresh fruit, cut the cherimoyas in half and remove the seeds. Scoop out the flesh and process it in a blender until you have a fairly smooth puree. You may want to follow this same process with thawed frozen fruit to reach a similar smooth consistency.

The heart-shaped cherimoya, sometimes called a custard apple for its juicy custardlike texture, has a green skin with rounded, tile-like indentations and a yellowish-white flesh dotted with larger dark seeds that look like coffee beans. As a kid, I used to bite into fresh slices of cherimoya and, like eating watermelon, spit out the seeds as I went.

Use the remaining recipe of Italian Meringue as a topping for ice cream or fresh fruit.

SERVES 10 TO 12

1 (¼-ounce) envelope unflavored
    gelatin powder
1½ cups cherimoya puree from about
    2 cherimoya   360 MILLILITERS
¼ cup water   60 MILLILITERS
½ recipe Italian Meringue (page 236)
1 cup heavy cream   240 MILLILITERS

◉ Sprinkle the gelatin over 2 tablespoons (30 milliliters) cold water and let stand for 5 minutes.

◉ Put the cherimoya puree in a medium bowl and set aside.

◉ In a small saucepan over low heat, warm 2 tablespoons (30 milliliters) water for 1 to 2 minutes. Remove from the heat and immediately add the gelatin mixture and stir until dissolved. Whisk the gelatin mixture into the cherimoya puree until incorporated, then slowly fold in the meringue.

◉ In the bowl of an electric mixer fitted with the whisk attachment, whip the cream until soft peaks form. Gently fold the whipped cream into the cherimoya mixture. Transfer the mousse to a covered container and chill in the refrigerator for at least 4 hours, preferably overnight. Serve chilled in bowls or parfait glasses.

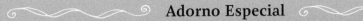

Adorno Especial

Suspiros de Coco

These garnishes add great contrasting texture to the mousse. The meringues are a good complement to other puddings or mousses or even chocolate ice cream. The fresh fruit garnishes add a bit of natural acidity to contrast the sweetness of the meringues and accentuate the flavor of the cherimoya.

Crisp Coconut Meringues 1 recipe (page 55)
Kiwi or strawberries, sliced

When ready to serve, place a meringue on a plate, followed by a scoop of the mousse. Top with another meringue and one more scoop of the mousse. Place a few slices of fresh kiwi or strawberries around the plate. Alternatively, spoon the mousse into decorative bowls or parfait glasses and serve the meringues on the side.

MANGO POPS
Paletas de Mango

½ cup granulated sugar   50 GRAMS

2 tablespoons freshly squeezed
   lemon juice

2 cups mango puree
   (from about 2 large mangoes;
   see page 185)   480 MILLILITERS

In a small saucepan over medium high heat, bring 1 cup (240 milliliters) water, the sugar, and lemon juice to a boil. Stir with a wooden spoon until the sugar dissolves. Remove from the heat and refrigerate until cool, about 30 minutes.

In a medium bowl, whisk together the mango puree and cooled syrup. Pour into pop molds and freeze for at least 4 hours. Alternatively, use 4-ounce plastic cups or even large ice cube trays and freeze the pops for about 30 minutes, then insert wooden sticks into the center of each mold. When ready to eat, run the bottoms of the pop molds under cold water for a few seconds to help unmold.

PINEAPPLE POPS
Paletas de Piña

1 cup granulated sugar   200 GRAMS

4 cups finely diced pineapple   680 GRAMS

In a small saucepan over medium-high heat, bring 1 cup (240 milliliters) water and the sugar to a boil. Stir with a wooden spoon until the sugar dissolves. Remove from the heat and place the pan in an ice bath (see page 195) to cool.

In a food processor or blender, puree half of the pineapple and the cooled syrup until smooth, about 2 minutes. Strain through a fine sieve set over a bowl, add the remaining 2 cups pineapple to the puree, and pour into ice pop molds. Follow the instructions for Mango Pops for freezing and unmolding.

Paletas

THE MEXICAN ICE POPS CART IS THE EQUIVALENT OF THE AMERICAN ICE
cream truck. From markets to side streets, beaches to buses, wherever you go
in Mexico there is always someone selling *paletas*. Every Sunday during my
childhood, I used to join my grandmother shopping at the market. That was her
only day off, and she would take me to one of the oldest *mercados* in Mexico City,
called Tacubaya. Before we went home, she would buy me a *paleta*. Since we
didn't have a freezer at home, it was always a nice treat to enjoy under the hot sun.

Typical American ice pops, with their manufactured flavors and food color-
ing-enhanced hues, are quite different from traditional Mexican pops, which are
more natural, made only with water, sugar, and big chunks of fresh fruit:
strawberry, guava, mamey (my favorite), and so on. There are even *horchata*-
flavored pops (made from the popular rice and cinnamon *agua fresca*, page 191),
ones dotted with pine nuts, ones made with *arroz con leche* (rice pudding),
or swirled with *queso fresco* and *zarzamora* (blackberry) or *frambuesa*
(raspberry). These days, most of the ice cream and pops in Mexico, and even the
Mexican inspired frozen treats in the United States, come from one company—
La Michoacana. Opposite are a couple of recipes to try at home.

MANGO CEVICHE
Ceviche de Mango

Ceviche refers to a Latin preparation of fish or shellfish that is "cooked" by the acid of a citrus marinade. Here I take the citrus marinade base of ceviche, translate it into an infused sugar syrup, and then add mangoes, sweet vanilla, and a punch of fresh ginger. It's the perfect refreshing complement to Dulce de Leche Brazo Gitano (page 92). Or try it alongside any simple chocolate cake or over vanilla ice cream. For a light dessert or great brunch side dish, add other fresh fruit—fresh berries work especially well—for a unique fruit salad, and serve with a scoop of lime or lemon sorbet. Be sure to choose firm mangoes. If they are too ripe and give to the touch, you will not be able to slice them and they will not hold up in the syrup.

MAKES ABOUT 4 CUPS

1 cup sugar　　　　　　　　　　200 GRAMS

1 vanilla bean, halved lengthwise, seeds
　scraped out and reserved
　(or 1½ tablespoons vanilla extract)

Peel of 1 lemon, cut into strips

1 tablespoon sliced fresh ginger

2 tablespoons freshly squeezed
　lemon juice

3 large, firm mangoes

◉ In a medium saucepan over medium-high heat, bring 2 cups (480 milliliters) water, the sugar, vanilla bean (including seeds), lemon peel, and ginger to a boil, stirring until the sugar is dissolved. Simmer, undisturbed, for 2 minutes. Let cool to room temperature. (An ice bath can speed up this process; see page 195.)

◉ Add the lemon juice and pour the syrup through a fine sieve into a clean bowl.

◉ Peel the mangoes, slice them very thinly (with a mandoline if you have one) or into long strips, and add them to the infused sugar syrup. Cover and refrigerate for at least 4 hours or up to 4 days.

How to Peel a Mango

CUT THE MANGO LENGTHWISE INTO THREE PIECES BY SLICING ALL THE way through on either side of the pit. You will end up with 2 dome-shaped pieces with only skin and fruit and 1 oval-shaped piece that is mostly pit. Score one of the dome-shaped pieces with a knife, cutting all the way through the flesh but being careful not to break the skin. If you want long strips of fruit, score only in one direction. If you want diced fruit, score both lengthwise and crosswise.

Press the rounded skin of the mango flat against a cutting board so that the pieces of fruit begin to separate. Carefully run a sharp knife along the underside of the skin, detaching the scored pieces of fruit. Repeat with the other dome-shaped piece. You may also be able to cut a bit of fruit from the top and bottom of the piece with the pit. To make mango puree, puree the flesh in a blender until smooth.

CARAMELIZED NECTARINES
Nectarinas Caramelizadas

These nectarines would be just as delicious cooked with a simple caramel, but the twists of vanilla, lemon, and Pisco make them extra special. Pisco, of the cocktail Pisco sour fame, is a grape brandy of Spanish origin, mainly produced today in Peru and Chile. The drink that made it famous has increased in popularity in the States along with the popularity of Latin cuisine and other Latin drinks like mojitos and caipirinhas. I like the added depth of flavor the brandy gives the nectarines. You can also use this same method with a variety of other fruits, such as apples, bananas, or pears. Serve leftovers over pancakes or pound cake, on their own with whipped cream or ice cream, or even with a fresh cheese.

5 ripe but firm fresh nectarines, quartered and pitted

1 cup granulated sugar   200 GRAMS

1 vanilla bean, halved lengthwise, seeds scraped out and reserved (or 1 to 2 tablespoons vanilla extract)

Juice of 2 lemons

¼ cup Pisco   60 MILLILITERS

◎ Cut each nectarine half into 4 slices and set aside.

◎ In a medium saucepan, stir together the sugar, 1 cup (120 milliliters) water, and the halved vanilla bean (including seeds) or extract and bring to a boil. Lower the heat to medium-high and boil, without stirring, for about 15 minutes, until the sugar dissolves and the mixture becomes a golden amber color. Carefully add the nectarines, lemon juice, and Pisco and stir until combined. Cook over medium heat for about 8 minutes, until firm-tender but not mushy. Remove from the heat and let cool.

LULO AND BERRY SALSA
Salpicón de Lulo y Fresas

Although you won't find fresh lulo here in the States, Latin markets will have either frozen lulo pulp or, most likely, jarred lulo fruit in syrup. Both will work and will let you experience the unique taste of lulo: what I think of as a sweet-sour, very refreshing combination of orange, mango, and passion fruit.

MAKES ABOUT 2 CUPS

1 cup lulo pulp (jarred fruit drained from syrup and flesh scooped out from skin)	240 MILLILITERS
½ cup blueberries	85 GRAMS
½ cup diced strawberries	85 GRAMS

◉ Toss the lulo pulp with the berries.

PRUNES MARINATED IN PASSION FRUIT SYRUP

Ciruelas Marinadas en Almibar de Maracuya

In America, prunes seem to get a bit of a bad rap. This recipe will certainly change your mind. Don't forget that prunes are actually dried plums, and when enrobed in this vibrant passion fruit syrup they are anything but dowdy. They are the perfect garnish in both flavor and texture for the Banana Tres Leches (page 84), and over vanilla ice cream as an easy, unique dessert.

MAKES ABOUT 5 CUPS

2 cups granulated sugar	400 GRAMS
2 cups passion fruit puree	370 MILLILITERS
2 cups halved pitted prunes	310 GRAMS

◎ In a large saucepan over medium heat, bring 1 cup (240 milliliters) water and the sugar to a boil, stirring until the sugar is dissolved and being careful not to burn. Let cool to room temperature. (An ice bath can speed up this process; see page 195.) Chill in the refrigerator.

◎ When the syrup is completely cool, stir in the passion fruit puree and the prunes, transfer to a mixing bowl, cover, and store in the refrigerator for up to 1 week.

TAMARILLOS IN SYRUP

Tomates de Arbol en Almibar

If you're lucky enough to find fresh tamarillos, simply peel off the bitter skin as you might with a plum, and enjoy. The yellow-orange variety tend to be milder and less acidic, so more appealing to enjoy fresh. Or you can blanch them like tomatoes by scoring the skin with a knife and dropping them into boiling water for about 3 minutes, then plunging them into ice water before peeling. Tamarillos' split fruit-vegetable personality makes them extremely versatile. You can of course use them like a fruit and eat them fresh, in desserts, blended into drinks, or made into preserves. Or you can use them like you might a sweeter tomato in stews, sauces, salads, or sliced on sandwiches.

Jarred, they have a texture similar to canned peaches and are best used as a component in a sweet or savory recipe, eaten alongside cheese, or served over waffles or on toast. Or puree them in a blender for a few seconds and use like a marmalade. I really like the La Fe brand. Look for them in the canned fruit section of Latin markets or online at www.lafe.com, a valuable source for many of the other ingredients I use in this book if you don't have access to a good market.

MAKES 6 PIECES

6 fresh tamarillos (see page 177)

4 cups sugar   800 GRAMS

◎ In a medium saucepan over high heat, bring 2 quarts (2 liters) water to a boil. Score an "X" on each end of the tamarillos with a knife and poach them in the boiling water for 3 minutes. Plunge into ice water until they are cool to the touch, then drain and peel.

◎ In the same saucepan over medium-high heat, bring 2 cups (480 milliliters) water, the sugar, and the peeled tamarillos to a boil. Reduce the heat and simmer for about 25 minutes, until the fruit is tender but not mushy and still holding its shape. To stop the cooking process, set the pan in an ice bath (see page 195).

PINEAPPLE CONFIT
Piña Confitada

I love the intensity that smoked paprika and cardamom bring to this simple confit. Make a show-stopping dessert that brings together the classic flavors of a piña colada by adding toasted coconut, a drizzle of Chocolate Ganache (page 254), and some Coconut Tuiles (page 62). Or serve with Toasted Coconut Ice Cream (page 196).

If you're feeling artistic, freeze the ice cream in the shape of miniature pineapples, covering each in the ganache and rolling in toasted coconut to resemble the real fruit. Serve over the confit.

If plating, puree half the confit in a blender. Top a circle of the smooth confit with the chunky confit, a scoop of ice cream, and a sprinkling of toasted coconut. Alternatively, layer the four components into parfait glasses. Drizzle with Chocolate Ganache and garnish with a coconut tuile.

SERVES 8 (ABOUT ½ CUP CONFIT PER PERSON)

1 medium golden pineapple

1½ cups granulated sugar,
   or more to taste   300 GRAMS

1 vanilla bean, halved lengthwise, seeds
   scraped out and reserved
   (or 1½ tablespoons vanilla extract)

½ teaspoon smoked paprika

1 teaspoon ground cardamom

◉ To peel the pineapple, cut off both ends. Stand the fruit up on a cutting board and run the knife down the sides to remove the skin, being careful to remove all the eyes. Remove the core and cut into ½-inch dice.

◉ In a medium saucepan over medium heat, bring the pineapple and the remaining ingredients to a boil (if using a vanilla bean, include both the halved bean and the seeds). (If the pineapple does not taste super sweet, you can increase the sugar by as much as 1 cup.) Lower the heat and cook until the pineapple is translucent, about 30 minutes. Watch carefully to make sure the liquid does not evaporate completely. If it gets low, add small amounts of water as necessary.

◉ Set aside and let cool to room temperature, then transfer to a bowl, cover, and refrigerate until cold, at least 1 hour. If using a vanilla bean, remove the halved bean before serving.

Aguas Frescas

SPANISH FOR "FRESH WATERS," *AGUAS FRESCAS* ARE REFRESHING INFUSIONS of fruits, grains, or flowers in water, sweetened with sugar and served over ice. *Agua de jamaica* made with hibiscus flowers, *horchata* made with rice and cinnamon, and *agua de tamarindo* made with tamarind are probably the most well-known flavors. But really *aguas frescas* can be made with any fruits: lime, pineapple (*piña*), watermelon, red currant (*grocella*). Lime *agua fresca* is much like limeade, but we add some zest and chunks of the fruit, not just the juice, while *grocella* is typically made with red currant syrup rather than the fresh berries. My favorite is probably *agua fresca* made with *guánabana*, or soursop (see page 169), a totally unique sweet-tart tropical fruit that's as recognizable to Mexicans as an apple is to Americans.

Agua de jamaica is made just like an iced tea. Boil water with hibiscus leaves, let steep off the heat, then strain and cool. Pour over ice and add sugar if desired.

To make *horchata*, cook rice in water as you normally would, adding a cinnamon stick, until it's about halfway done. Cool and blend the rice, cinnamon stick and all, along with some milk in a blender until smooth. In Mexico, our cinnamon sticks (actually canela) have more of a paperlike texture, so if you have trouble blending the stick, you can just add ground cinnamon. The result is like drinking a deliciously cold, liquid rice pudding. If you prefer a thicker, sweeter drink, you can use evaporated milk instead. Be careful not to overcook the rice, as it will become sticky and too thick to blend.

Agua de tamarindo is made with fresh tamarind (see page 111). The fresh pods are fairly easy to find in ethnic markets these days. Cook in boiling water until the pod releases the seeds, about 10 minutes, then let cool. Press the cooked pulp through a sieve, leaving behind any hard fibers and the seeds. Stir the strained pulp back into the water (don't miss the strained pulp that might stick to the bottom of the sieve), add sugar to taste, and serve over ice.

Just as with iced tea, soda, or lemonade in the United States, you'll find both fresh juices and *aguas frescas* for sale in Mexico everywhere from casual restaurants and markets to tacquerias and street stalls. At Mexican *mercados*, there's always a spot where they sell tacos, quesadillas, and *aguas frescas* for a snack or light lunch.

6

ICE CREAM, SORBET, AND GRANITA

Helado, Crema Helada, Nieve, y Granizado

In This Chapter

MAMEY ICE CREAM

Helado de Mamey

SERVES 6

1 cup heavy cream	240 MILLILITERS
1 cup whole milk	240 MILLILITERS
½ cup sugar	100 GRAMS
1 cinnamon stick	
½ tablespoon vanilla extract	
4 large egg yolks	
¾ cup mamey puree (from about	
1 pound fresh fruit, see page 213)	
	180 MILLILITERS

In a large saucepan over medium-high heat, bring the cream, milk, sugar, cinnamon stick, and vanilla extract to a boil. Reduce the heat and stir until the sugar is completely dissolved. Remove from the heat and let rest for 5 minutes.

In a medium bowl, whisk the egg yolks together. Continue whisking while pouring a small amount of the hot cream mixture into the yolks. This will temper the yolks and keep them from curdling. While whisking the hot cream mixture, gradually add the tempered yolks. Stir with a wooden spoon over medium-low heat until the custard coats the back of the spoon, being careful not to boil, about 4 minutes.

Strain the custard through a fine sieve into a clean bowl to remove the cinnamon stick and any bits of cooked yolk.

Chill the custard in the refrigerator until very cold, about 3 hours, or use an ice bath (see opposite). Stir in the mamey puree. Pour the custard into an ice cream maker and freeze according to the manufacturer's instructions.

MILK-CARAMEL ICE CREAM

Helado de Dulce de Leche

SERVES 6

1 cup heavy cream	240 MILLILITERS
1 cup whole milk	240 MILLILITERS
4 large egg yolks	
1 cup Dulce de Leche	
(page 52)	225 GRAMS
¼ cup dark rum	60 MILLILITERS

◎ In a large saucepan over medium-high heat, bring the cream and milk to a boil. Remove from the heat and let rest for 5 minutes. Follow the instructions in the Mamey Ice Cream recipe (opposite) for finishing and straining the custard.

◎ Whisk in the Dulce de Leche and rum.

◎ Chill the custard in the refrigerator until very cold, about 3 hours, or use an ice bath (see below). Pour the custard into an ice cream maker and freeze according to the manufacturer's instructions.

Cooling in an Ice Bath

WE RECOMMEND COOLING ALL MILK-BASED ICE CREAM MIXTURES IN AN ice bath before refrigerating to help speed the cooling process and prevent the growth of bacteria, especially when dealing with egg-based custard ice creams. Once the mixture has been cooled slightly, allowing the mixture to finish cooling more slowly (in the refrigerator versus an ice bath) before placing it in your ice cream maker will give it a fluffier texture and more developed flavors. If you have time, allowing the mixture to cool in the refrigerator overnight will produce the very best end result. To make an ice bath, start with a pan or bowl larger than the one you are trying to cool down. You can even use the kitchen sink. Fill it about halfway with cold water and ice cubes and gently set the pan or bowl containing the mixture to be cooled in the water, being careful not to get any water into the mixture. Stir gently and occassionally until the mixture is cool to the touch.

TOASTED COCONUT ICE CREAM

Helado de Coco Tostado

I recommend using unsweetened shredded coconut for this recipe, but if you can't find it sweetened will work as well.

SERVES 8

2	cups unsweetened shredded coconut	150 GRAMS
2	cups heavy cream	480 MILLILITERS
1½	cups whole milk	360 MILLILITERS
½	cup granulated sugar	100 GRAMS
1	(8.5-ounce) can coco Lopez cream of coconut	255 MILLILITERS
7	egg yolks	

◉ Preheat the oven to 250°F.

◉ Spread the coconut out in a single layer on a nonstick baking sheet or one lined with parchment paper. Bake until the coconut is golden and crunchy, 45 minutes to 1 hour.

◉ In a large saucepan over medium-high heat, bring the cream, milk, sugar, cream of coconut, and 1½ cups (115 grams) toasted coconut to a boil. Reduce the heat and stir until the sugar is completely dissolved. Remove from the heat and let rest for at least 15 minutes and up to overnight (refrigerated) to allow the coconut flavor to saturate the mixture. Strain through a fine sieve to remove the coconut. (Don't discard the shredded coconut—you can dry it and use it to sprinkle over the ice cream: Put the drained coconut on a baking pan lined with parchment paper. Dry it in the oven at 300°F for 15 minutes, or until golden brown.)

◉ Follow the instructions in the Mamey Ice Cream recipe (page 194) for finishing the custard.

◉ Chill the custard in the refrigerator until very cold, about 3 hours, or use an ice bath (see page 195). Pour into an ice cream maker and freeze according to the manufacturer's instructions. Serve sprinkled with the remaining toasted coconut.

VANILLA BEAN ICE CREAM
Helado de Vainilla

SERVES 6

1 cup heavy cream	240 MILLILITERS
1 cup whole milk	240 MILLILITERS
½ cup granulated sugar	100 GRAMS
1 vanilla bean, halved lengthwise, seeds scraped out and reserved (or 1½ tablespoons vanilla extract)	
4 egg yolks	

◉ In a large saucepan over medium-high heat, bring the cream, milk, sugar, and halved vanilla bean (including seeds) or extract to a boil. Reduce the heat and stir until the sugar is completely dissolved. Remove from the heat and let rest for 5 minutes. Follow the instructions in the Mamey Ice Cream recipe (page 194) for finishing and straining the custard.

◉ Chill the custard in the refrigerator until very cold, about 3 hours, or use an ice bath (see page 195). Pour the custard into an ice cream maker and freeze according to the manufacturer's instructions.

LUCUMA ICE CREAM

Helado de Lucuma

If frozen lucuma puree is unavailable, substitute 2 cups lucuma powder. The puree is very thick, so no additional liquid will be needed—simply add the 2 cups lucuma powder to the milk mixture once the sugar has completely dissolved.

SERVES 8

2	cups heavy cream	480 MILLILITERS
1	cup whole milk	240 MILLILITERS
¾	cup granulated sugar	150 GRAMS
1	cinnamon stick	
7	egg yolks	
1½	cups lucuma puree (see page 198)	
		360 MILLILITERS

⊚ In a large saucepan over medium-high heat, bring the cream, milk, sugar, and cinnamon stick to a boil. Reduce the heat and stir until the sugar is completely dissolved. Remove from the heat and let rest for 5 minutes. Follow the instructions in the Mamey Ice Cream recipe (page 194) for finishing and straining the custard.

⊚ Chill the custard in the refrigerator until very cold, about 3 hours, or use an ice bath (see page 195). Stir in the lucuma puree. Pour into an ice cream maker and freeze according to the manufacturer's instructions.

WHITE CHOCOLATE MOCHA ICE CREAM

Helado de Mocha

SERVES 8

2½ cups whole milk	600 MILLILITERS
½ cup heavy cream	120 MILLILITERS
6 tablespoons granulated sugar	75 GRAMS
7 egg yolks	
6 ounces white chocolate (preferably El Rey), chopped (about 1 cup chips)	170 GRAMS
¼ cup Kahlúa	60 MILLILITERS
3 tablespoons coffee extract	

◉ In a large saucepan over medium-high heat, bring the milk, cream, and sugar to a boil. Reduce the heat and stir until the sugar is completely dissolved. Remove from the heat and let rest for 5 minutes. Follow the instructions in the Mamey Ice Cream recipe (page 194) for finishing and straining the custard. Stir in the white chocolate, Kahlúa, and coffee extract and stir until the chocolate is melted.

◉ Chill the custard in the refrigerator until very cold, about 3 hours, or use an ice bath (see page 195). Pour into an ice cream maker and freeze according to the manufacturer's instructions.

CHEESE ICE CREAM

Helado de Queso

SERVES 8

2 cups whole milk	480 MILLILITERS
¾ cup heavy cream	180 MILLILITERS
1 cup granulated sugar	200 GRAMS
10 egg yolks	
1 pound cream cheese, softened	455 GRAMS

◎ In a large saucepan over medium-high heat, bring the milk, cream, and sugar to a boil. Reduce the heat and stir until the sugar is completely dissolved. Remove from the heat and let rest for 5 minutes. Follow the directions in the Mamey Ice Cream recipe (page 194) for finishing and straining the custard.

◎ Chill the custard in the refrigerator until very cold, about 3 hours, or use an ice bath (see page 195). In a food processor or blender, blend the cream cheese and the chilled custard until smooth. Pour into an ice cream maker and freeze according to the manufacturer's instructions.

CARAMELIZED BANANA ICE CREAM

Helado de Platano Caramelizado

SERVES 8

2 tablespoons butter

1 cup packed dark
  brown sugar   225 GRAMS

¼ cup dark rum
  (preferably Meyer's)   60 MILLILITERS

1 tablespoon vanilla extract

1 teaspoon ground cinnamon

3 ripe bananas, cut into
  ¼-inch-thick rounds

2 cups heavy cream   480 MILLILITERS

2 cups whole milk   480 MILLILITERS

½ cup granulated sugar   100 GRAMS

7 egg yolks

In a sauté pan over medium heat, melt the butter. Stir in the brown sugar, rum, vanilla extract, and cinnamon and cook just until the sugar begins to caramelize, about 3 minutes. Add the bananas and cook until the bananas have caramelized and softened, 3 to 5 minutes depending on their ripeness. Set aside to cool.

In a large saucepan over medium-high heat, bring the cream, milk, and sugar to a boil. Reduce the heat and stir until the sugar is completely dissolved. Remove from the heat and let rest for 5 minutes. Follow the instructions in the Mamey Ice Cream recipe (page 194) for finishing and straining the custard.

If you prefer a smoother texture, stir in the caramelized bananas now. Chill the custard in the refrigerator until very cold, about 3 hours, or use an ice bath (see page 195). Pour the custard into an ice cream maker and freeze according to the manufacturer's instructions. If you prefer a chunkier texture, freeze the plain custard first, then blend the caramelized bananas into the frozen ice cream before serving.

TAMARIND ICE CREAM

Helado de Tamarindo

SERVES 8

2 cup heavy cream	480 MILLILITERS
1 cup whole milk	240 MILLILITERS
¾ cup sugar	150 GRAMS
7 egg yolks	
1 cup tamarind puree	
(see page 111)	240 MILLILITERS

◎ In a large saucepan over medium-high heat, bring the cream, milk, and sugar to a boil. Reduce the heat and stir until the sugar is completely dissolved. Remove from the heat and let rest for 5 minutes. Follow the instructions on page 194 for finishing the custard.

◎ Chill the custard in the refrigerator until very cold, about 3 hours, or use an ice bath (see page 195). Stir in the tamarind puree. Pour into an ice cream maker and freeze according to the manufacturer's instructions.

HAZELNUT ICE CREAM

Helado de Avellanas

SERVES 8

2 cups heavy cream	480 MILLILITERS
2 cups whole milk	480 MILLILITERS
½ cup plus 2 tablespoons granulated sugar	125 GRAMS
¼ cup light corn syrup	60 MILLILITERS
6 tablespoons hazelnut paste	85 GRAMS
8 egg yolks	

◎ In a large saucepan over medium-high heat, bring the cream, milk, sugar, corn syrup, and hazelnut paste to a boil. Reduce the heat and stir until the sugar and hazelnut paste are completely dissolved. Remove from the heat and let rest for 5 minutes. Follow the instructions on page 194 for finishing the custard.

◎ Chill the custard in the refrigerator until very cold, about 3 hours, or use an ice bath (see page 195). Pour into an ice cream maker and freeze according to the manufacturer's instructions.

CHOCOLATE JALAPEÑO ICE CREAM

Helado de Chocolate con Jalapeño

SERVES 8

2½ cups whole milk	600 MILLILITERS
½ cup heavy cream	120 MILLILITERS
6 tablespoons granulated sugar	75 GRAMS
1 large green jalapeño chile, seeded and finely diced	
7 egg yolks	
8 ounces bittersweet chocolate (El Rey "Bucare" 58.5%), chopped	225 GRAMS

◉ In a large saucepan over medium-high heat, bring the milk, cream, sugar, and chile to a boil. Reduce the heat and stir until the sugar is completely dissolved. Remove from the heat and let rest for 5 minutes. Follow the instructions from the Mamey Ice Cream recipe (page 194) for finishing and straining the custard. Stir in the chocolate until melted.

◉ Chill the custard in the refrigerator until very cold, about 3 hours, or use an ice bath (see page 195). Pour into an ice cream maker and freeze according to the manufacturer's instructions.

SOUR CREAM ICE CREAM

Crema Helada de Crema Nata

SERVES 6

½ cup light corn syrup	120 MILLILITERS
½ cup granulated sugar	100 GRAMS
2 cups sour cream	455 GRAMS
1 tablespoon freshly squeezed lemon juice	

◉ In a small saucepan over medium-high heat, bring ½ cup (125 milliliters) water, the corn syrup, and sugar to a boil. Reduce the heat and stir until the sugar is completely dissolved. Remove from the heat and chill in the refrigerator until very cold, about 3 hours, or use an ice bath (see page 195).

◉ Stir in the sour cream and lemon juice. Pour into an ice cream maker and freeze according to the manufacturer's instructions.

CHERRY ICE CREAM
Crema Helada de Cereza

Most *cremas heladas* are made with just milk and cream, while the more popular *helado*, or what we think of as traditional ice cream, uses egg yolks as well. In this recipe, due to the acidity of the cherries and the amount of puree needed to get a pronounced cherry flavor, *crema helada* works better and turns out a smoother frozen treat. Don't use canned cherries or a pie filling product here. Rather, use fresh, pitted sweet cherries or frozen sweet cherries that have been thawed and pureed until smooth.

Nonfat dry milk powder is usually found in the baking aisle of the supermarket, or with the instant cocoa drinks.

SERVES 8

¾ cup whole milk	180 MILLILITERS
⅓ cup heavy cream	80 MILLILITERS
½ cup nonfat dry milk powder	45 GRAMS
1 cup granulated sugar	200 GRAMS
2¼ cups cherry puree (from about 1½ to 2 pounds fresh cherries or 1 pound frozen cherries)	540 MILLILITERS

In a large saucepan over medium-high heat, bring the milk, cream, milk powder, and sugar to a boil. Reduce the heat and stir until the sugar is completely dissolved. Remove from the heat and chill in the refrigerator until very cold, about 3 hours, or use an ice bath (see page 195).

Stir in the cherry puree. Pour the mixture into an ice cream maker and freeze according to the manufacturer's instructions.

CHOCOLATE ICE CREAM

Crema Helada de Chocolate

SERVES 6

2	cups whole milk	480 MILLILITERS
1	cup heavy cream	240 MILLILITERS
1½	cups granulated sugar	300 GRAMS
6	ounces bittersweet chocolate (El Rey "Bucare" 58.5%), chopped	170 GRAMS
¾	cup unsweetened cocoa powder	85 GRAMS

◎ In a large saucepan over medium-high heat, bring the milk, cream, and sugar to a boil. Reduce the heat and stir until the sugar is completely dissolved. Remove from the heat and stir in the chocolate and cocoa powder until melted.

◎ Chill the custard in the refrigerator until very cold, about 3 hours, or use an ice bath (see page 195). Pour into an ice cream maker and freeze according to the manufacturer's instructions.

SPICED ICE CREAM

Crema Helada de Especias

I highly recommend using whole spices to make this ice cream, for their more delicate flavor. Boiling the whole spices with water, rather than milk, fully infuses the mixture with their flavors (similar to creating a spiced "tea"). Using ground spices can easily overpower the recipe. By adding low-fat milk powder to the recipe, it produces a creamy end product with a sorbet-like texture that is still light enough to complement rich Quinoa Pudding (page 44).

SERVES 6

3 cinnamon sticks

3 pieces star anise

3 whole cardamom seeds

1 cup granulated sugar   200 GRAMS

1 tablespoon light corn syrup

½ cup nonfat dry milk powder   45 GRAMS

◎ In a large saucepan over high heat, bring 2¼ cups (540 milliliters) water and the spices to a boil. Lower the heat and simmer for 5 minutes to release the flavors. Add the sugar and corn syrup and stir until the sugar is dissolved. Remove from the heat, whisk in the milk powder, and chill in the refrigerator until very cold, about 3 hours, or use an ice bath (see page 195). Transfer the spiced milk to a covered container and refrigerate for at least 8 hours or overnight.

◎ Strain the mixture through a fine sieve into a large bowl to remove the whole spices. Pour into an ice cream maker and freeze according to the manufacturer's instructions.

YOGURT ICE CREAM
Crema Helada de Yogurt

SERVES 6

½ cup light corn syrup   120 MILLILITERS

½ cup granulated sugar   100 GRAMS

2 cups plain yogurt   455 GRAMS

1 tablespoon freshly squeezed
   lemon juice

In a medium saucepan over medium-high heat, bring ½ cup (120 milliliters) water, the corn syrup, and sugar to a boil. Reduce the heat and stir until the sugar is completely dissolved. Remove from the heat and chill in the refrigerator until very cold, about 3 hours, or use an ice bath (see page 195).

Stir in the yogurt and lemon juice. Pour into an ice cream maker and freeze according to the manufacturer's instructions.

Morir Soñando

I LEARNED HOW TO MAKE *MORIR SOÑANDO* FROM THE DOMINICAN FRIENDS I met during my first U.S. kitchen stint. When I first saw them make it, I didn't believe it would actually taste good. Milk and citrus together? But believe me, it's a miraculous combination and remains one of my very favorite refreshments on hot summer days. The secret to keeping the milk and citrus (lime is my favorite) from curdling is having them both ice cold before blending them together.

The exact ingredients of this traditional Dominican drink vary by region. Some people prefer to use fresh orange juice instead of lime juice, or evaporated milk instead of milk, or add a dash of vanilla extract. I've even tried this drink with pineapple juice to rave reviews. As you can imagine, the orange juice and vanilla extract version turns out like a drinkable Creamsicle. What could be better?

MAKES ABOUT 2 (12-OUNCE) GLASSES

¼ cup freshly squeezed lime juice
(from about 2 limes)   60 MILLILITERS
½ cup granulated sugar (or to taste) 100 GRAMS
1½ cups whole milk   360 MILLILITERS
½ cup evaporated milk   120 MILLILITERS
1 tablespoon vanilla extract
Ice

In a large glass, stir the lime juice and the sugar until the sugar has dissolved. Add ice and stir until the lime juice mixture is well chilled.

Working quickly, pour the milks and vanilla extract over ice in a separate large glass and stir until well chilled. Continue stirring while pouring the cold lime juice and ice mixture into the milk. Or strain the cold lime juice into the milk and ice mixture.

Serve as is or strain into clean chilled glasses and serve immediately.

"TO DIE DREAMING" ICE CREAM

Crema Helada de Morir Soñando

This recipe is inspired by one of my favorite drinks, called *morir soñando* or "to die dreaming." It sounds a bit more romantic in Spanish and is a sentiment I hold close to my heart: one should keep dreaming big dreams from your first day until your last. But the name is just as appropriate as a description of the "to die for" flavor of this traditional Dominican beverage. I suggest serving this ice cream with my Almond Flan (page 6) topped with a few crunchy Coconut Tuiles (page 62).

Chill the lime juice in the refrigerator until ready to use. It must be cold to avoid curdling when added to the cream mixture.

SERVES 6

2½ cups whole milk	600 MILLILITERS
¼ cup heavy cream	60 MILLILITERS
1 cup granulated sugar	200 GRAMS
Grated zest of 2 limes	
2 tablespoons nonfat dry milk powder	
1 cup freshly squeezed lime juice (from 6 to 8 limes), chilled	240 MILLILITERS

In a large saucepan over medium heat, bring the milk, cream, sugar, and lime zest to a simmer. Add the milk powder slowly, whisking to avoid lumps, and bring to a boil. Remove from the heat and chill in the refrigerator until very cold, about 3 hours, or use an ice bath (see page 195).

Slowly pour in the cold lime juice, whisking constantly to avoid curdling. Pour into an ice cream maker and freeze according to the manufacturer's instructions.

COCONUT SORBET

Nieve de Coco

I prefer to make this recipe with coconut puree, usually found in the freezer section of your local supermarket. If you have any difficulty finding the frozen puree, you can substitute 2 cups canned coconut milk with very little change in the flavor or texture. One warning: Do not purchase low-fat coconut milk, as the final product will be too thin and won't freeze properly.

SERVES 6

½ tablespoon light corn syrup

½ cup granulated sugar   100 GRAMS

1 cup coconut puree   240 MILLILITERS

1 tablespoon freshly squeezed lemon juice

1 cup unsweetened coconut milk   240 MILLILITERS

◉ In a large saucepan over medium-high heat, bring 1 cup (240 milliliters) water, the corn syrup, and sugar to a boil and, being careful not to burn, stir until the sugar is completely dissolved. The mixture will thicken, but should remain clear and not caramelized.

◉ Remove from the heat and chill in the refrigerator until very cold, about 3 hours, or use an ice bath (see page 195).

◉ Stir in the coconut puree, lemon juice, and coconut milk. Pour into an ice cream maker and freeze according to the manufacturer's instructions.

COLOMBIAN FRUIT SALAD
(page 163)
*with Coconut Sorbet (page 210) and
Coconut Tuile (page 62)*

BANANA FRITTERS
(page 174)
with Fresh Strawberry
Sauce (page 174)

213

PASSION FRUIT TART
(page 166)
with Italian Meringue (page 236)

LATIN-AMERICAN
FRUITS
Clockwise from top right:

PAPAYA
(page 151)

COCONUT
(page 98)

PASSION FRUIT
cut, in center right
(page 168)

TAMARIND
in center (page 111)

GUAVA
in long bowl, at bottom
and in round bowl, at left
(page 9)

PASSION FRUIT
yellow-skinned, at back
left (page 168)

MAMEY
(page 43)

AVOCADO PANNA COTTA *(page 176)*
with Chocolate Butter Cookie (page 61)
and Tamarillos in Syrup (page 189)

**TOASTED COCONUT
ICE CREAM** *(page 196)*

TANGERINE SAFFRON SORBET *(page 220)*
with Sour Orange Granita (page 222)

218

SOURSOP SORBET
Nieve de Guanábana

SERVES 6

2¼ cups guanábana
   pulp   540 MILLILITERS
 2 tablespoons freshly
   squeezed lemon juice

⊚ Follow the instructions in the Coconut Sorbet recipe (page 210), using 1¼ cups (300 milliliters) water and stirring in the guanábana pulp and lemon juice just before pouring the sorbet mixture into the ice cream maker.

GUAVA SORBET
Nieve de Guayaba

To make the guava puree from fresh fruit, using a paring knife, remove the stems and skin from the guava and cut each piece into 4 segments. Puree in a blender until smooth. Strain the mixture through a fine sieve to remove any seeds.

SERVES 6

¾ cup granulated sugar   150 GRAMS
 2 tablespoons light corn syrup   30 MILLILITERS
 2 cups guava puree (from about
   1 pound frozen pulp or
   fresh fruit)   480 MILLILITERS
 1 tablespoon freshly squeezed lime juice

⊚ Follow the instructions in the Coconut Sorbet recipe (page 210), using 1 cup (240 milliliters) water and stirring in the guava puree and lime juice just before pouring the sorbet mixture into the ice cream maker.

LULO SORBET
Nieve de Lulo

SERVES 8

1 cup granulated sugar	200 GRAMS
2¼ cups lulo pulp (see page 214)	
	540 MILLILITERS
¼ cup freshly squeezed orange juice	60 MILLILITERS

◎ Follow the instructions in the Coconut Sorbet recipe (page 210), using 1¼ cups (300 milliliters) water and stirring in the lulo pulp and orange juice just before pouring sorbet mixture into ice cream maker.

TANGERINE SAFFRON SORBET
Nieve de Mandarina con Azafran

SERVES 6

1 teaspoon saffron threads	
1 cup granulated sugar	200 GRAMS
1 tablespoon freshly squeezed lime juice	
2 cups freshly squeezed tangerine juice	480 MILLILITERS

◎ Follow the instructions in the Coconut Sorbet recipe (page 210), boiling the saffron with 2½ cups (600 milliliters) water and the sugar and stirring in the lime and tangerine juices just before pouring the sorbet mixture into the ice cream maker.

MANGO GINGER SORBET
Nieve de Mango con Genjibre

SERVES 6

1½ tablespoons minced fresh ginger	
1 cup granulated sugar	200 GRAMS
2 cups mango puree (from about 2 pounds frozen pulp or 4 large, fresh mangoes)	480 MILLILITERS
1 tablespoon freshly squeezed lime juice	

◎ Boil the ginger with 2½ cups (600 milliliters) water and the sugar and pour through a fine sieve after cooling to remove the ginger. Follow the instructions in the Coconut Sorbet recipe (page 210), stirring in the mango puree and lime juice just before pouring the sorbet mixture into the ice cream maker.

Sorbets and Granitas

SORBET IS CREAMIER AND SOFTER THAN GRANITA, WITH A SMOOTHER, almost silky texture, compared to granita's hard icy crunch. Since granita is more like shaved ice, it adds light, refreshing texture and flavor to a dessert without the use of flour, as with a cookie, crust, or streusel-type topping. Granita recipes are almost always a three-to-one ratio of liquid to solid ingredients in order to get the right amount of ice crystallization, while sorbet amounts vary widely depending on the ingredients used.

Granita is ideal for the home cook, since it doesn't require any special equipment, such as an ice cream maker. Granita paired with a fresh fruit *salpicón* (fruit salsa) is one of the simplest summertime desserts, both delicious and impressive.

Scraping the granita with a fork every hour during the freezing process will create additional ice crystals and will give your granita a crunchier texture.

Granita is extremely popular in Latin America. In Puerto Rico, it's called *piragua,* combining the Spanish words for "pyramid" (*piramide*) and "water" (*agua*), and is sold by pushcart vendors known as *piragüeros*. It's basically the Latin version of the American snowcone, shaped like a pyramid instead of a snowball. The *piragüeros'* cart holds a huge chunk of ice, which is shaved to order into a paper cone, shaped, and topped with flavored syrups (lime, tamarind, mango, passion fruit, anise, and many more) and sometimes fresh fruit. In Mexico, the same concoction is called *raspado,* meaning "scraped ice," and my favorite flavor is tamarind. In Columbia and Peru, you will find a similar treat topped with sweetened condensed milk. My *granizado* recipes are really the same concept.

CUCUMBER GREEN APPLE GRANITA

Granizado de Pepino con Manzana Verde

You don't have to have a juicer to juice the fresh cucumber and green apple. Peel and roughly chop the cucumber, and core and roughly chop the apple. Puree in a blender until smooth, then pass the resulting puree through a fine sieve.

SERVES 6

1 cup granulated sugar		200 GRAMS
1 cup freshly squeezed cucumber juice (from about 1 medium cucumber)		240 MILLILITERS
1½ cups freshly squeezed green apple juice (from about 2 large apples)		360 MILLILITERS

⊚ Follow the instructions in the Passion Fruit Granita recipe (page 225), using 1 cup (240 milliliters) water and stirring in the juices just before freezing.

SOUR ORANGE GRANITA

Granizado de Naranja Agria

SERVES 6

1 cup granulated sugar		200 GRAMS
1 cup freshly squeezed sour orange juice (or half orange juice and half lime juice)		240 MILLILITERS

⊚ Follow the instructions in the Passion Fruit Granita recipe (page 225), using 2½ cups (600 milliliters) water and stirring in the juice just before freezing.

Naranja Agria

SOUR ORANGES, ALSO KNOWN AS BITTER ORANGES IN THE UNITED STATES and Seville oranges around the Mediterranean, are used extensively in Cuban cuisine from cocktails and marinades to mojos and marmalades. You should be able to find them fresh at your local Latin grocery depending on the season and where you live, and these days they even crop up at traditional grocery stores.

The first time I spotted a *naranja agria* was at the Palacio de Los Jugos ("fruit palace"), a produce market popular with the Hispanic community of Miami. At first glance, I thought the fruit was a giant lemon, but on closer inspection I noticed the thicker, bumpier rind. After trying it at home, I was instantly hooked. Although it's not an eating orange, bitter oranges have high acidity and a powerful aroma perfect for adding balance to rich sweet or savory dishes—my Coconut Three Milks Cake with Sour Orange Granita (opposite), for example. Orange blossom water, which I use to flavor *pan dulce* dough for my *pan de muerto* (page 70), is distilled from the flowers of the sour orange tree. And sour oranges are also the fruit used to flavor the popular orange liqueurs triple sec and Grand Marnier.

Flavor-wise, a sour orange is something like a cross between orange, lime, and grapefruit. In fact, if you have trouble finding the fresh fruit, a half and half combination of freshly squeezed orange juice and lime juice is a good approximation.

SOURSOP GRANITA
Granizado de Guanábana

I like using a complementary *granizado* to add interesting depth to some of my more involved dessert preparations. With the Dulce de Leche Brazo Gitano (page 92), the smooth texture of the cake contrasts with the cool crunch of this shaved ice. And the creamy richness of the *dulce de leche* is intensified by the sweet-tart flavor of *guanábana*.

Before preparing this recipe, you will want to slice the *guanábana* fruit in half lengthwise, pull or scoop the white, juicy segments out of the rind, remove all the seeds, and puree the pulp in a blender. If you can only find the pulp frozen, you will just need to thaw it before adding it to the water and sugar mixture in the recipe. You can also freeze the pulp if you don't have time to use it before the fruit spoils. In a pinch, even *guanábana* juice will work (in the same measure as the pulp)—Goya or La Fe brands are easily found.

SERVES 6

1 cup granulated sugar	200 GRAMS
2 cups *guanábana* pulp	480 MILLILITERS

⦾ Follow the instructions in the Passion Fruit Granita recipe (page 225), using 1½ cups (360 milliliters) water and stirring in the *guanábana* pulp just before freezing.

PASSION FRUIT GRANITA

Granizado de Maracuya

This intensely flavored ice is a wonderful contrasting garnish to Banana Tres Leches (page 84), a refreshing palate cleanser, or a simple ending to a light summer meal. You can make it with passion fruit puree, as described here—the puree can be found frozen in many specialty food shops—or with countless other fruits.

SERVES 6

1 cup granulated sugar	200 GRAMS
1 tablespoon light corn syrup	
1¾ cups passion fruit puree	420 MILLILITERS

⑨ In a large saucepan over medium-high heat, bring 4 cups (960 milliliters) water, the sugar, and corn syrup to a boil and, being careful not to burn, stir until the sugar is completely dissolved. The mixture will thicken, but should remain clear and not caramelized. Remove from the heat and chill in the refrigerator until very cold, about 3 hours, or use an ice bath (see page 195). Transfer the syrup to a freezer-safe bowl, stir in the passion fruit puree, and freeze for at least 3 hours or overnight, scraping every hour if you choose.

⑨ Remove the granita from the freezer and, using a fork, scrape the mixture until you have a light, airy, icy consistency. The granita can be stored, covered tightly, in the freezer for up to 3 days but should always be scraped again just before serving.

COFFEE GRANITA

Granizado de Café

Tía Maria has a lighter coffee flavor than Kahlúa, which is also slightly sweeter. Both will produce a good final result.

SERVES 8

1 cup granulated sugar	200 GRAMS
2 cups coffee beans, crushed	130 GRAMS
½ cup Tía Maria, Kahlúa, or other coffee liqueur	120 MILLILITERS

⊚ Put the coffee beans in a plastic bag and roughly crush them with the bottom of a pan. Follow the instructions in the Passion Fruit Granita recipe (page 225), boiling the crushed beans with 4 cups (950 milliliters) water and the sugar. Strain the crushed beans out of the liquid and stir in the liqueur just before freezing.

CHERIMOYA GRANITA

Granizado de Cherimoya

For a light and refreshing dessert that is a study in both flavor and texture contrasts, place the icy granita in parfait glasses or chilled bowls and top with fresh passion fruit pulp and a few crisp Walnut Coconut Cookies (page 53).

SERVES 6

1 cup granulated sugar	200 GRAMS	
3 cups cherimoya puree	720 MILLILITERS	
½ cup sweetened condensed milk	120 MILLILITERS	

Follow the instructions in the Passion Fruit Granita recipe (page 225), using 1 cup (240 milliliters) water and stirring in the cherimoya puree and sweetened condensed milk just before freezing.

FROZEN MOJITO SOUFFLÉ
Soufflé de Mojito Frio

Translating a cocktail into a frozen soufflé makes for a wonderfully refreshing and light dessert or even just a cool treat to enjoy on a warm summer afternoon. Don Q white rum from Puerto Rico is my preference, but use whatever you like. If you want to try the margarita version, simply substitute *tequila blanco* (white tequila) for the white rum and replace the crème de menthe with additional lime juice.

SERVES 6

- ½ (¼-ounce) envelope unflavored gelatin powder
- ¼ cup Don Q white rum   60 MILLILITERS
- 1½ tablespoons freshly squeezed lime juice
- 1½ teaspoons crème de menthe
- ½ cup granulated sugar   100 GRAMS
- 2 eggs, separated
- ¾ cup heavy cream   180 MILLILITERS
- Fresh mint
- 1 recipe Pomegranate Reduction (page 259)

◉ If you'd like to mimic the presentation of a true baked soufflé, prepare 6 (4-ounce) ramekins with parchment paper collars that rise about 1 inch above the top of the ramekins. Alternatively, you can just use parfait glasses or any freezer-safe individual serving vessels of your choice.

◉ Sprinkle the gelatin over 2 tablespoons of the rum and let stand for 5 minutes.

◉ In a small bowl, combine the gelatin mixture and the remaining rum. Add the lime juice and crème de menthe and let set slightly.

◉ In a medium saucepan over medium heat, bring 2 tablespoons water and the sugar to a boil. Continue cooking without stirring, until the temperature on a candy thermometer reaches 248° F (the "soft ball" stage). If you don't have a candy thermometer, take a bit of the sugar mixture with a spoon and submerge it in a bowl of ice water for a few seconds. Grab the sugar with your fingertips. You should be able to form it into a small, soft ball. Remove from the heat and set aside.

While the sugar syrup is cooking, beat the egg whites in the bowl of an electric mixer fitted with a whisk attachment until soft peaks form. Add the egg yolks and beat until pale in color and tripled in volume. Turn the mixer down to medium speed and slowly add the hot syrup, a little at a time, to prevent the eggs from curdling. Continue to beat the tempered mixture as it cools, about 10 minutes. When finished, the egg and sugar mixture should be a pale lemon color and very light in texture, similar to a meringue. Transfer to a medium bowl and whisk in the rum mixture.

Wash the mixer bowl and whisk attachment. In the bowl of the electric mixer fitted with a whisk attachment, whip the cream until stiff peaks form. Gently fold the whipped cream into the mousse and divide it among 6 serving vessels. Freeze until set, at least 6 hours or overnight. (Well covered, the mousses will keep in the freezer for up to 1 month.)

When ready to serve, remove the parchment paper collars, if used, and garnish with the mint and pomegranate reduction. Serve immediately.

FRIED ICE CREAM

Helado Frito

Ice cream is everywhere in Mexico. And at many of the small ice cream shops in Mexico City, you'll find them offering crunchy, creamy scoops of fried ice cream. I've also enjoyed fried ice cream when out to dinner with my kids. Daniel and Layla wouldn't let me rest until I re-created something similar at home. They were the ones who suggested the brilliant corn flakes coating. I even use a similar coating for my liquid chocolate croquettes (page 130) to rave reviews.

After a few attempts, I discovered that a double coating of the cereal is necessary to keep the ice cream from melting away while frying in the hot oil. I'd suggest making this recipe with Dulce de Leche (page 195), Mamey (page 194), or Chocolate Ice Cream (page 205), but you can just use your favorite flavor. The quantity of coating in this recipe is enough to cover scoops of ice cream from 1 batch of ice cream. If you want to be extra decadent, you can top these with Caramel Sauce (page 259) or Chocolate Sauce (page 253) or both.

1 **recipe of your favorite flavor ice cream** **(or ½ gallon of your favorite purchased** **ice cream)**	
1 **(18-ounce) box corn flakes**	510 GRAMS
1 **cup unsweetened** **shredded coconut**	150 GRAMS
1 **tablespoon ground cinnamon**	
5 **eggs**	
2 **quarts canola oil for frying**	2 LITERS
Confectioners' sugar for garnish	
Unsweetened cocoa powder for garnish	

⊚ Scoop the ice cream with a 2-ounce scoop onto a baking sheet and freeze until very firm, at least 2 hours or overnight.

⊚ Pour the corn flakes into a plastic bag and crush them with your hands into small pieces. Don't use a blender, or you'll end up with powder and no texture. In a large bowl, combine the corn flakes, coconut, and cinnamon. In a separate medium bowl, beat together the eggs.

⊚ Remove the ice cream scoops, a few at a time, from the freezer. Dip in the egg wash, then roll in the corn flake mixture, pressing gently to help the coating stick. Put the coated scoops onto a sheet pan and repeat until all the scoops are coated. Freeze until very firm, at least 2 hours or overnight. Repeat the entire process, dipping each scoop into the egg wash and rolling it into the corn flake mixture again. Return the coated scoops to the sheet pan and freeze again until very firm, at least 2 hours or overnight. Once frozen, you can consolidate the coated scoops into a plastic bag or container if you're not frying the ice cream right away.

◎ In a large, deep, heavy pot, heat the oil to 350°F. Fry the coated ice cream scoops in small batches straight from the freezer, 2 or 3 at a time, for 20 to 30 seconds or until golden brown. The egg wash and double coating creates a seal around the ice cream that should protect it from the heat of the oil. If you notice the coating cracking, remove the scoops from the hot oil.

◎ Dust with confectioners' sugar and cocoa powder and serve immediately.

7

COMPONENTS

In This Chapter

CARAMEL FOR FLAN
Caramelo por Flan

WHIPPED CREAM
Crema Batida

COFFEE WHIPPED CREAM
Crema Batida de Café

ITALIAN MERINGUE
Merengue Italiano

SIMPLE SYRUP
Almibar Neutro

CHOCOLATE MOCHA MOUSSE
Mousse de Mocha

WHITE CHOCOLATE MOUSSE
Mousse de Chocolate Blanco

CHOCOLATE MOUSSE WITH HAZELNUTS
Mousse de Chocolate con Avellanas

CHOCOLATE MOUSSE WITH RUM
Mousse de Chocolate con Ron

GUAVA FOAM
Espuma de Guayaba

LITCHI FOAM
Espuma de Litchi

LEMON FOAM
Espuma de Limon

RICE PUDDING FOAM
Espuma de Arroz con Leche

ALMOND FOAM
Espuma de Almendra

YELLOW CORN FOAM
Espuma de Choclo

COCONUT FOAM
Espuma de Coco

PASSSION FRUIT GELEE
Geletina de Maracuya

AMARETTO GELEE
Gelatina de Amaretto

CANDIED ALMONDS
Almendras Caramelizadas

SUGAR-COATED NUTS
Nueces Garapiñadas

CRANBERRY SAUCE
Salsa de Arandano

LITCHI SAUCE
Salsa de Litchi

CHOCOLATE SAUCE
Salsa de Chocolate

CHOCOLATE GANACHE
Ganache de Chocolate

IBARRA CHOCOLATE GANACHE
Ganache de Chocolate Ibarra

CHOCOLATE KIRSCH SAUCE
Salsa de Chocolate con Kirsch

VANILLA CRÈME ANGLAISE
Salsa de Vainilla

CILANTRO OIL
Aceite de Cilantro

AMARETTO CREAM
Crema de Amaretto

CINNAMON CREAM
Crema de Canela

PISTACHIO CREAM
Crema de Pistache

CHAMOMILE CREAM
Crema de Manzanilla

COFFEE REDUCTION
Reduccion de Café

POMEGRANATE REDUCTION
Reduccion de Granada

CARAMEL SAUCE
Salsa de Caramelo

CARAMEL FOR FLAN
Caramelo por Flan

You will use this entire recipe if you prepare one of my flans. But since most people think the caramel is the best part, you may want to make extra to drizzle over the tops of the flans once they are unmolded. Leftovers can also be stored in an airtight container in the refrigerator for a couple of months, or even at room temperature for a few weeks. Reheat the caramel in the microwave, in a bain-marie, or in a pan set over gently simmering water before using it. I love it on fruit: Simply sauté the fruit of your choice (such as bananas, nectarines, or apples) in a little butter, finish off with the caramel (I like to add another squeeze of fresh lime juice) and some toasted almonds, and use the mixture to top cakes, pancakes, or ice cream.

3 **cups granulated sugar**   600 GRAMS
1 **teaspoon freshly squeezed lime juice**

◎ In a small saucepan, stir together the sugar, 1 cup (240 milliliters) water, and the lime juice and bring to a boil. Lower the heat to medium-high and boil, untouched, for about 15 minutes, until the sugar dissolves and the mixture becomes a golden amber color.

◎ To stop the cooking process and avoid burning the caramel, remove the pan from the heat and cool it in an ice bath (see page 195). Alternatively, add ¼ cup (60 milliliters) cold water very slowly into the caramel and stir until it is incorporated. Be careful, as it will spatter a bit.

WHIPPED CREAM
Crema Batida

Either of these whipped creams work great with a slice of pound cake and berries.

2 cups heavy cream   480 MILLILITERS
½ cup granulated sugar   100 GRAMS
1½ teaspoons vanilla extract

◎ Stir all the ingredients together in the bowl of an electric mixer fitted with a whisk attachment. Beat on medium-high speed until stiff peaks form, about 3 to 4 minutes. The whipped cream can be made a couple of hours in advance and kept, covered, in the refrigerator, until ready to use.

Coffee Whipped Cream

◎ Replace the vanilla extract with 1 tablespoon coffee extract or cool brewed espresso or 1½ tablespoons instant coffee granules. If you are using instant coffee, heat a little bit of the cream and stir in the instant coffee to dissolve, then slowly add it to the rest of cream.

ITALIAN MERINGUE
Merengue Italiano

If using this meringue as an ingredient in a mousse, refrigerate it for no more than 20 minutes. It will need to stay soft in order to fold it into a mousse mixture, as in my Chocolate Cigar and Chocolate and Hazelnut Bombe recipes (pages 132 and 136). If using it as a recipe component on its own, as in my Banana Three Milks Cake and Baked Patagonia recipes (pages 84 and 96), it can be made ahead, covered, and refrigerated for up to 10 hours.

 2 tablespoons light corn syrup
3¼ cups granulated sugar   650 GRAMS
 10 egg whites

⊚ In a large saucepan, combine 1 cup (240 milliliters) water, the corn syrup, and 2½ cups of the sugar and bring to a boil. Continue cooking, without stirring, until the temperature on a candy thermometer reaches 248° F (the "soft ball" stage). If you don't have a candy thermometer, take a bit of the sugar mixture with a spoon and submerge it in a bowl of ice water for a few seconds. Grab the sugar with your fingertips. You should be able to form it into a small, soft ball.

⊚ Soak the bowl and the whisk attachment of an electric mixer in warm water and dry thoroughly. This will ensure that the egg whites gain enough volume during beating. While the syrup is cooking, beat the egg whites and the remaining ¾ cup sugar in the bowl of an electric mixer until soft peaks form. You will get the most volume if the egg whites are brought to room temperature and the bowl and beaters are soaked in warm water and dried thoroughly before beating. Turn the mixer to high speed and slowly and carefully add the hot syrup to the egg white mixture. Continue beating at high speed until the meringue becomes glossy, about 10 minutes, or until the outside of the mixing bowl no longer feels hot to the touch. Cover and set aside in the refrigerator for no longer than 20 minutes if folding it into a mousse, or for up to 10 hours if you are using it on its own.

SIMPLE SYRUP

Almibar Neutro

2 cups granulated sugar   400 GRAMS

1 tablespoon glucose or corn syrup
(to prevent crystallization)

◎ In a small saucepan, bring 1 cup (240 milliliters) water to a boil. Add the sugar, then reduce the heat, and simmer, stirring occasionally until dissolved. Remove from the heat and let cool completely. Store, tightly covered, in the refrigerator until ready to use. It will keep for 3 to 4 weeks and is a great sweetener for iced tea or coffee. No more waiting for sugar crystals to dissolve.

CHOCOLATE MOCHA MOUSSE
Mousse de Chocolate Mocha

If you choose to make the mousse in advance and freeze it, you can even enjoy it on its own. Just like my white chocolate mousse, eat it straight from the freezer for a silky, ice creamlike treat.

SERVES 10

- ½ (¼-ounce) envelope unflavored gelatin powder
- 9 ounces semisweet chocolate, finely chopped (about 1½ cups chips)   255 GRAMS
- 3 eggs
- ½ cup granulated sugar   100 GRAMS
- 3 tablespoons brewed espresso or coffee liqueur
- 2 cups heavy cream   480 MILLILITERS

Sprinkle the gelatin over 2 tablespoons of cold water and let stand for 5 minutes.

In the top of a double boiler over gently simmering water, melt the chocolate, stirring constantly. Remove from the heat, pour into a large bowl, and set aside.

Clean the double boiler well. Again, set it over gently simmering water, add the eggs and sugar, and whisk for about 5 minutes, until the mixture has doubled in volume. It should be pale and thick—cook to the ribbon stage: When you lift the whisk out of the batter, it should flow from it in smooth, even ribbons. Add the espresso and the gelatin mixture and heat until the gelatin dissolves. Remove from the heat and gently fold the mixture into the chocolate. The mixture should look smooth and shiny.

In the bowl of an electric mixer fitted with a whisk attachment, beat the cream until soft peaks form. Fold the whipped cream into the chocolate mixture until well incorporated, transfer to a plastic container, and place in the refrigerator for at least 2 hours, until up to 2 days. The mousse can be frozen for up to 2 months—defrost overnight in the refrigerator before serving or enjoy it frozen.

WHITE CHOCOLATE MOUSSE
Mousse de Chocolate Blanco

This mousse shows up in my Peach Three Milks Cake recipe (page 82), except there white rum replaces the tequila. Remember that white chocolate is quite delicate, so when making this mousse be sure to keep a close eye on it while it's melting, as it can easily break or become lumpy. If it does, you will need to make a fresh batch.

SERVES 10

1 (¼-ounce) envelope unflavored
gelatin powder

¼ cup tequila blanco
(preferably Don Julio)   60 MILLILITERS

12 ounces white chocolate, chopped
(preferably El Rey)
(about 2 cups chips)   340 GRAMS

¼ cup (½ stick) butter   55 GRAMS

3 egg yolks

3 whole eggs

2 tablespoons granulated sugar

2 vanilla beans, halved lengthwise,
seeds scraped out and reserved
(or 3 tablespoons vanilla extract)

2½ cups heavy
cream, chilled   600 MILLILITERS

◉ Sprinkle the gelatin over 2 tablespoons of the tequila and let stand for 5 minutes.

◉ In the top of a double boiler over gently simmering water, melt the white chocolate and butter, stirring constantly. Remove from the heat, pour into a large bowl, and set aside.

◉ Clean the double boiler well. Again, set it over gently simmering water, add the egg yolks, whole eggs, and sugar, and whisk rapidly for about 5 minutes, until the mixture has doubled in volume. Remove from the heat, pour into a medium bowl, and set aside.

◉ Use a fresh bowl over the double boiler. Again, set it over gently simmering water, pour in the remaining tequila, the gelatin mixture, and the halved vanilla beans (including seeds) or extract, and heat until the gelatin is dissolved. Add to the egg mixture and whisk until well incorporated. Fold the egg mixture into the chocolate mixture.

◉ In the bowl of an electric mixer fitted with a whisk attachment, beat the cream until soft peaks form. Gently fold the whipped cream into the chocolate mixture. Transfer to a bowl, cover, and freeze for at least 6 hours, until set, or up to 1 month.

CHOCOLATE MOUSSE WITH HAZELNUTS

Mousse de Chocolate con Avellanas

SERVES 12

18	ounces bittersweet chocolate, chopped (El Rey "Bucare" 58.5%)	510 GRAMS
1	cup (2 sticks) butter	225 GRAMS
3	tablespoons unsweetened cocoa powder	
11	egg yolks	
¾	cup granulated sugar	150 GRAMS
3	cups heavy cream	720 MILLILITERS
2	cups Italian Meringue (page 236)	200 GRAMS
2	cups hazelnuts, toasted (opposite)	285 GRAMS

◎ In the top of a double boiler over gently simmering water, melt the chocolate, butter, and cocoa powder. Pour into a large bowl and let cool to room temperature.

◎ In a medium bowl, beat the egg yolks.

◎ In a medium saucepan over medium-high heat, bring the sugar and 1 cup of the cream to a boil, then remove from the heat. While whisking, pour a small amount of the hot cream mixture into the yolks. This will temper the yolks and keep them from curdling. While whisking the cream mixture in the saucepan, gradually add the rest of the yolks.

◎ Transfer the pan to an ice bath (see page 195), and, when the egg and cream mixture is completely cool, add it to the chocolate mixture and stir to combine.

◎ Slowly fold the meringue into the chocolate mixture, about one third at a time.

◎ In the bowl of an electric mixer fitted with the whisk attachment, beat the remaining 2 cups cream until soft peaks form. Gently fold the whipped cream into the chocolate mixture. Fold in the hazelnuts. Transfer to a bowl, cover, and freeze for at least 6 hours, until set, or up to 1 month.

◎ If preparing the *bombe* recipe (page 136), transfer the mousse to 10 circular molds (I use 4½-ounce Flexipan half spheres) or 4-ounce ramekins rather than one large bowl. If you don't have either, use cupcake tins with paper liners.

To Toast Hazelnuts

DEPENDING ON WHAT YOU CAN FIND AT YOUR LOCAL SUPERMARKET OR bulk food store, hazelnuts, also known as filberts, may have a brownish skin that should be removed before adding them to a recipe. The skin is most easily removed after toasting. Plus, toasting will bring out the flavor of the nut and give it a crisper crunch in any dessert. Whether the hazelnuts you find are raw or roasted, toasting still adds an extra layer of flavor. Be sure to purchase unsalted nuts.

To toast on the stovetop, put the hazelnuts in a dry sauté pan that will hold them in a single layer. Heat over medium-high heat, stirring or swirling the pan often to avoid burning. The nuts are done when you can smell their aroma and they have begun to turn a darker golden brown, about 8 to 10 minutes. To toast in the oven, put the hazelnuts in a shallow baking pan and bake at 350°F for 10 to 15 minutes.

If necessary, remove the skins by rubbing the nuts, a handful at a time, in a clean dishtowel.

CHOCOLATE MOUSSE WITH RUM
Mousse de Chocolate con Ron

SERVES 16

9 ounces bittersweet chocolate, chopped
  (El Rey "Bucare" 58.5%)   255 GRAMS

6 ounces bittersweet chocolate, chopped
  (El Rey "Gran Saman" 70%)   170 GRAMS

4 cups heavy cream   950 MILLILITERS

2 (¼-ounce) envelopes unflavored
  gelatin powder

2 tablespoons rum

1 pinch salt

2 egg yolks

2 cups Italian Meringue
  (page 236)   200 GRAMS

⊚ In the top of a double boiler over gently simmering water, melt the chocolate with 1 cup of the cream. Remove from the heat and let cool.

⊚ Meanwhile, sprinkle the gelatin over the rum and let stand for 5 minutes.

⊚ When the chocolate is cool, add the salt and the egg yolks, one at a time, and stir until smooth.

⊚ In a small saucepan, heat the gelatin mixture and stir until dissolved. Stir into the chocolate mixture until well incorporated. Gently fold the meringue into the chocolate mixture, about one third at a time, making sure not to deflate the mixture. In the bowl of an electric mixer fitted with a whisk attachment, beat the remaining 3 cups cream until soft peaks form. Gently fold the whipped cream into the chocolate mixture. Spoon the mousse into a large bowl, cover, and chill for at least 2 hours, until set or up to 2 days. The mousse can be frozen for up to 2 months—defrost overnight in the refrigerator before serving or enjoy it frozen.

GUAVA FOAM

Espuma de Guayaba

You'll find fresh or frozen guava puree at most Latin American markets or in the imported section of your local supermarket. I prefer using guava puree or paste rather than marmalade, as marmalade is usually too sweet. If you can only find paste rather than puree, blend 1 to 1½ cups paste with water in a blender until you reach about 2 cups and a decent pureed consistency. The foam may be a little heavier if made with paste, but it will taste just as good.

MAKES 3 CUPS

1 (¼-ounce) envelope unflavored
   gelatin powder
½ cup Simple Syrup
   (page 237)   120 MILLILITERS
2 cups guava puree   480 MILLILITERS

Sprinkle the gelatin over 2 tablespoons cold water and let stand for 5 minutes.

Put the syrup in a small saucepan and cook over low heat until warm. Remove from the heat, immediately add the gelatin mixture, and stir until dissolved. Stir in the guava puree. Pour the mixture into a whipped cream dispenser. Follow the instructions for your particular dispenser. Most recommend only filling the dispenser about half full and inserting 1 or 2 nitrous oxide cartridges to pressurize the contents (depending on the size of your dispenser and the quality of the cartridges). Just make sure to work quickly. You want to fill the dispenser and insert the cartridge(s) before the gelatin sets. Put the dispenser in the refrigerator for 24 hours, or until ready to use.

LITCHI FOAM

Espuma de Litchi

Look for fresh litchis in specialty or Asian markets. To make the puree for this recipe, you simply need to slice the litchi in half, pop out the large, brown center seed, and remove the rough, red rind, leaving only the translucent white flesh. The flesh can be easily pureed in a blender. If you can't find fresh litchis, canned will do. These are readily available in most grocery stores these days. Just drain them of their liquid before pureeing.

MAKES 3 CUPS

1 (¼-ounce) envelope unflavored
  gelatin powder

½ cup Simple Syrup
  (page 237)   120 MILLILITERS

1 cup litchi puree   240 MILLILITERS

⑨ Follow the instructions in the Guava Foam recipe (page 243).

LEMON FOAM
Espuma de Limón

MAKES 2½ CUPS

1½ (¼-ounce) envelopes unflavored gelatin powder	100 GRAMS
Grated zest of 2 lemons	
½ cup granulated sugar	200 GRAMS
½ cup freshly squeezed lemon juice (from about 4 lemons)	120 MILLILITERS

◉ Sprinkle the gelatin over 2 tablespoons cold water and let stand for 5 minutes.

◉ Combine 1½ cups (360 milliliters) water, the lemon zest, and sugar in a small saucepan and cook over low heat until the sugar dissolves. Remove from the heat and pour the syrup through a fine sieve into a clean bowl, preferably one with a spout, to remove the zest. Immediately add the gelatin mixture and stir until dissolved. Stir in the lemon juice and pour the mixture into a whipped cream dispenser. Follow the instructions for your particular dispenser. Most recommend only filling the dispenser about half full and inserting 1 or 2 nitrous oxide cartridges to pressurize the contents (depending on the size of your dispenser and the quality of the cartridges). Just make sure to work quickly. You want to fill the dispenser and insert the cartridge(s) before the gelatin sets. Put the dispenser in the refrigerator for 24 hours, or until ready to use.

RICE PUDDING FOAM
Espuma de Arroz con Leche

If you don't want to use a whipped cream dispenser to make the foam, make a rice pudding whipped cream instead. Start by pureeing the rice pudding, then whip the cold cream with the sugar until stiff peaks form and fold it into the rice pudding puree.

MAKES 3 CUPS

1 cup heavy cream	480 MILLILITERS
¼ cup granulated sugar	50 GRAMS
¼ recipe Rice Pudding, cold (page 24)	

◉ In a small saucepan over high heat, combine the cream and sugar and bring to a boil. Remove from the heat and let cool. Stir the cold rice pudding into the cream mixture, then puree in a blender until the mixture is smooth and there are no chunks of rice.

◉ Pour the mixture into a whipped cream dispenser. Follow the instructions for your particular dispenser. Most recommend only filling the dispenser about half full and inserting 1 or 2 nitrous oxide cartridges to pressurize the contents (depending on the size of your dispenser and the quality of the cartridges). Put the dispenser in the refrigerator for 24 hours, or until ready to use.

ALMOND FOAM

Espuma de Almendra

MAKES 3 CUPS

½ cup sliced almonds, toasted   125 GRAMS

½ cup granulated sugar   100 GRAMS

1½ (¼-ounce) envelopes unflavored gelatin powder

¼ cup Simple Syrup
(page 237)   60 MILLILITERS

In a plastic container, combine 1 quart (1 liter) cold water and the almonds. Let sit overnight at room temperature to soften the almonds. Put the almonds, water, and sugar in a blender and blend until smooth, 2 to 3 minutes, to make the almond milk.

Sprinkle the gelatin over 2 tablespoons cold water and let stand for 5 minutes.

Put the syrup in a small saucepan and cook over low heat until warm. Remove from the heat, immediately add the gelatin mixture, and stir until dissolved. Stir in the almond milk until well combined. Pour the mixture into a whipped cream dispenser. Follow the instructions for your particular dispenser. Most recommend only filling the dispenser about half full and inserting 1 or 2 nitrous oxide cartridges to pressurize the contents (depending on the size of your dispenser and the quality of the cartridges). Just make sure to work quickly. You want to fill the dispenser and insert the cartridge(s) before the gelatin sets. Put the dispenser in the refrigerator for 8 to 24 hours.

YELLOW CORN FOAM

Espuma de Choclo

If you want to make this a sauce to serve with Chocolate Flan (page 143) rather than a foam, don't add the gelatin. Simply cool the corn mixture, blend until smooth, and pour through a fine sieve to remove any bits of corn.

MAKES 3 CUPS

1 (¼-ounce) envelope unflavored gelatin powder	
2½ cups yellow corn kernels	600 GRAMS
½ cup granulated sugar	100 GRAMS
½ cup heavy cream	240 MILLILITERS

Sprinkle the gelatin over 2 tablespoons cold water and let stand for 5 minutes.

In a large saucepan over medium-high heat, bring the corn, 1 cup (240 milliliters) water, the sugar, and cream to a boil. Lower the heat and simmer for 5 minutes, or until the corn is tender. Remove from the heat, add the gelatin mixture, and stir until dissolved. Let cool for 15 minutes.

Blend in a food processor or blender until smooth. Pour the mixture into a whipped cream dispenser. Follow the instructions for your particular dispenser. Most recommend only filling the dispenser about half full and inserting 1 or 2 nitrous oxide cartridges to pressurize the contents (depending on the size of your dispenser and the quality of the cartridges). Just make sure to work quickly. You want to fill the dispenser and insert the cartridge(s) before the gelatin sets. Put the dispenser in the refrigerator for 24 hours, or until ready to use.

COCONUT FOAM
Espuma de Coco

I use this Coconut Foam in place of whipped cream in my version of the banana split; one that preserves the look of the traditional masterpiece but is inspired by Latin flavors. Top the requisite sliced bananas with scoops of both *guanábana* (page 219) and lulo (page 220) sorbets, Chocolate Sauce (page 253), Coconut Foam, and a sprinkling of Candied Almonds (page 250). Perfect for the summertime, this dessert is very light and surprisingly healthy. Great for kids, it presents fruit in a fun and playful way.

You'll find frozen coconut puree at most Latin American markets or in the imported section of your local supermarket. While I prefer using the puree for this foam, coconut milk in a can will also work just as well.

MAKES 3 CUPS

1 (¼-ounce) envelope unflavored gelatin powder	
½ cup Simple Syrup (page 237)	120 MILLILITERS
2 cups coconut puree	480 MILLILITERS

⊚ Sprinkle the gelatin over 2 tablespoons of the syrup and let stand for 5 minutes.

⊚ Put the remaining syrup in a small saucepan and cook over low heat until warm. Remove from the heat, immediately add the gelatin mixture, and stir until dissolved. Stir in the coconut puree until well combined. Pour the mixture into a whipped cream dispenser. Follow the instructions for your particular dispenser. Most recommend only filling the dispenser about half full and inserting 1 or 2 nitrous oxide cartridges to pressurize the contents (depending on the size of your dispenser and the quality of the cartridges). Just make sure to work quickly. You want to fill the dispenser and insert the cartridge(s) before the gelatin sets. Put the dispenser in the refrigerator for 24 hours, or until ready to use.

PASSION FRUIT GELEE
Gelatina de Maracuya

MAKES 2 CUPS

- ½ (¼-ounce) envelope unflavored gelatin powder
- 1¼ cups passion fruit puree   *300 MILLILITERS*
- 1 cup Simple Syrup (page 237)   *240 MILLILITERS*

◎ Sprinkle the gelatin over ¼ cup of the fruit puree and let stand for 5 minutes.

◎ In a small saucepan over low heat, heat the syrup. Remove from the heat, add the gelatin mixture, and stir until dissolved. Add the remaining passion fruit puree and transfer the mixture to a small, square plastic container and put it in the freezer for a least 2 hours, or until the gelee is completely frozen, or up to 1 week.

AMARETTO GELEE
Gelatina de Amaretto

Use these gelee cubes in a special presentation of my peach *tres leches* (page 77). Or sprinkle pieces over chocolate or vanilla ice cream. They are like little amaretto-flavored gummy candies.

MAKES 1 CUP

- 1 (¼-ounce) envelope unflavored gelatin powder
- 1 cup amaretto liqueur   *240 MILLILITERS*

◎ Sprinkle the gelatin over 2 tablespoons cold water and let stand for 5 minutes.

◎ In a small saucepan over low heat, heat the amaretto, being careful not to boil. Remove from the heat, add the gelatin mixture, and stir until dissolved. Transfer the mixture to a small, square plastic container and put it in the refrigerator for a least 1 hour or up to 1 week.

◎ When ready to serve, remove the gelee from the refrigerator and either scoop out small teaspoonfuls or cut it into small squares using a paring knife warmed with a bit of warm water and wiped dry before cutting.

CANDIED ALMONDS

Almendras Carmelizadas

MAKES 1 CUP

¾ cup granulated sugar   150 GRAMS

1 cup whole
   blanched almonds   130 GRAMS

In a small saucepan over medium-high heat, stir together ¼ cup (60 milliliters) water and the sugar and bring to a boil. Boil, untouched, for about 15 minutes, until the sugar dissolves, the mixture becomes a pale caramel color, and a candy thermometer measures 245° F.

Remove from the heat, add the almonds, and stir with a wooden spoon until the caramel coats the nuts. Put the saucepan back over medium heat and stir continuously until the sugar turns a golden amber color. Working quickly, spread the warm almonds out on parchment paper, a Silpat mat, or aluminum foil and let cool.

When completely cool, break the candied almonds apart and store in an airtight container at room temperature until ready to use. Do not put the container in the refrigerator, as the humidity will make them lose their crunch. They will keep for about 2 weeks, and in addition to a great garnish, they make an addictive snack.

SUGAR-COATED NUTS

Nueces Garapiñadas

*G*arapiñadas means "coated with sugar," making these nuts different from the candied almonds that I recommend with Flan de Queso (page 8). These are like the nuts you might find sold in paper cones on the streets of New York, with a grainy, sugary coating. The former are made with sugar that has been completely melted into a smooth caramel, whereas these are made with sugar that is still slightly granular, coating the nuts like a crunchy breading of sorts. Toss them into salads or just eat them out of hand for a snack.

MAKES 1½ CUPS

½ cup granulated sugar	100 GRAMS
1½ cups pecan halves or	
whole cashews	160 GRAMS
½ teaspoon freshly grated nutmeg	

◎ In a small saucepan over medium-high heat, stir together ¼ cup (60 milliliters) water and sugar and bring to a boil. Boil, untouched, for about 15 minutes, until the sugar dissolves, the mixture becomes a pale caramel color, and a candy thermometer measures 245° F.

◎ Remove from the heat, add the nuts, and stir with a wooden spoon until the caramel coats the nuts. Put back over medium heat, continuing to stir until the sugar in the caramel again becomes crystallized and grainy, 2 to 5 minutes. Do not allow the caramel to melt again and become a smooth, glassy coating, as in my Candied Almonds (opposite). Working quickly, spread the warm almonds out on parchment paper, a Silpat mat, or aluminum foil, sprinkle with the nutmeg, and let cool.

◎ When completely cool, break the sugar-coated nuts apart and store in an airtight container at room temperature until ready to use. Do not put the container in the refrigerator, as the humidity will make them lose their crunch. They will keep for about 2 weeks.

CRANBERRY SAUCE

Salsa de Arandano

MAKES 4 CUPS

- 2 cups white wine — 480 MILLILITERS
- 1 vanilla bean, halved lengthwise, seeds scraped out and reserved (or 1½ tablespoons vanilla extract)
- 2 cups freshly squeezed orange juice — 480 MILLILITERS
- 2 cups fresh cranberries — 340 GRAMS
- ½ cup granulated sugar — 100 GRAMS

◉ In a medium saucepan, combine the wine, the vanilla bean (including seeds) or extract, 1 cup of the orange juice, the cranberries, and sugar and bring to a boil. Lower the heat and simmer for 20 minutes. Remove from the heat, add the remaining cup orange juice, and let cool for at least 15 minutes.

LITCHI SAUCE

Salsa de Litchi

MAKES 1 CUP

- 8 ounces fresh litchis, peeled and pitted (or 1½ cups canned litchi fruit, drained) — 225 GRAMS
- ½ cup granulated sugar — 100 GRAMS

◉ Put the litchis, 1 cup (240 milliliters) water and the sugar in a small saucepan and bring to a boil. Cook until the mixture is reduced by half, about 5 minutes. Lower the heat, simmer for 3 more minutes, remove from the heat, and let cool. In a food processor or blender, blend the sauce until it is smooth. Pass the sauce through a fine sieve to remove any lumps and refrigerate until ready to use.

CHOCOLATE SAUCE

Salsa de Chocolate

MAKES 5 CUPS

1 cup dark corn syrup	240 MILLILITERS
3 cups granulated sugar	600 GRAMS
1 pound unsweetened chocolate, chopped	455 GRAMS
6 tablespoons butter	85 GRAMS

In a medium saucepan over medium-high heat, bring 3 cups (720 milliliters) water, the corn syrup, and sugar to a boil. Lower the heat and simmer until reduced to a thick syrup that coats the back of a spoon, about 10 minutes. Remove from the heat and let rest for at least 20 minutes. Stir in the chocolate and butter until melted. Set aside and let cool.

The sauce can be stored in an airtight container in the refrigerator for up to 1 week. To serve, remove from the refrigerator 1 hour in advance and let the sauce come to room temperature.

CHOCOLATE GANACHE
Ganache de Chocolate

MAKES 1½ CUPS

6 ounces semisweet chocolate	
(about 1 cup chips)	170 GRAMS
1 cup heavy cream	240 MILLILITERS

◎ Put the chocolate in a medium bowl.

◎ In a small saucepan over medium-high heat, bring the cream to a boil. Pour it over the chocolate and stir until melted. Pour into a gravy boat or creamer for ease of pouring.

◎ The ganache will keep in the refrigerator for 2 days. Do not freeze. Bring to room temperature or heat gently in a bowl over simmering water before serving.

Ibarra Chocolate Ganache

Ibarra-brand chocolate from Mexico is flavored with cinnamon and vanilla, and is typically used to make chocolate *á la taza*, or drinking chocolate (hot chocolate). You will find it in Latin markets in a cute hexagonal 19-ounce red and yellow box of large round tablets, about 3 inches in diameter. The Abuelita brand is equally good. You'll get 6 (3-ounce) rounds in a box, so use the other 4 to enjoy traditional chocolate *á la taza*: Melt 1 round with about 4 cups milk in a saucepan, adding sugar to taste, and blend in a blender if you want the classic foamy top.

◎ Follow the instructions in the chocolate ganache recipe, replacing the chocolate with Ibarra chocolate.

Chocolate Kirsch Sauce

12 ounces milk chocolate, chopped	
(about 2 cups chips)	340 GRAMS
1 cup heavy cream	240 MILLILITERS
Grated zest of 1 lemon	
¼ cup kirsch	60 MILLILITERS

◎ Follow the instructions in the chocolate ganache recipe, boiling the lemon zest with the cream and straining it over the chocolate. Stir until the chocolate is melted and then stir in the kirsch. Serve immediately.

VANILLA CRÈME ANGLAISE

Salsa de Vainilla

MAKES 2 CUPS

1½ cups heavy cream   360 MILLILITERS

½ cup whole milk   120 MILLILITERS

1 vanilla bean, halved lengthwise,
   seeds scraped out and reserved
   (or 1½ tablespoons vanilla extract)

¼ cup granulated sugar   50 GRAMS

4 egg yolks

◉ In a large saucepan over medium heat, bring the cream, milk, halved vanilla bean (including seeds) or extract, and 2 tablespoons of the sugar to a boil.

◉ In a medium bowl, whisk together the egg yolks and the remaining sugar. Continue whisking while pouring a small amount of the hot cream mixture into the yolks. This will temper the yolks and keep them from curdling. While whisking the hot cream mixture in the saucepan, gradually add the rest of the tempered yolks. Stir with a wooden spoon over medium-low heat until the custard coats the back of the spoon, being careful not to boil, about 4 minutes.

◉ Let cool slightly, then strain the cream mixture through a fine sieve into a clean bowl to remove the vanilla bean and any bits of cooked yolk. Chill the custard in an ice bath (page 195), then pour into a gravy boat or creamer for ease of pouring.

CILANTRO OIL
Aceite de Cilantro

Use fresh cilantro or, even better, fresh cu-lantro for this oil. Culantro is similar to cilan-tro, but with a more robust flavor and sturdier leaves. You can find it readily in Latin markets.

MAKES 1 CUP

1 cup fresh cilantro	
or culantro leaves	55 GRAMS
1 cup vegetable oil	240 MILLILITERS

In a small saucepan, bring 1 quart (1 liter) water to a boil. Lower the heat, add the cilan-tro, and blanch it for just 10 seconds. Remove from the heat, strain out the cilantro leaves, and plunge them in ice water to stop the cook-ing process. This will help the herb maintain its vibrant green color. Drain the leaves again and squeeze any excess water out with your hands. Put the cilantro in a blender with the oil and blend together for 1 minute until emulsi-fied. Store the oil in a tightly covered container in the refrigerator until ready to use, or up to 2 days.

AMARETTO CREAM
Crema de Amaretto

MAKES 3 CUPS

1½ **cups heavy cream**	360 MILLILITERS
½ **cup whole milk**	120 MILLILITERS
¼ **cup granulated sugar**	50 GRAMS
4 **egg yolks**	
¼ **cup amaretto liqueur**	60 MILLILITERS

In a medium saucepan over medium heat, bring the cream, milk, and sugar to a boil. Low-er the heat and simmer for 5 minutes, whisk-ing constantly, being careful not to burn the cream. Remove from the heat.

In a medium bowl, whisk the egg yolks to-gether. Continue whisking while pouring a small amount of the hot cream mixture into the yolks. This will temper the yolks and keep them from curdling. While whisking the hot cream mixture, slowly add the yolks. Stir with a wooden spoon over medium-low heat until the custard coats the back of the spoon, being careful not to boil, about 4 minutes.

Strain the custard through a fine sieve into a clean bowl to remove any bits of cooked yolk. Whisk in the amaretto. Cover and refrigerate until very cold, about 3 hours or up to 2 days. An ice bath can speed up this process (see page 195).

CINNAMON CREAM
Crema de Canela

MAKES 2½ CUPS

1 cup heavy cream	240 MILLILITERS
1 cup whole milk	240 MILLILITERS
¼ cup granulated sugar	50 GRAMS
5 cinnamon sticks	
5 egg yolks	

⊚ Follow the instructions in the Amaretto Cream recipe (opposite), adding the cinnamon sticks to the cream mixture before boiling and discarding them before serving.

PISTACHIO CREAM
Crema de Pistache

MAKES 2½ CUPS

¼ cup pistachio paste	55 GRAMS
1 cup whole milk	240 MILLILITERS
1 cup heavy cream	240 MILLILITERS
¼ cup granulated sugar	50 GRAMS
4 egg yolks	

⊚ Follow the instructions in the Amaretto Cream recipe (opposite). In a food processor or blender, puree the pistachio paste with the milk and add it to the cream and sugar before boiling.

CHAMOMILE CREAM

Crema de Manzanilla

MAKES 2½ CUPS

1½ cups heavy cream	360 MILLILITERS
1 cup milk	240 MILLILITERS
6 tablespoons sugar	75 GRAMS
4 chamomile tea bags	
5 egg yolks	

◉ Follow the instructions in the Amaretto Cream recipe (page 256). When you lower the heat to simmer the cream mixture, add the tea bags and simmer for 10 minutes rather than 5. With a large spoon, carefully squeeze the tea bags against the side of the pan before discarding them.

CARAMEL SAUCE

Salsa de Caramelo

MAKES 4 CUPS

2 cups granulated sugar	400 GRAMS
¼ cup light corn syrup	60 MILLILITERS
3 cups heavy cream	720 MILLILITERS

◉ In a medium saucepan over medium heat, combine 1 cup (240 milliliters) water, the sugar, and corn syrup, bring to a boil, and cook, untouched, until golden brown, 10 to 15 minutes. Slowly add the cream, stirring constantly until well incorporated. Let the sauce cool before serving. The sauce will keep, stored in a well-sealed container in the refrigerator, for up to 1 month.

COFFEE REDUCTION

Reduccion de Café

MAKES ½ CUP

1 cup brewed espresso   240 MILLILITERS
  (or ½ cup instant coffee granules
  dissolved in 1 cup water)
½ cup granulated sugar   100 GRAMS
1 tablespoon light corn syrup

◎ In a small saucepan over medium-high heat, bring all the ingredients to a slow boil. Reduce the heat and simmer, stirring occasionally and being careful not to burn, until the mixture becomes a thick syrup with a honeylike consistency, about 15 minutes.

POMEGRANATE REDUCTION

Reduccion de Granada

MAKES ½ CUP

1 cup pomegranate juice   240 MILLILITERS
½ cup granulated sugar   100 GRAMS

◎ In a small saucepan over medium heat, bring the juice and sugar to a boil. Reduce the heat and cook until a candy thermometer reaches 135° F, about 15 minutes. The syrup will be slightly thickened, but will still pour in a thick ribbon from a spoon. Let cool to room temperature. Refrigerate, tightly covered, for up to 2 months. Bring to room temperature before serving.

ACKNOWLEDGMENTS

I would like to thank my friends and colleagues who have offered their time, encouragement, and many talents to this book. Their invaluable help made this dream a reality. To my family—Claudia and my two beautiful children, Layla and Daniel—you give me the love and support that I need to strive for perfection in life. I am proud to be the father of such great children. In particular, I am grateful to Laura Zimmerman Maye, my co-author; Christopher Steighner, our editor, and everyone at Rizzoli; Lisa Ekus, our agent; Ben Fink, our photographer; Chalkley Calderwood, our designer; Douglas Rodriguez, my mentor and friend; Christina Sirtak; Ed Lieberman; Rosemary Staltare; Kathleen O'Toole; Gail Pretzfelder; Jorge Adriazola; Beatriz and Rodrigo Zurita; Adrian Leon; Jose Garces; Bruni Bueno; and Donna Marie.

INDEX

Page references in *italic* refer to illustrations.